I0983194

SALVAGE

The New Face of War

The New Face of War

MALCOLM W. BROWNE

The Bobbs-Merrill Company, Inc.
A Subsidiary of Howard W. Sams & Co., Inc., Publishers
Indianapolis • Kansas City • New York

First Printing, 1965

PRINTED IN THE UNITED STATES OF AMERICA

TO LE LIEU

Contents

Preface

As The Associated Press representative in Viet Nam, Malcolm W. Browne has recorded history in the making and, in so doing, he has, on occasion, actually made history himself. One example of this was his coverage of the self-immolation of the Buddhist monk, Quang Duc, in 1963 who burned himself alive in one of the great public squares of Saigon.

Mr. Browne's description of this event and the photograph which he took of it attracted world-wide attention. They also started a wave of thoughts and feelings which unquestionably strengthened the forces which had already put the then government of Viet Nam into its terminal phase.

Mr. Browne has thus fairly won his spurs as an enterprising and courageous journalist on an assignment which carries with it many risks: of being sick or wounded or kidnapped or killed— or some combination of these various states. The Viet Nam assignment is also one where the truth is hard to ascertain and where some persons deliberately promote untruths. He, therefore, also ran the risk—which is perhaps the most unwelcome of all to a conscientious journalist—of reporting something which turns out not to be so. Mr. Browne has done well in avoiding all of these pitfalls.

What is particularly valuable about this book is the way in which it conveys what people in Viet Nam truly think and feel. The crisis in Viet Nam would be rapidly ended if people thought in a certain way. The feelings of the people and the circumstances of their daily lives are therefore of prime importance and on them hinge military success.

One need not agree with all of Mr. Browne's opinions to recognize that in his book is the flavor of the struggle in Viet Nam. Where one man will say: "This glass of water is half full," another will say: "This glass of water is half empty." Thus it is that Mr. Browne says: "There is a distinct possibility that this war may be lost." Whereas I would probably say: "There is a distinct possibility that this war may be won."

But these are differences of phraseology. What is important is that this war, as Mr. Browne says, has a "new face"—certainly as far as Americans are concerned. There is, for one thing, a brand-new type of fighting man—the terrorist, who is just as distinct as the infantryman or the aviator. And he fights in a war with no front, no rear and no flanks in which his "base" is right among the people. He finds concealment, rest, recreation, food, care for his wounds and vital information right in the hut of the everyday Vietnamese citizen.

There are many other examples of this "new face." Mr. Browne gives them in all their vivid reality: the smell of the cooking, the blazing heat of the sun, the look in the eye. In so doing, he enables the reader to understand the fundamentals of this far-away struggle in which the vital interest of the United States is so heavily engaged.

And this understanding by America is vital, for if we in America persist, the outlook is good. But if we in America are impatient and easily discouraged, the outlook is bad. The answer to this new kind of war lies partly in Viet Nam, but it also lies greatly in the United States. In the work which he has done to inform American opinion Mr. Browne has made a contribution of value to his own country, to Viet Nam and to the free world. He does so once again in this book.

HENRY CABOT LODGE

Author's Preface

The United States is fighting a war in South Viet Nam which is proving increasingly costly in blood and treasure. There is a distinct possibility that this war may be lost, for one reason or another.

Vietnamese communist leaders are proud of the techniques of war they have developed. Building from the traditions of Marx, Lenin and Mao Tse-tung, they have refined the art of revolutionary warfare for their small, underdeveloped nation to a degree that they regard as unbeatable.

Each inventor likes to apply the apparatus he has designed to new situations and new challenges. The Viet Cong expects to win its war in South Viet Nam. But it is also offering the techniques it developed here to all other communist revolutionary groups in underdeveloped nations throughout the world, especially in Africa and Latin America. A growing number of these nations are showing interest in the Vietnamese patent, and before long, many of them may be paying royalties to Hanoi, Peking and Moscow.

The prospects are that the United States may be fighting wars in the Vietnamese pattern in many places, for many years to come.

Accordingly, South Viet Nam is a laboratory. The results of the struggle here are important not only in terms of Viet Nam itself. They may prove to have much the same relationship to the new face of war that the Spanish Civil War of the late 1930s had to World War II.

I have written this book in the hope that it may contribute in some way to American understanding of how this kind of war is fought. The experiences of two World Wars and the Korean conflict, indeed, the experiences of most of America's military tradition, seem almost completely inapplicable in Viet Nam. America was not prepared for Viet Nam, and is now painfully trying to learn something entirely new.

This is the book of a reporter, not a scholar. As such, its observations are highly personal, in that I have been an observer at close range. In writing the book, I have scarcely referred to notes at all, but have relied on experiences and impressions burned into my consciousness over a period of three stormy years. I have made no attempt to arrange things chronologically, and I have omitted many aspects of the Vietnamese situation that the reader might have found interesting, but which I felt did not bear directly on the subject. Other observers of Viet Nam may disagree with my criteria of selection, but this is all to the good. Many views are needed.

Accordingly, this should not be read as history, although I have slipped in some dates and names here and there. One of the better historical sources to which the reader might apply is the files of The Associated Press. I think, also, that Americans may profit by reading the basic writings of the communist tacticians themselves. They do not make pleasant reading, but neither did Hitler's *Mein Kampf.* Any soldier is in grave danger who does not know what weapons his enemy is using.

Viet Nam is dangerous, confusing and frustrating. There is a sinister fascination about the country into the grip of which most foreigners fall who stay here any length of time. I am no exception.

At the same time, it is a beautiful and sometimes noble little country, which I have come to love. As a citizen of the Free World, I hope the challenge represented by Viet Nam is met. But beyond this, in a very personal sense, I hope Viet Nam itself pulls through. Its people deserve something better than what they have had for all too long.

I shall be forever grateful to all my Vietnamese, American, French, Australian, Canadian, New Zealand, English, Indian, German, Cambodian and other friends, who are a part of this book. Many will recognize themselves, and I hope they will not be angry seeing themselves through my eyes.

My special gratitude goes to The Associated Press, whose correspondent for South Viet Nam I have been since 1961. Without the continuous guidance and unstinting assistance of hundreds of AP people all over the world, this book would have been out of the question. Of all these people, I owe the most to Wes Gallagher, who sent me here.

Finally, my admiration and thanks go in general to all my colleagues everywhere who have to do with news, whether they work for news agencies, newspapers, radio, television, magazines, or whatever. They all are the eyes and ears of the Free World, without whom there would not be a Free World.

M. W. B.
Saigon
October, 1964

The New Face of War

Chapter 1

Paddy War

A drenching, predawn dew had settled over the sloping steel deck of the landing craft, and I slipped several times climbing aboard in the inky darkness.

Soldiers cursed sleepily as they heaved heavy mortar base plates and machine guns from the pier onto their field packs on the deck.

The night was still and moonless, and the air would have been warm except for that unpleasant dew, sometimes laced with raindrops. The French used to call it "spitting rain."

This was December, 1961, and I was going out for my first look at an operation against the Viet Cong. There were no American field advisors in those days (and no helicopters and almost no communications), and I tried to stay close to soldiers or officers who could speak French. Most of them could.

The place was a town called Ben Tre in the heart of the flat, fertile Mekong River Delta, about fifty miles south of Saigon. Ben Tre, the capital of Kien Hoa Province, still takes pride in the fact that it has produced some of Viet Nam's top Communists. Ung Van Khiem, former Foreign Minister of the Hanoi government, came from here. Kien Hoa is also famous for its pretty girls.

It was about 4 A.M., and I was dead tired. I had been up late with the province chief, Colonel Pham Ngoc Thao, a catlike man with short-cropped hair and a disconcerting walleye.

Thao had been an intelligence officer in the Viet Minh during the Indochina War, and had gone over to Diem after independence in 1954.

The night before, Thao had invited me to the opening of a theater he had had built in Ben Tre, and the curious town residents had turned out in their holiday best. The bill of fare was a traditional Vietnamese drama and some comedians, jugglers and singers. It lacked the glamour of a Broadway opening night, but it was about the fanciest thing Ben Tre had ever seen.

Two masked actors in ornate classical costume were intoning verses about a murder they were planning and the audience was murmuring expectantly when Thao leaned toward me.

"My troops are going out in the morning. We have intelligence that a battalion of Viet Cong is moving through one of my districts. I'm not going, but would you be interested?"

Just then, the action on stage reached a high point. Several actors in stilted, oriental poses were supposed to portray violence, their brilliantly colored robes swishing. Applause rushed through the theater, and children put down their pop bottles to chatter. Thao, obviously pleased, warmly joined the applause.

He always liked the theater. A year or so later, when Diem sent him on a special mission to the States, he made a special point of visiting Hollywood, where he was photographed with actress Sandra Dee. The picture was sent back to Viet Nam by news agencies, but Diem's censors prohibited its publication, presumably because they felt it would be detrimental to fighting spirit.

The 300 or so troops on the pier that morning were an oddlooking bunch, a mixture of civil guards and self-defense corpsmen. Some were in neat fatigue uniforms with helmets, others in the loose, black garb of the Vietnamese peasant, topped with old French bush hats. There were no troops from the regular army on this operation. The commander was a crusty, Frenchtrained captain with several rows of combat ribbons on his faded olive drab uniform.

The diesel engines of the three landing craft carrying our makeshift task force belched oily smoke and we were moving, the black silhouettes of palm trees sliding past along the edges of the narrow canal. Here and there a dot of light glimmered through the trees from some concealed cluster of huts.

For a few minutes, the commander studied a map with a neat plastic overlay, making marks with red and black grease pencils, under the light of a pocket flashlight.

One of the few things Western military men have taught Vietnamese officers to do really well is mark up maps. The Vietnamese officer studies his sector map like a chessboard. Even if he has only a squad or two of men under his command, he uses all the ornate symbols of the field commander in marking his deployment on maps. This love of maps has often infuriated American advisors, who feel more time should be spent acting and less on planning.

After a while the light flicked out. A few of the troops were smoking silently, but most had arranged their field packs as pillows and had gone to sleep amid the clutter of weapons. We were not scheduled to reach our objective until several hours after sunrise.

I finally dropped off to sleep, and must have been asleep about an hour when a grinding lurch and the sound of splintering wood roused me.

It was still pitch dark, but people were screaming, and on the deck of the landing craft, troops were rushing around. In the darkness, we had somehow collided with and sunk a large, crowded sampan. Twenty or thirty sleeping occupants had been thrown into the canal, with all their worldly possessions. A few of them apparently were hurt.

The two other landing craft were chugging on down the canal, but we had stopped. Troops holding ropes were helping swing the people in the water over to the shore. When everyone had reached safety, we started up again, people still yelling at us in the distance. We must have destituted several large families at a blow, but there was no thought of getting their names so that they could be compensated by the government. I couldn't help feeling that their feelings for the government must be less than cordial.

The sky began to turn gray, and at last we left the maze of narrow canals and turned into a branch of the great Mekong itself.

The sun rose hot and red, its reflection glaring from the sluggish expanse of muddy water. We were moving slowly ("We don't want to make too much engine noise or the Viet Cong will hear us coming," the commander told me), and the dense wall of palm trees on both banks scarcely seemed to move at all.

It was nearly 9 A.M. when our little flotilla abruptly turned at right angles to the left, each vessel gunning its engines. We had reached the objective and were charging in for the beach. As we neared the shore we could see that the beach actually was a mud flat leading back about fifty yards to the palm trees, and it would be arduous hiking getting ashore.

The other two landing craft were going ashore about one mile farther up the river. The idea of this exercise, it was explained to me, was to seize two sets of hamlets running back from the river front, trapping the reported Viet Cong battalion in the wide expanse of rice fields in between.

We slammed into the mud, and the prow of our clumsy ship clanked down to form a ramp. We leapt into waist-deep water and mud and began the charge toward higher ground.

If the Viet Cong had even one machine gun somewhere in the tree line, they certainly could have killed most of us with no danger of encountering serious fire from us. Each step in that smelly ooze was agonizingly slow, and at times both feet would get mired. Little soldiers carrying heavy mortars and machine guns sank nearly to their necks. It happened that no one was shooting at us that day.

The first squads clambered up to high ground and began firing. Two light machine guns began thumping tracers across the open rice field, and mortars began lobbing shells at random. Individual soldiers with Tommy guns (I was surprised how many of our group were equipped with submachine guns) were emptying their magazines into a string of huts or into the field. Off a mile or so to our right, noises told us that our companion party was similarly employed. It really sounded like a war.

I was standing on a high path running parallel to the river near a machine-gun position, looking out over the field where our Viet Cong battalion was supposed to be trapped. The green rice was nearly waist high, and there might easily be a battalion concealed in this field for all anyone knew.

Suddenly, a man leapt up about fifty yards away and began to run. This was it!

Every machine gun, Tommy gun, rifle and pistol in our sector poured fire at that man, and I was amazed at how long he continued to run. But finally he went down, silently, without a scream.

Our little army continued to pour intense fire into the field and several huts until it occurred to someone that no one was shooting back, and it might be safe to move forward a little.

Some of the troops began to move into the huts, shooting as they went.

Near me was a cluster of five Dan Ve (local Self-Defense Corpsmen) dressed in ragged black uniforms with American pistol belts and rusty French rifles. The group was detailed to go into the field to look for the man we had seen go down, and I went with them.

We found him on his back in the mud, four bullet holes stitched across the top of his naked chest. He was wearing only black shorts. He was alive and conscious, moving his legs and arms, his head lolling back and forth. There was blood on his lips.

The Dan Ve squad, all young peasant boys, looked down at the man and laughed, perhaps in embarrassment. Laughter in Viet Nam does not always signify amusement.

Perhaps as an act of mercy, perhaps as sheer cruelty, one of the men picked up a heavy stake lying in the mud and rammed one end of into the ground next to the wounded man's throat. Then he forced the stake down over the throat, trying to throttle the man. The man continued to move. Someone stamped on the free end of the stake to break the wounded man's neck, but the stake broke instead. Then another man tried stamping on the man's throat, but somehow the spark of life still was too strong. Finally, the whole group laughed, and walked back to the path.

The firing had stopped altogether, and several old peasant men were talking to the officers of our party. Two of the old men had a pole and a large fish net.

The peasants—I think they were hamlet elders—walked out to the wounded man, rolled him into the fish net, and with the net slung between them on the pole, carried him back to the path. As they laid him out on the ground, two women, both dressed in baggy black trousers and blouses, ran up from one of the huts. One of them put a hand to her mouth as she saw the wounded man, whom she recognized as her husband.

She dashed back to her hut and returned in a moment carrying a bucket, which she filled with black water from the rice field. Sitting down with her husband's head cradled in her lap, she poured paddy water over his wounds to clean off the clotting blood. Occasionally she would stroke his forehead, muttering something.

He died about ten minutes later. The woman remained seated, one hand over her husband's eyes. Slowly, she looked around at the troops, and then she spotted me. Her eyes fixed on me in an expression that still haunts me sometimes. She was not weeping, and her face showed neither grief nor fury; it was unfathomably blank.

I moved away some distance to where the operation commander was jabbering into a field telephone. When his conversation ended, I handed him a 500-piastre note (worth about $5.00), asking him to give it to the widow as some small compensation.

"Monsieur Browne, please do not be sentimental. That man undoubtedly was a Viet Cong agent, since these hamlets have been Viet Cong strongholds for years. This is war. However, I will give her the money, if you like."

I don't know what happened to that money, and I didn't go near the place where the woman was sitting, but I walked into the hut I had seen her leave.

It was typical of thousands of Mekong Delta huts I have seen. The framework was bamboo, and the sides and roof were made of dried, interlaced palm fronds with a layer of rice straw thatch on top. The floor was hardened earth. A large, highly polished wooden table stood near the door. Peasants eat their meals on these tables, sleep on them and work on them. There were four austerely simple chairs. In a corner were several knee-high earthen crocks filled with drinking water. Just inside the door was the family altar, extending all the way to the ceiling. Pinned to it were yellowed photographs and some fancy Chinese calligraphy. On a little shelf a sand pot containing incense sticks smoldered fragrant fumes.

To the right, from behind a woven bamboo curtain, two children were peering with wide eyes. The eyes were the only expressive elements in their blank, silent little faces. Incongruously, one of them was standing next to a gaily painted yellow rocking horse, one rocker of which was freshly splintered by a bullet hole.

I walked out of the hut and down the path. By now, troops were strung all along the path between the two hamlets about a mile apart, and were stringing telephone wire and performing other military chores.

Snaking through the palm trees, a water-filled ditch about twenty feet across obstructed my progress. But a few yards away, a soldier had commandeered a small sampan from an old woman and was ferrying troops back and forth. I went across with him. As I continued down the path, scores of mud walls about five feet high obstructed progress. All were obviously freshly built, and most had gun slots. It was strange that no one had decided to defend these good emplacements against us.

I came to a small hut straddling the path, consisting only of upright bamboo spars and a roof. The little building was festooned with painted banners, the largest of which read "*Da Dao My-Diem*" ("Down with U.S.-Diem"). A group of young women were dismantling the hut as soldiers trained rifles at them. I was told that this was a Viet Cong "information center."

Finally, the troops began moving out from the tree line into the field itself, converging from three sides: the two hamlets and the path itself. The battle would come now, if ever.

We moved single file along the tops of the dykes that divided the field into an immense checkerboard. The thought struck me that if there were guerrillas hiding in the tall rice we would make fine targets as we moved along, but no one seemed worried.

Progress was slow. The mud dykes were slippery as grease, and every time a soldier toppled into the muddy paddy, the whole column halted as he was pulled out. I was reminded some-how of the White Knight in Lewis Carroll's *Through the Look-ing Glass*. Superficially, we combed the field from one end to the other, our various forces finally meeting in the middle.

A little L19 spotter plane droned overhead, radioing what was no doubt useful information to the ground commander.

It would be difficult to search that field more completely than we did, and we found not the slightest trace of a human being. Of course, the rice could easily have concealed a thousand or even ten thousand guerrillas, without our knowing.

Viet Cong guerrillas have developed the art of camouflage to an incredible degree. In rice fields, they often remain com-pletely submerged under the muddy water for hours, breathing through straws.

But by now the sun stood like a blast furnace in the sky, and the troops were tired. A few had tied to their packs live ducks and chickens they had pilfered from the hamlets, and were looking around for level ground on which to prepare lunch.

"It looks as though the Viet Cong got away again," the com-mander told me. "It's time to go. It's not a good idea to be moving around out here when the sun starts going down."

By noon, 300 mud-drenched, tired troops were boarding the landing craft, and silence had settled over the hamlets again. We had suffered one wounded—a Civil Guard who had stepped on a spike trap, which had pierced his foot.

The three landing craft churned their way out into deep water, and the tension disappeared. Soldiers lighted cigarettes, talked and laughed, and spread their sopping clothing on the deck to dry.

All of them had a warm feeling of accomplishment, of hav-ing done a hard day's work under the cruel sun. The irregularity in the palm-lined shore that marked our hamlet receded into the distance.

And I couldn't help thinking of the old travelogues that end, "And so we leave the picturesque Mekong River Delta, palm trees glimmering under a tropic sun, and happy natives on the shore bidding us 'aloha.'"

Chapter 2

Mechanized Paddy War

Marshy rice fields for years were the bane of South Vietnamese government forces and a blessing for the Viet Cong. Somehow the guerrillas could always move swiftly across this terrible terrain, while government troops loaded with tons of heavy weapons got hopelessly mired down. Even helicopters were only a partial answer.

The Viet Cong for years had used a little one-man boat, shaped like a saucer and made of woven palm fronds and bamboo. A man with one knee on the little saucer could scoot across the gooiest mud, propelling himself with his free leg.

In late 1962, the United States brought its own secret paddy weapon to Viet Nam—a five-ton monster called the M113.

The M113 is an armored, amphibious personnel carrier. It moves on tank tracks, and is supposed to be equally mobile on land, on water, or in mud. The thing is squat and square as a cracker box, and its crew consists of a driver and a man to operate the heavy .50-caliber machine gun on top. There is a large hatch in the upper deck, in which ten or twelve men can stand with their heads and shoulders sticking out. If the vehicle is fired on, the troops can sit inside on steel benches, holding on with nylon straps suspended from the ceiling. It is not unlike the inside of a New York City subway car.

The first thirty M113s arrived in Viet Nam in mid-1962, and were promptly sent to war in the Mekong River Delta.

This time, American advisors were sure, the Vietnamese Army would be the match of the wily Viet Cong.

It happened that I went along with one of the first M113 combat operations, and by coincidence, the operation was in almost exactly the same part of Kien Hoa Province where I had witnessed my first operation a year earlier.

The battle plan for this particular exercise was an enormous pincers—two salients of fifteen vehicles each—converging from north and south on the target area. Troops on foot, some fifteen hundred of them, as I recall, were to set up blocking forces to the east and west, to complete the trap.

I went with the southern group of M113s. They had been traveling and maneuvering for several days to get into the jumping-off position, and when I joined them, they were clustered in a thicket of palms and young bamboo.

The crews, young and freshly trained, were eager for combat. Several American advisors were chanting warlike Vietnamese slogans they had learned, acting like college cheerleaders. Crew-cut American Army captains leapt in the air, waving their arms, and yelling "*Sat cong!*" ("Slaughter communists!") as their Vietnamese trainees took up the chant.

The M113s themselves had been "spit shined," and looked as beautiful in their fresh olive brown paint as they ever can be. There was scarcely a speck of mud in the tracks.

As the sun set, troops were still making last-minute adjustments and checks on their machines. We were to start before dawn.

We headed out of the thicket with running lights on but headlights off. We were moving along a narrow dirt road, and drivers were taking it easy, even though there was a bright moon. This road, like many others in the Mekong Delta, had no shoulders, and dropped off sharply into paddies on both sides. The rainy season had nearly ended, but the paddies were still flooded.

It struck me at the time as a little ominous that the drivers were being so careful to stay on the road. After all, this vehicle was designed to go on any kind of terrain.

We traveled about fifteen miles, and the sky began to brighten. Viet Nam is only a few degrees north of the Equator, and sunrises and sunsets are abrupt.

The whole column clanked to a stop. We had reached the point at which we were to leave the road and cut across country.

Paralleling the road to our right was an irrigation ditch some thirty feet wide with rather steep sides dropping about five feet to the water level. The water itself was probably about neck deep.

We paused perhaps ten minutes while the column commander surveyed the situation through field glasses. At length, the first M113 nosed down into the ditch, sliding sideways as it went. Tracks churning wildly, it made for the other shore, momentum carrying it about halfway up the opposite bank. Then it stopped. The tracks were still going full speed, but they were only hacking deep furrows into the soft mudbank.

The driver finally gave up and backed out for another try. The same thing happened. And again and again.

The sun was higher, and troops on the other fourteen waiting vehicles had stretched out on the top decks for a snooze. The driver now was trying to make the stranded M113 climb back the bank he had come down, but with no more success than he had had on the opposite bank.

The column commander (and his irritated American advisor) finally decided some kind of remedial action was necessary, and headed off down the road to try to find a more propitious fording place. In forty minutes or so, they were back, on the other side of the ditch. Evidently they had found the spot.

The column started off down the road, and we reached a place where the banks were almost level with the water. Spray flying, we plunged into the ditch, and the whole column made it across.

By now, we were badly behind schedule, and the column commander ordered more speed as we headed across the flooded paddies.

Incidentally, M113s are probably the most uncomfortable vehicles ever devised. They do not ride along smoothly like tanks, which are usually longer and weigh up to eight times as much. Edges and corners on M113s are sharp and hard, and the nylon hand straps with which troops hang on begin to cut the skin after a while. The comfort quotient reaches its lowest point when you are moving at high speed (about twenty-five miles an hour) across a rice field.

Paddies are laid out with dykes every hundred yards or so, and slamming into one of these dykes nearly halts the M113 and upends it, all in one shattering movement. Then the nose swoops down and slams into the paddy on the other side, usually at an oblique angle. A man standing in the hatch is easily caught unaware by one of these maneuvers and is banged into all kinds of sharp objects before he recovers his balance. I have seen seasoned personnel-carrier troopers lose eight inches of flesh off legs and arms as the result of such encounters.

A moving M113, by the way, also makes a very unstable platform for the .50-caliber machine gun mounted on top. It is possible to fire a long burst under such conditions and miss a target only 100 yards distant. I will come back to this deficiency in a later chapter, in which the lives of two children were saved as the result of poor gunnery.

But at any rate, we were moving, no longer in a column, but in a ragged line of scrimmage, like a herd of charging rhinoceroses.

The commander of the operation, meanwhile, had radioed our troop that he was not pleased with our slow progress. The northern pincer, it seemed, was ready for the final charge, and we were still nowhere in range.

It was probably with this message in mind that our plucky little commander decided we should not waste time reconnoitering when we came to another canal, about fifty feet wide.

Delta canals in Viet Nam, all of them man-made, are straight as arrows. Even from the air, they stretch all the way to the horizon, like glittering slashes across the verdant plain.

Like the first big obstacle we had come to, this canal had steep banks that looked solid enough but were actually merely coagulated ooze. Like lemmings racing for the sea, our little armada charged into the canal.

That, as far as I was concerned, was the end of the operation.

I waited around for a few hours while drivers churned at the banks on both sides, without success. But by now, the crews and our troops had begun to lose interest in the operation. With typical Vietnamese fatalism, some drivers had given up altogether and were idly smoking. A few crew members, including the commander, had climbed into the water, and were knowingly poking at the bottom with sticks. The American advisor with us was hurling obscenities.

In due course, the radio message came that the operation had decided to go on without us, and we were to go somewhere else if the M113s were finally rescued from the canal. A helicopter arrived after a while with some angry Vietnamese officers on board, and I talked them into giving me a seat.

I understand the M113s finally got out of the canal, although I was not informed how or when.

As a matter of fact, the northern force got to its objective only an hour or two behind schedule, partly, I suppose, because it had fewer difficult canals to cross. They found no Viet Cong, however.

I don't want to imply, in any case, that the M113s were a complete fiasco.

Since the early operations, there have been improvements in the machines themselves and in techniques for using them. For one thing, most M113s now are equipped with cable winches that are useful in pulling themselves out of mire.

For another, drivers and commanders both have a more realistic idea of the limitations of the M113. They know that the M113 runs very well on dry ground or in deep water, but has trouble in mud of a certain depth. Drivers look for good fording places, as a rule, and generally cross one at a time. Often the first vehicle across a canal becomes a belaying point for the others, which are towed across by cable. Still, progress across rain-soaked delta terrain is often painfully slow.

The personnel carrier has another defect: it is very vulnerable to heavy weapons fire. It is armored, but the armor is thin, and will stop little more than rifle bullets. Heavy machine-gun slugs will penetrate the slab sides, and recoilless cannon shells easily demolish vehicles.

The first M113s sent to Viet Nam lacked any kind of armor for the machine gunner, who was exposed from the waist up to fire.

It didn't take the Viet Cong long to begin capitalizing on these things.

On January 2, 1963, near a cluster of huts called Ap Bac ("Northern Hamlet") in the delta forty miles southwest of Saigon, the Viet Cong decided to try its strength against the best gadgets the Free World had to offer—including the M113.

The communist force involved was and still is probably the most dangerous fighting unit in the country—the notorious 514th Battalion. Word that the 514th is operating nearby is considered very bad news. American GIs have written and sung rambling folk songs, including one called "On Top of Old Ap Bac," in which the 514th is prominently mentioned.

The 514th had prepared its positions at Ap Bac well. The guerrillas had dug good fortifications behind a tree line, looking out over a wide expanse of rice field. They had a number of machine guns in positions to lay grazing fire across the muddy field. And, most important, the Viet Cong had received orders for the first time in the war to stand and fight a major government operation.

Troops of nearly every description were involved on the government side; there were regular army troops, paratroopers, civil guards, self-defense corpsmen and others. There were American advisors and pilots, three of whom were killed during the day.

There were fifteen helicopters carrying troops into the assault, fourteen of which were hit by Viet Cong fire. Several were downed.

There also was a troop of M113s, which arrived appallingly late for the fight because of problems negotiating a canal.

As has happened so many times since, the M113s were sent into the fray as tanks—a role for which they were not designed. The big machines charged up to the tree line and moved along it, firing into the Viet Cong positions.

Eight of the unprotected M113 machine gunners were killed outright by the fusillade that met them, and the whole troop of M113s was forced back.

The foot soldiers were pinned down, and it was apparent the

government forces were in serious trouble. Several hundred paratroopers were dropped into the area from Saigon at about sunset, but missed the drop zone.

The next day, government forces cleaned up the carnage in the rice field and "liberated" Ap Bac without a shot. The Viet Cong had melted away in the night.

For the Viet Cong, Ap Bac became the victory cry. The hamlet's name, in gold letters, was affixed to the 514th's battle flags. Communist propaganda posters, professionally printed in four colors, bloomed throughout the delta, all glorifying the fighters at Ap Bac.

Statistically, Ap Bac could hardly be considered a real victory or defeat for either side. Government fatalities ran to more than sixty, but numbers like that have become common.

Ap Bac was closely studied, however. A section of the U.S. Military Assistance Command responsible for battle research was turned loose on the M113 and its flaws.

This section, headed by a brigadier general, reached the conclusion that M113 gunners should have some armor. Field engineers in Saigon soon designed and built makeshift armored cupolas for nearly all the M113s in the country, and the death rate of gunners dropped sharply.

New helicopter landing tactics were devised, with variable success.

Still seeking the ideal paddy vehicle, the United States began bringing hundreds of Fiberglas dinghies to Viet Nam.

These little watercraft, called "swimmer support boats," could hold about twelve men, were equipped with large outboard motors, and were unsinkable. They worked fine in shallow canals and ditches, and brought a new dimension to amphibious warfare. Of course, they still could not travel across paddies.

New uses were found for the M113s.

Someone discovered that they are useful in crushing concealed guerrillas. By driving fifteen M113s in an irregular zigzag pattern across a flooded paddy a few hundred yards square, a commander can be fairly sure there are no living enemies left in the field. On several occasions, I have seen blood oozing into muddy track marks as the big machines swiveled through fields, and have even seen pieces of bodies thrust to the surface.

Another and unexpected use for the M113s evolved. They turned out to be very good for use in Saigon during coups, both by rebel forces and loyalists.

Of course, every tactic has a countertactic when resourceful adversaries are pitted against each other. The Viet Cong has been known to lure M113 units into fields that have been well laced with land mines.

South Viet Nam's former Premier, Major General Nguyen Khanh, narrowly escaped death in 1964 when an M113 near him ran over a mine in just such a field.

America quickly settled down in earnest to learn the art of fighting in rice fields.

Chapter 3

Viet Cong Gadgets

On my desk in Saigon is an object that seems to me an almost perfect symbol of the factors that have made the Viet Cong a potent and feared fighting force.

It is a brass cartridge case about one-half inch in diameter and three inches long. I picked it up after a clash in the Mekong River Delta near the riddled body of a government soldier, and it is probable this cartridge was the instrument of his death.

It is no ordinary cartridge case. The cylindrical part of the case is made of brass plumber's tubing. The base of the case, soldered to the tube, is an old French ten-centime coin, the kind with a hole in the middle. A percussion cap was crimped into the hole, and the whole thing made an effective shotgun shell. The cartridge was made to fit a weapon the Viet Cong calls the "sky horse gun," made of scraps of plumbing and wood. These guns often blow up, killing their users. But more often, they project a deadly hail of buckshot into some hapless squad of government troops.

I wonder how many of those old French colonial coins found their way into communist ammunition factories in the jungle for use first against the French and then the Americans?

Viet Cong armament plants are marvels of ingenuity and "field expediency," to use an American military phrase. Occasionally, government forces find them and I have seen several.

One such factory, a long hut with a thatched roof, contained a homemade lathe turned by an ancient Japanese marine diesel engine. Electric power for the plant came from a generator hooked to the motor of a Vespa motor scooter. In one corner, near a brick chimney, was a charcoal-fired forge, to which was connected a system of bellows. The big bellows were operated by bicycle pedals, and three small boys pedaling at top speed could easily keep the forge glowing brightly.

This plant had only two products—rifle grenade launchers and 60-millimeter mortars. Finished or partly finished products were neatly crated in one corner of the hut when the government unit I was with seized the plant.

The grenade launchers were ingenious and effective. They were steel cups exactly the diameter of an American hand grenade, each fitted with a threaded hole into which a rifle muzzle could be screwed. A steel loop was welded to the outside of the cup. To fire one, the user puts a blank cartridge in his rifle, screws the cup to the barrel, and puts an ordinary grenade in the cup, the grenade's safety handle stuck through the cup's steel loop. The pin of the grenade is then pulled, and the guerrilla aims and fires. The gas from the cartridge drives the grenade forward, and as it leaves the cup, the safety handle is automatically released. Compared with American grenade launchers, the thing is remarkably simple and cheap. Best of all, it is perfectly adapted to the use of captured equipment.

Over the years, this plant had turned out tens of thousands of grenade launchers.

The mortar works were more complicated. The mortar tubes themselves were precisely bored from heavy steel tubing legally purchased in Saigon. Each tube was reinforced by welded bands of steel. Mortar bipods and base plates were made of scrap steel, all welded neatly together. Finished mortars were professionally painted and oiled.

American 60-millimeter mortar shells are abundant in Viet Nam and easy to capture, and that was why this was the caliber of choice for the homemade guns.

The former chief of An Xuyen Province, Lieutenant Colonel Pham Van Ut, thought so highly of these Viet Cong mortars that he issued them to his own troops whenever they were captured.

"They're every bit as good as American or French mortars,"

he told me. "They lack optical sighting devices, but good mortar-men don't need gadgets like that. We can't afford to be proud about using enemy weapons, even if they're homemade."

Viet Cong armorers are notoriously poor chemists and prefer whenever possible to use captured explosives rather than make their own. But they can and do make effective explosives.

Nitroglycerin, TNT, plastic, blasting gelatin and so on are beyond the competence of jungle factories. But explosives chemically akin to gunpowder are not. The basic ingredient, called an oxidizing agent, is normally sodium or potassium chlorate or nitrate.

To these are added substances called reducing agents, such as sulphur and powdered charcoal.

The great advantage of these materials, from the Viet Cong standpoint, is the fact that they are all legal to buy and possess. Sodium nitrate is extensively used by the Saigon meat processing industry as a preservative, for example.

On February 16, 1964, terrorists placed a bomb in the lobby of Saigon's Capital Kinh-Do Theater, the "Americans-only" movie theater. The front wall of the building was demolished, two American servicemen were killed, and fifty-one other Americans were injured—many of them women and children.

U.S. security agents analyzed fragments of the bomb, and found that the explosive was a mixture of potassium chlorate and arsenic sulfide. Potassium chlorate can be purchased legally at Western-style pharmacies in Saigon, and arsenic sulfide is available at Chinese pharmacies.

Most of the terrorist explosions in South Viet Nam are caused by such improvised bombs.

The famous "Saigon bicycle bomb" described in Graham Greene's novel *The Quiet American* is worth special mention. The lethal potency of these specially modified bicycles led to a law under which any purchaser of an electric timing device must register the device and obtain a license for it. The law even extends to the little self-timers built into some electric stoves, and to the timers used on photographic enlargers.

The standard Viet Cong bicycle bomb is made by filling the

entire frame tubing with explosive. In French colonial days, plastic was the explosive of choice, but in recent years this has become hard to get.

Wires attached to blasting caps inside the frame are led out small holes and tied to the brake cables, which camouflage them. The wires lead to the electric headlamp, in which has been mounted a stopwatch which has an electric contact attached to one of the hands. A small flashlight battery furnishes the detonating power.

A bicycle bomb parked with hundreds of other bicycles is very difficult to spot. A policeman must either notice extra wires connected to the brake cables, or must take the headlamp apart —an operation that may cost him his life.

Workmanship on these bombs is sometimes slipshod, of course. Every month or so, a man is mysteriously blown to fragments while peacefully pedaling along. Whenever this happens it is presumed the Viet Cong has lost another agent.

Somewhere in the Mekong Delta, a Viet Cong plant has been turning out tens of thousands of hand grenade cases for years. These cases are made of cast aluminum, and are very effective.

For years, the Viet Cong has laid special stress on the capture of American 105-millimeter howitzer shells. At this writing, the guerrillas are not believed to own any 105 guns, but the shells are put to another use. The nose fuse of these shells is easily unscrewed, and an electric blasting cap can be tamped into the fuse well instead.

Thus rigged, the 105 shell becomes an excellent mine that can be concealed in a pile of rice straw on the shoulder of a road, with wires running back several hundred yards to a foxhole or tree line. The first American combat death in Viet Nam in 1961 resulted from one of these mines, and many other Americans have been killed or wounded by them since.

Viet Cong gadgetry extends to fortifications as well. The communist guerrilla in Viet Nam probably spends more time on digging than on any other military pursuit.

About twenty miles north of Saigon is an area covered mostly with jungle and rubber plantations, which Americans have dubbed "the Iron Triangle." It is a roughly triangular tract of wilderness about a hundred square miles in area in which all efforts to drive out the Viet Cong so far have proved ineffective.

One of the reasons is a vast network of tunnels the guerrillas have dug throughout the area. The tunnels are interconnected in a huge maze, with camouflaged ventilation holes extending to the surface every fifty yards or so.

All efforts to wipe out this tunnel system have failed. Tanks have sometimes crushed sections of tunnel, but never all the tunnels. Smoke generators operated by diesel engines have been ducted into the tunnel works, but they never seem to smoke out all the enemy. Demolition charges have blown out long stretches of tunnel. Entrance holes have been found under stoves in peasants' huts, and sealed.

But with molelike perspicacity, the guerrillas go on digging, and the tunnels continue to expand.

"It wouldn't surprise me to learn," an American officer told me, "that one of these damn tunnels leads right under my desk in Saigon."

The idea is far-fetched, but not as impossible as it sounds.

At the end of World War II, French colonial forces reoccupied the North Vietnamese capital of Hanoi, which, they had every reason to believe, was militarily secure. But Ho Chi Minh's guerrillas had an ugly surprise for the French. One day, the guerrillas came pouring into the heart of Hanoi from a tunnel system the French had never known existed, and all at once Hanoi was at war. The French quickly crushed the city insurrection, and it was to be nine years before the guerrillas again took the city— this time for good.

The digging philosophy of the Vietnamese guerrilla extends to any area through which he passes, even if he is not fighting. Over the years, the Viet Cong has built solid, cleverly concealed fortifications in many thousands of hamlets, against the day when it may have to use them. Innocent-seeming paddy dykes are studded with gun ports; apparently accidental holes in the corners of fields actually are machine-gun emplacements; tall trees contain snipers' nests, and even graveyards become enormous bunker systems.

More often than not today, government operations chase enemy guerrillas into areas where they feel the Viet Cong is cornered, only to find the Viet Cong has moved into one of its own bastions.

At this point the Viet Cong fights with the terrain all on his side. As a rule, government forces then react by hurling artillery, aerial bombs, rockets and napalm at the enemy fortification. Finally, government troops move into the hamlet or thicket (often the following day) and find no Viet Cong anywhere. Sometimes enemy bodies or evidence of casualties have been left behind, but more often there is nothing.

Meanwhile, the young American pilots of the helicopters and fighter bombers return to their bases with rosy reports of the havoc they have wrought on the enemy.

"Nothing could have lived down there," a young Skyraider pilot said once as he stepped from his cockpit. "Considering the concentration of the enemy down there and the sheer volume of stuff we threw at him, we must have killed at least two hundred. That's my estimate, and I think it's a good one."

Seasoned infantrymen rarely agree with these reports, which often are submitted in the form of official enemy casualty statistics.

"I was at Tarawa," an old Marine officer told me once. "All of us thought there couldn't be a Jap left alive on that little island after all the shells and bombs we poured in to soften it up. But I guess you can remember what happened when we hit the beach. You'd think people would have learned from that that bombs and shells and napalm don't necessarily knock out a well-prepared enemy."

Assaulting a Viet Cong tunnel network is normally an exhausting and bloody business, resulting in heavy friendly casualties. The ground over and near the tunnels is invariably studded with thousands of concealed spike foot traps—another specialty of Viet Cong ingenuity. These traps, made of upright nails with barbed points, easily penetrate the sole of a combat boot, and painfully incapacitate a soldier stepping on one. Sometimes they are treated with tetanus-infected buffalo urine to make their wounds even more dangerous.

Recently, the Viet Cong announced that it had manufactured three million of these spiked traps in one small quadrant of the Mekong Delta alone.

Mines and booby traps add to the difficulty of clearing a tunnel field, and snipers are invariably posted at ventilation holes.

"One of them stood up and shot at me," a wounded American captain told me once. "I saw him and drew a bead, but he ducked down just as I fired. I started moving cautiously toward the place I saw him disappear, when another shot came from another spot about fifty yards away. That was the one that got me. I believe it was the same sniper, using another hole."

Entrance holes to tunnels or weapons depots are sometimes underwater in the bank of a canal or water hole, and are accessible only to swimmers who know where to look.

Viet Cong weaponry tends to harmonize with terrain and the soldiers who use the weapons.

In the jungle-covered mountain range extending from fifty miles north of Saigon all the way to North Viet Nam, the war is combat by stealth, characterized by privation and discomfort.

Conventional weapons and ammunition are hard to capture or make in the desolate rain forest, but the primitive tribesmen of the area know well the uses of simpler weapons.

The mountain crossbow is native to the area, and kills silently. This can be important when ambushing with only a small force of guerrillas. The Vietnamese mountain crossbow is very small and light. The bow is about two and a half feet long, but a pull of about a hundred pounds is required to cock its leather string. Its arrows are short spikes of bamboo, fletched with palm fronds. Crossbow arrows have enormous penetration at short range, and often are tipped with a poison chemically similar to curare.

I have heard of cases in which Viet Cong tribesmen carried as many as ten crossbows laced together to make one weapon, firing ten arrows at a single shot.

The Viet Cong in the mountains also have built spear catapults, which they sometimes use even as antiaircraft weapons. In 1963, a U.S. Army helicopter operating in the mountains staggered back to its base with a spear in its belly.

For the disciplined and intelligent Viet Cong guerrilla, any material object is a potential weapon. Slivers of scrap steel are fashioned into daggers and swords. Not long ago, a Viet Cong squad preceded a successful assault on a government outpost by hurling thirty well-filled hornets' nests into the fortification.

Of course, as the Viet Cong fighting organization has grown, it has needed better weapons. Some of these, notably carbines of Russian design, a few Chinese communist SKZ recoilless cannon, machine guns and Czech or Chinese ammunition have reached the Viet Cong by infiltration from North Viet Nam.

Some communist weapons used by the Viet Minh during the Indochina War were left in secret caches when the war ended in 1954, and capture of a communist-made weapon from a Viet Cong guerrilla is not necessarily proof of recent infiltration. Communist-made weapons rarely carry proof marks that would positively identify the year in which they were made.

But substantial quantities of Czech submachine-gun ammunition have turned up in Viet Cong hands near the southern tip of Viet Nam, and ammunition normally is dated. The bases of many of these cartridges are dated 1962 and 1963, furnishing absolute proof of infiltration.

Nevertheless, intelligence experts feel less than 10 per cent and probably more like 2 per cent of the Viet Cong's stock of modern weapons is communist-made. The rest are all captured American weapons.

In his memoirs of the Indochina War, General Vo Nguyen Giap, overlord of the Vietnamese communist armed forces, wrote:

"The sole source of supply could only be the battle front:

to take the material from the enemy to turn it against him. While carrying on the aggression against Viet Nam the French Expeditionary Corps fulfilled another task: it became, unwittingly, the supplier of the Viet Nam People's Army with French, even U.S. arms."

Giap's philosophy is applied exactly the same way today by the Viet Cong, the successor to the army he led to victory at Dien Bien Phu.

There is another aspect of Viet Cong military gadgetry, probably more important than all the others combined: the art of camouflage.

Many writers on Indochina have discussed the proficiency of Vietnamese guerrillas at camouflage, and many of these writings are standard texts, read by senior Vietnamese and American military officials.

It is probably safe to say, nonetheless, that camouflage continues to receive more lip service than application by the Saigon forces and their American advisors.

It is difficult, of course, to camouflage a modern conventional army on the move. Conventional troop units move in masses even when their columns are stretched out, and they cannot avoid detection. Guerrilla units move only in groups of two or three men each, coalescing into battalions and regiments only at the precise time and place at which they have decided to do battle.

The American-equipped and -trained soldier (including the Vietnamese government soldier) wears a steel helmet covered with a camouflage net, and his uniform is sometimes printed in a camouflage pattern. But compared with a well-camouflaged Viet Cong guerrilla, he is a sitting duck.

The Viet Cong often wears a helmet made of wicker and plastic sheeting that looks like an inverted pie tin. It is a much better platform for camouflage foliage than the American helmet. But the guerrilla is not content to pin a few leaves to his hat. His whole body is very often swathed in foliage, and he changes his foliage as he moves from one type of terrain to another.

The black clothing worn by most regional guerrillas is exactly the same clothing as that worn by all Vietnamese peasants, and is, in itself, a form of camouflage.

Guerrillas sometimes dress as women selling fruit and vegetables when infiltrating a hamlet or post.

"When you're not sure, grab 'em between the legs," a U.S. Army Special Forces man told a Vietnamese guard at the gate of one of these hamlets.

Good camouflage is the most important factor in setting up ambushes.

The pilot of a U.S. Army L19 spotting plane recently watched in horror as the Viet Cong ambushed a large government unit moving along a road.

"I was flying low over the convoy, and could see everything perfectly. Everything looked normal, and the fields on the side of the road seemed empty," he said.

"All at once, the whole shoulder of the road, about a half mile long, seemed to lift up and turn into about two hundred men, all of them shooting into the convoy at point-blank range. After the first volley of shots, they charged in and mixed up with the government troops in such close hand-to-hand fighting it all looked like one group. I couldn't have strafed them even if I'd been armed, because I'd have killed government troops too. It was all over quickly, long before reinforcements even got rolling."

The experts agree there is no magic or genius involved in camouflage. Camouflage, they say, is the infinite capacity for taking pains and a psychological outlook that thinks of concealment before anything else. These qualities, in turn, are dependent on military discipline. A unit must be so well disciplined that it does the right things instinctively, without requiring separate orders each time.

More than anything else, this, I believe, is what often gives the Viet Cong the edge over government troops. The Viet Cong regular has many deficiencies as a fighting man, but I believe there can be no argument that he is, in general, a much better disciplined soldier than his government counterpart.

Both communist and anticommunist troops make extensive

use of military gadgetry in Viet Nam. In the following chapter, I shall discuss some of the gadgets working for the Free World.

But I would like to note here what I regard as the essential difference between Viet Cong gadgetry and ours.

Viet Cong gadgetry begins and ends on the battlefield, while ours begins in America and is adapted, for better or worse, to the Vietnamese jungle. When the American gadget proves inadequate for the task, it is sent back to the drawing boards, some of which are in Saigon, but most of which are 10,000 miles away. Supply lines are attenuated, and the American military designer lives in a different world from Viet Nam. This is in no way a criticism of American guerrilla weapons, some of which are excellent. But it seems to me that men who can design Polaris missiles must have the greatest difficulty adjusting their frames of reference to crossbows. And, unfortunately for us, the crossbow is an eminently more practical weapon in Viet Nam than the ballistic missile.

There is another dangerous aspect to the differences between our gadgetries.

Viewed in a certain sense, an American Thompson submachine gun is a work of art. Its hundreds of precision-made parts move together in an efficient, reliable concert of sudden death. If the reader has never examined a Tommy gun close up, I can assure him that it is a very impressive mechanism indeed—the more so, if the beholder has spent the past five years making shotguns out of pieces of pipe.

Consider the guerrilla who has nothing but a water canteen made from a bamboo log, a cloth sleeve over his shoulder containing rice, a pair of cloth shorts, a coolie hat made of palm fronds, sandals made of slabs cut from a rubber tire and fitted with leather thongs, and a dagger made from an old butcher knife.

This guerrilla is a man who must live by his wits and who knows the uses of everything he carries as well as he knows his own body. He cherishes all his possessions.

He may, if he is a clever machinist or has a good friend in the party organization, have obtained a "sky horse gun." If so, he regards it as a wonderful weapon—much more effective than the dagger. It is also a matter of prestige to own a firearm, since only about one out of every three Viet Cong guerrillas has his own gun.

It is not difficult to imagine how this guerrilla would feel if, in the heat of a battle, he managed to capture a Tommy gun and were allowed by his squad leader to keep it. All at once, our guerrilla would have a superb weapon and the prestige of owning the best of all possible battle trophies.

The Tommy gun in his hands becomes a treasured object, to be used against the enemy, but most of all, to be cleaned and cared for, and never, under any circumstances, to be lost.

The Viet Cong do, in fact, take excellent care of the weapons they capture, and use them with the skill that speaks of unstinting practice. In short, they treat their weapons the way all soldiers are supposed to.

Guerrilla gadgetry moves from privation and necessity through ingenuity, and finally to sophisticated weapons.

The tendency in an American-trained and -equipped army is exactly the reverse. When a soldier is issued a weapon, he knows that it is exactly like the weapons issued to everyone else. It would never occur to him to marvel at its efficiency, because he has never been faced with the necessity of making weapons on primitive lathes.

He is trained to take care of his gun, and is theoretically subject to discipline if he breaks it or loses it. But he knows that if something does happen to it, he will merely get a scolding and another weapon will come from America to replace it.

It is not surprising, therefore, that Vietnamese government troops have lost staggering numbers of American weapons and ammunition to the Viet Cong. Vietnamese units, unless they have unusually tough officers (or tough American advisors), often carry new weapons that already are pitted with rust, full of sand, and filthy. A heavy weapon is a heavy burden for a small Vietnamese soldier, and he is apt to dislike it, especially after lugging it for years over waist-deep mud, across canals and through jungle.

In summary, I feel that Viet Cong gadgetry has evolved as part of its fighting spirit and is ideally suited to its human materiel. The guerrillas have learned to take on American helicopters—at first, by putting up millions of bamboo helicopter traps in likely landing areas, later by antiaircraft batteries of captured .50-caliber machine guns.

But even with the captured machine guns, the guerrillas have taught themselves, building mock-up helicopters towed along cables between trees, for gunnery practice.

The whole training and equipping of the communist force is a naturally evolving process, carried on continuously under fire.

Our program, on the other hand, has been geared to adapting the wealth of American technology and military experience to a new and foreign environment. The evolutionary process in some cases has gone backward, as the people who first introduced helicopters now study ways of making better foot traps.

With varying degrees of success, America's armed forces are painfully adapting themselves to the new and often primitive face of war.

Chapter **4**

American Gadgets

There is a proposal current in the United States at this writing calling for the use of America's ultimate military gadget, the atomic bomb, in South Viet Nam's war. As I understand it, the application of this idea would involve either using The Bomb to strip a 900-mile swath of vegetation from South Viet Nam's border, or to so contaminate the entire frontier with radioactive material that no living thing could cross the "hot zone" without lethal results.

Apart from technical considerations, the proposal sheds interesting light on American thinking about Viet Nam, I think. I have known many Americans who feel somehow frustrated and angry that the cream of U.S. military gadgetry has somehow never been adapted for use in this strange war.

Whether or not nuclear weapons ever are used for somewhat exotic purposes here, the thinking behind the nuclear bomb proposals certainly extends to other advanced American gadgets that have been tried here. While many of these ideas have had only indifferent success, others have worked out fairly well.

A case in point has been countercamouflage.

As discussed in the last chapter, the Viet Cong have developed camouflage to a high art—one that government forces in Viet Nam have never been able to match. Discipline and guerrilla warfare techniques have never been developed to the extent that government troops can "see through" Viet Cong camouflage, so U.S. gadgets have been invoked.

One of these is aerial reconnaissance.

In 1962, the U.S. Air Force brought a handful of speedy RF101 jet fighter-reconnaissance planes here, equipped with very ingenious photographic devices.

Batteries of automatic cameras in these planes were rigged to take good pictures at speeds near 400 miles an hour, at various altitudes.

Some of these cameras are timed to take pictures at intervals of several hundred yards, which can later be viewed in a device not unlike the old-fashioned stereopticon. The ground in these pictures is brought into sharp, three-dimensional relief, as it would look to some monstrous observer whose two eyes were a quarter mile apart.

In some cases, normal photographs taken by these planes have shown open rice fields, apparently suited as helicopter landing assault points. But the 3-D pictures have shown the fields studded with camouflaged Viet Cong helicopter stakes, laid out in patterns designed to trap any craft landing in the area.

Other RF101 pictures have revealed, under the scrutiny of experts, underwater bridges across mountain rivers, used as concealed fording places by the guerrillas.

But perhaps the most interesting development is a new type of film, capable of differentiating between normal foliage and camouflage foliage.

Plates developed from this film show normal, living foliage in bright red. But foliage that has been cut more than a few hours ago while still green to the naked eye shows up as a purplish brown on the new film.

Splotches of this telltale color on pictures of jungle taken from 10,000 feet high often have led to air strikes and claims of destroyed communist arms factories and bases.

Obviously, this film cannot be used for spotting camouflaged human beings, because reconnaissance missions and film processing and evaluation take several hours, giving guerrillas plenty of time to move. Still, Air Force photo-evaluation men feel they have a useful gadget.

American jet combat planes so far have not been used on actual strafing and bombing runs in South Viet Nam, but they have found some odd alternate uses.

A tradition that dates back to the dawn of history and is as much a part of Vietnamese national life as rice is the midday siesta.

Throughout Viet Nam, government offices, businesses and shops close up for lunch periods up to three hours long every day. The throbbing, noisy streets of Saigon are dead and deserted at a few minutes past noon every day, taxi drivers slumped over their wheels, and sidewalk vendors curled up on newspaper in doorways.

Farmers stop toiling, water buffalo close their eyes, and even soldiers stop fighting, when they have a chance.

Viet Cong guerrillas themselves, according to captured enemy training documents, try to sleep at least an hour in the middle of the day, if not pressed too hard.

With this in mind, U.S. Air Force jet pilots began flying a siesta-spoiling campaign against the Viet Cong. Operating over known communist base areas in the jungle, American jets would peel off at about 35,000 feet, screaming straight down at full power, faster than the speed of sound, to a pullout at 8,000 or 9,000 feet.

The result of this maneuver is to send a shock wave called a sonic boom straight down. On the ground, this shock wave sounds like a titanic explosion. It shatters glass, raises clouds of dust, panics animals and children, and presumably wakes people up.

There are no indications that siesta-busting jet missions have significantly damaged Viet Cong fighting morale, but such flights must be a satisfaction to pilots used to nothing but official complaints about sonic booms.

Airplanes and helicopters have been rigged with all kinds of interesting gadgets in Viet Nam. The special role of helicopters in Viet Nam has warranted a separate chapter, which follows this one.

But among the more spectacular devices hooked to planes

is a loudspeaker setup so powerful that programs broadcast from 3,000 feet high are clearly audible on the ground. Broadcasts are often pleas to guerrillas in the jungle to surrender. It is an eerie thing to hear a DC-3 droning high overhead, from which a monstrous, celestial voice is enjoining sinners to repent.

Some Air Force tactics are applied to ground operations.

As a rule, when a Vietnamese hamlet or outpost is attacked by enemy guerrillas, it must stand or fall on the strength of its own defenders, since it is almost always impossible to send in reinforcements before sunrise.

American statisticians have calculated, in fact, that the likeliest time for a Viet Cong attack on any given post is 2 A.M.—the worst possible time from the defenders' viewpoint. So the Air Force created a small organization of pilots and planes called the "Dirty Thirty," whose special mission was to drop parachute flares over outposts and hamlets under attack.

Sometimes, fighter planes try to strafe the attackers under the ghostly light of the flares. Virtually every government hamlet and outpost in Viet Nam now has a large wooden frame shaped like an arrow, studded with several dozen fire pots, and mounted on a swivel. During attacks, the arrows are lighted up and pointed in the direction of the attackers, as a guide to the fighter pilots.

Sometimes the tactic works. In some cases, the mere presence of the flare planes has been enough to scare off the guerrillas. In too many cases, however, planes cannot strafe without hitting the hamlets themselves, since the Viet Cong have penetrated too far.

American gadgetry is sometimes held up to scorn in Viet Nam, even by Americans themselves.

The U.S. Air Force organized a group of pilots into a specially trained tactical force called the "Air Commandos," which long was a subject of ridicule by army men. The Air Commandos were permitted to wear all kinds of fancy, nonregulation headgear, often French bush hats with red pompons attached.

"If we could get rid of all the 'Air Gorillas,' all the combat planes and all the artillery pieces," a senior American Army advisor said once, "we'd be a long way toward winning this war.

This war is an infantryman's war, where the rifle is king, and the squad leader is the most important officer."

But the army, too, has come in for its share of gadgets.

A particularly controversial one was the introduction of lie detectors in Viet Nam, as a means of distinguishing innocent farmers from Viet Cong—one of the thorniest problems of the war.

The lie detectors brought to Viet Nam, mostly assigned to military police outfits, were a very simple version of the Winston-Keeler polygraph, depending on the sweating and consequent electrical conductivity of the palms.

Radio Moscow broadcast a fifteen-minute satire in Vietnamese on the use of American lie detectors in Viet Nam, the theme of which was a mythical interrogation of General Paul D. Harkins, the U.S. commander in Saigon.

Surprisingly, American soldiers in the field were less critical. One American felt the lie detector gave military interrogators more a psychological than scientific tool.

"What we do," he said, "is attach the lie detector electrodes to our suspect's hands, and then tell him the gadget will blow his hands off if he tells a fib. The trick often works."

Most of the weapons in Viet Nam are basic World War II types, but there have been some innovations. America's new AR-15 "Armalite" rifle was sent here by the thousand, even though the weapon is not issued to American troops. The Armalite is made mostly of aluminum and Fiberglas, and is correspondingly light and convenient for small Vietnamese soldiers. It fires a special .223-caliber cartridge with a muzzle velocity so high a wound anywhere in the body is often fatal. The weapon can be fired like a submachine gun, with devastating effects.

Another weapon in combat for the first time in Viet Nam is the American M-79 grenade gun. Resembling a shotgun, this weapon fires a 40-millimeter explosive shell which has nearly the same explosive force as a hand grenade. The M-79 was designed to replace both the obsolete light mortar and the old rifle grenade launcher. Soldiers in Viet Nam think highly of it.

American servicemen in Viet Nam love odd personal weapons, which they buy by the thousand from mail order houses, to replace their issued equipment. It is a mark of prestige to own a Colt .45 frontier revolver, a two-barreled derringer pistol of the Jesse James type, a pearl-handled Berretta .25-caliber automatic, or a Swedish "K" submachine gun. Such weapons seem to go well with the odd headgear and specially cut fatigue uniforms favored by Americans in Viet Nam. They seem compatible with the peculiar character of the war itself.

American designers have experimented with pocket flame throwers no larger than aerosol cans, and are working on a new kind of uniform die designed to change colors automatically to match surrounding terrain.

American arms designers have produced a mine called the "Claymore," which has found wide use here. The Claymore, curved like a horseshoe, has an optical sighting device, and hurls a blast of shrapnel directionally at the point toward which it has been pre-aimed. Such mines are useful in mounting ambushes along jungle trails, and the Viet Cong has taken great pains to capture as many of them as possible.

But by far the most widely publicized and controversial bit of American gadgetry in Viet Nam has been defoliation—the destruction of trees and plants by aerial spraying.

The idea of chemical plant destruction occurred to someone after it had been noted that many bloody Viet Cong ambushes jump off from roadside or canalside shrubbery.

Defoliation in Viet Nam began during the French Indochina War. The French often sent out crews of road workers to chop and burn foliage fifty yards or so back from the highway. There were no conclusive results. In any case, Viet Minh propagandists made as much capital as possible from the fact that French crews sometimes destroyed orchards in their defoliation sweeps along roads.

But America adapted planes for the job. A fleet of two-engine C123 transport planes was fitted with large steel tanks, and a herbicide spray made of kerosene and weed-killing chemicals was developed.

For more than a year, the spraying technique was largely

unsuccessful. It turned out that defoliating sprays are only effective when the sap is running, that is, for a relatively brief time each year.

"If only we could pave this whole country over," an American soldier said, "we could start from scratch, with no ambushes to worry about ever again."

Finally, successful spraying began, and a few roads and canals were bared of foliage. Daring C123 pilots hugged the ground as they swept through mountain passes in some of the most dangerous flying this country has seen. The big planes also dumped their spray along a new power line leading from a hydroelectric plant at Danhim 140 miles southwest to Saigon.

Vietnamese Air Force helicopters and planes took to using the spray for another purpose—killing crops in Viet Cong territory.

The idea was to deprive guerrillas in the relatively poor areas of the country from food.

There was an immediate propaganda backlash from all this, which continues every day on Radio Hanoi and other communist outlets.

Defoliation spray, while harmless to animals and plants, is an evil-looking, purple fluid with a bad smell. Dropping such things from the sky generally seems unnatural to the Vietnamese peasant, even when he has been told by government leaflets what to expect and that he should not worry. Viet Cong agents had little difficulty convincing much of the population that America had launched a diabolical new kind of chemical warfare.

Outbreaks of food poisoning and epidemics, which are common in the Vietnamese countryside, were blamed on the American spray.

The Viet Cong issued helpful pamphlets, explaining how to avoid the bad effects of spray. By digging holes at least six feet deep, contaminated produce (anything over which an American plane had flown) could be taken out of harm's way, the leaflets said. Otherwise, anyone near the poisoned vegetables (especially nursing mothers and children) would be subject to horrible diseases and death.

To counteract such propaganda, government psychological warfare teams roamed the countryside eating bread soaked in defoliant spray, washing their faces in it, and so on. But the Vietnamese peasant is apt to look at such demonstrations as mere trickery.

I have many an educated Vietnamese friend who speaks knowingly and matter-of-factly about the American "chemical poison campaign," even after having seen the facts of the situation.

The American poison myth grew. In one community, an old woman sat moaning on a curb one day. Passers-by asking what was wrong were told that an American military advisor had touched her basket of vegetables with a special poison stick, thereby destroying her market stock.

In July, 1964, Cambodia charged that Vietnamese planes had dropped a "deadly yellow powder" over Cambodian hamlets near the border, resulting in the death of seventy-six persons. The charge and all the others like it had a familiar ring to Americans who had served in Korea.

North Korean charges of American germ warfare became so elaborate that visitors to the Kaesong "Peace Pagoda" north of Panmunjom can see to this day a purported photostat of a document authorizing "germ bombs."

Charges like this sound outlandish to American ears, but to an Asian peasant they are apt to seem no less plausible than the existence of airplanes dropping purple spray themselves, of which there is visible evidence.

From a technical standpoint, defoliation is said to destroy about 60 per cent of the vegetation in the affected area. I have yet to see conclusive evidence that defoliation has materially reduced the danger of Viet Cong ambush along roads. Cleared roads give defenders a better field of fire, but they also give guerrillas a better field of fire.

In any case, the Viet Cong guerrilla makes his own foliage—as often as not, a little stack of rice straw to hide under in a foxhole.

Whether or not aerial defoliation will prove to have had

military value in Viet Nam, along roads, canals, national frontiers or anywhere else, is a question that will no doubt be argued for years. But there is no question that defoliation gives the communists a perfect propaganda hook on which to hang a campaign that has hurt the Free World cause badly. On balance, I think the communists got the better of the deal.

America has sought unconventional weapons to fight an unconventional war. The Viet Cong, on the other hand, has been content to fight the war with weapons that are so conventional as to be downright primitive in many cases. I feel that many Americans have failed to grasp the fact that the really unconventional part of this war is that its major weapons are words, not gadgets.

During the Indochina War, the Viet Minh—father of the modern Viet Cong—had no air force, no helicopters, no armor, no battleships, no heavy artillery, no road-building machinery, very few trucks and limited supplies of everything else. Despite this, the Viet Minh defeated the French Army, which had all these things.

Even in the field of propaganda, America and its Vietnamese ally have relied more on propagation techniques than rice-roots political action.

Saigon propaganda ministry reports are filled with the statistics on how many tons of leaflets have been dropped over enemy territory, how many radios and loudspeakers have been installed in how many hamlets, and how many times a propaganda movie has been shown by a mobile team. American experts have fitted out hundreds of little scooter trucks with movie projection equipment, sound systems and leaflet bins at a huge cost. But the emphasis invariably seems to have been on the gadgetry rather than the content.

Meanwhile, the United States has invested vast sums in the design of "counterinsurgency equipment"—special gadgets for fighting the Vietnamese war, especially aircraft.

The Air Force A1E fighter-bomber and the Army's Mohawk fighter-bomber were both more or less specially adapted for this kind of war. Every year, American industry comes up with new "counterinsurgency" gadgets.

Some of them have proved successful in Viet Nam. But a Vietnamese friend told me recently, "Special equipment is a useful adjunct to our war, but it is no substitute for correct military thinking and execution. Let us hope we are not headed into traps like those the French faced in Algeria and here."

Chapter 5

Helicopters

The column of trucks had rumbled through the gate and was parked on the airport's concrete apron. The shadowy forms of troops were organizing themselves into groups of about a dozen each. It would be an hour until dawn, and there were shouting and confusion as Vietnamese NCOs shepherded their men from the trucks into columns in front of the dark forms of the helicopters.

Inside the ready room of the 57th Transportation Company (Helicopter), pilots in their gray-blue nylon coveralls were strapping on pistol belts, checking sector maps and reading notices on the operations board. Mostly young men they were, although a few were balding. Many sported handle-bar mustaches. They were warrant officers and lieutenants, mostly, with a few captains. The enlisted gunners already were out at the helicopters checking fuel levels, instruments and controls.

The pilots yawned from time to time, but listened closely as a major briefed them on the landing zone, the suspected presence of several enemy heavy machine guns that must be skirted, a dangerous tree line, and the other little things that mean life or death for a helicopter pilot.

The thirty pilots pulled their navigation maps with plastic overlays from a big rack and chattered briefly about communications for the day, with frequent references to "Paris Control," Saigon's radar navigation center.

"With any luck we'll be back in time for martini hour," a pilot told his copilot.

"Yeah, if we keep our dog tags together this trip," the copilot said. "I hear Old Vic has two companies of hard hats two clicks from the LZ, and they have reckless rifles. We're going to have to zap a few or they'll really spoil our day."

(Viet Nam, like all the wars in America's history, has produced military jargon. The above remarks mean: "Yes, if we live through this operation. I hear the Viet Cong has about two hundred hard-core, regular guerrillas two kilometers from the landing zone, who have recoilless cannons. We're going to have to shoot a few or they'll hit us badly, kill us.")

Pilots pulled on heavy flak vests lined with bullet-resistant, Fiberglas plates, and slogged along the muddy path to the dark flight line.

Inside the big, banana-shaped H21s, dull blue cabin lights glowed. Pilots climbed up into their plexiglass-surrounded cockpits and slipped on heavy, white flight helmets. Switches were flicked, and red instrument lights glowed from dashboards.

At each helicopter, both gunners waited outside for the starting signal from the two pilots.

"We pull pitch [take off] in ten [minutes]," somebody yelled.

There was a tinkling of metal as resting troops stood up, rearranging their field packs. The packs were loaded with cooking utensils, and here and there a live duck hung by its feet from a soldier's pistol belt. The Vietnamese army, perhaps more than other armies, travels on its stomach.

It was time. Somewhere in the night, a pilot yelled to his gunner outside, "Clear?" "Clear, sir," the answer came back. The engine in the tail of the big machine churned as the starter cut in, a blast of smoke surged from the huge exhaust pipe, and a plume of blue flame shot into the night. All along the flight line, engines started with an ear-shattering roar.

Pilots adjusted themselves in their seats, changed their engine mixtures, and tuned up radios for communications checks. Forward gunners took their positions at the open doors on the right side of the H21s, just behind the cockpit. They fed belts of ammunition into their guns, and swung the gun mounts around into firing position. Rear gunners gestured from their positions at open doors on the left side near the tail for the troops to come aboard. Each of the little Vietnamese soldiers got a helping hand up the high step from the door gunner.

Idling motors speeded up, transmission shafts along the ceiling of each craft began to whine, and the twin rotors began to turn. Red signal beacons on each helicopter were now blinking along the flight line.

The troops sat or squatted on the aluminum floor, since there were no seats. A few lighted cigarettes.

Pilots were tuned to several communications frequencies, and listening to all of them simultaneously. To pass the remaining few minutes before take-off, some had tuned in the armed forces radio station in Saigon as well, and were listening to an undertone of jazz along with the messages.

The helicopters were rolling forward now, out on a runway, one behind the other.

Pilots revved up their engines and pulled up gently on levers in the floor left of their seats, coarsening the pitch of their rotors just enough to "feel" whether the engine was putting out enough power to lift the machine. All the helicopters were up to par this morning.

The signal came, and the helicopters roared off down the runway, much like conventional airplanes taking off. Hovering or taking off vertically puts too much load on the engine of a loaded H21.

The predawn lights of Saigon sparkled below the wheeling fleet of helicopters as they maneuvered into formation, and the first tint of approaching sunrise gleamed in reflection from the curving Saigon River. The ungainly machines labored up to 3,000 feet, and the city was gone. The moon had come from behind clouds now, and sparkled brilliantly in the flat, flooded rice fields below. Through the oval portholes along the sides of the helicopters, the red of sunrise began to flood the cabins with light.

The operation was on its way now, flying at about eighty miles an hour southwest of Saigon to a target about a half hour away. There was time for cigarettes all around. Three thousand feet is a safe altitude where nothing much can go wrong.

The objective, a hamlet in the northern part of the Mekong River Delta, reportedly was currently occupied by about two companies of regular Viet Cong troops, that is from 200 to 400 well-armed professionals.

Like most hamlets in the delta, this one was strung for a half mile or so along a canal, hedged in by palm and pineapple trees the bamboo. A dense tree line separated the hamlet from the planned landing zone, an open rice field. Since the rear door where the troops must unload is on the left side of helicopters, the whole formation would have to land with its left flank facing the tree line. The landing must not be so close to the tree line that enemy fire would cut the helicopters to pieces, nor must it be so far as to exhaust the troops running through the thick mud and water toward their objective. For this operation, a landing spot 200 yards from the tree line seemed appropriate. The pilots had their fingers crossed.

The watery, green patchwork of rice fields, canals and stands of palm trees slid by below. The homes of farmers stood out as neat, green squares dotted across the plain. Vietnamese peasants plant their fruit trees and pineapples in perfect rectangles surrounding their huts, affording both privacy and a pleasant break in the featureless, flat, rice terrain.

Ten minutes to go, and time to let down to contour flying. Helicopter pilots in Viet Nam have found that by far the most dangerous altitude from the standpoint of enemy ground fire is 700 feet. They like to pass through this particular height as fast as possible and as far away from enemy concentrations as possible.

The nose of the helicopter dipped down abruptly, and troops put their hands to their ears in pain from the sudden change in altitude air pressure. The ground leapt up until the entire formation had leveled out a scant ten feet high, charging at top speed across the paddies.

Herds of water buffalo swept into the pilots' field of vision, stampeding out of the way of the roaring H21s. Pilots squeezed their pitch control levers just enough to pull their machines over trees and huts, then back down "on the deck." Gunners no longer smoked, but crooked their fingers over the triggers of their .30-caliber machine guns, swinging the guns toward spots that might conceal snipers. At this altitude, the sound of an approaching helicopter does not travel far, and there were high hopes of catching the enemy by surprise.

Five miles away, four miles, three miles, and the tree line was now visible ahead. Suddenly, the whole formation banked steeply to the right, skimming along parallel to the tree line.

"We're drawing fire from those huts about ten o'clock from the flight," one of the lead helicopters radioed. The guns began to chatter, and orange tracers floated in toward the huts. Bushels of spent cartridges and machine-gun belt links spewed from the door guns over the tensely waiting troops inside.

Outside, the crackling of small arms fire was audible from the tree line, and an occasional puff of smoke marked the spot where one of the Viet Cong had fired.

It was time to land. The nose tilted up, and the big helicopter slowed and settled toward the ground like an ungainly bird. The troops were standing now, bunched near the rear door, close to the smoking hot machine gun.

The tall rice lashed in wild waves across the field and clouds of spray rose near the helicopters, as their beating rotors blasted a hurricane downward.

A noise like that of a sledge hammer against a kettledrum sounded in the helicopter, and a few troops were speckled with blood spots where slivers of metal had hit them. The slug had left a silvery, jagged hole in the side of the machine and torn scores of flying fragments from an aluminum structural beam.

The helicopter jounced down into the paddy, water coming up nearly to the doorframe. The troops began leaping out, each getting a friendly whack on the shoulder from the American door gunner. As they jumped, they ran, hip deep in mud and water, holding their rifles high. The fifth soldier out of the helicopter took only ten steps before his face abruptly turned into a mass of red jelly, and he slumped to the ground. All twelve soldiers were out now, and the machine gun was back in firing position. The first few shots headed toward the tree line, and then the arc of fire swept aimlessly up into the sky. The gunner was hit.

Its rotors flapping wildly, the H21 heaved itself from its berth into the air, its dangling nose wheel skimming through the water. A few hundred yards away a column of orange flame and dense black smoke erupted from the field. One of the other H21s was down and out, perhaps hit by a recoilless cannon shell.

The rice field was dropping away now. Black-clad figures, some of them carrying rifles, were out in the open here, apparently caught by surprise by the helicopters. Now it was the turn of the right door gunner, who kept his finger locked on the trigger until the cabin was choking with the sweet-acid smell of burned powder.

One after another, the little black figures fell and lay still as geysers of mud and water flicked up around them.

The helicopter climbed painfully to 1,000 feet, and the right gunner dashed back to his wounded buddy. The round had gone through the soldier's chest near his shoulder, but he was alive and conscious.

Keeping his balance by holding metal beams, the right gunner moved back along the lurching helicopter, braced himself from slipping on the blood-slick floor, and hauled his wounded crew mate away from the door.

Flak jackets can stop spent bullets and shrapnel fragments, but they do not stop direct hits. The right gunner unzipped his buddy's pierced flak jacket and unbuttoned the bloody fatigue shirt underneath. Using the pressure dressings from both the wounded man's pistol belt and his own, the gunner pressed to stop the blood. The wounded man groaned, and his buddy lighted a cigarette and stuck it between his lips. It would be thirty minutes back to Saigon, with nothing else to do.

The latest American casualty would soon be on his way to the U.S. Army field hospital at Nha Trang, a coastal town northeast of Saigon once known as the finest ocean resort in South Viet Nam.

On the ground, the troops were pinned down and scarcely moving at all. For a half hour they had tried to inch forward, half-swimming, half-crawling toward the tree line. A number of soldiers had been hit, no one knew just how many. Another helicopter group would soon be bringing reinforcements, and meanwhile, four single-engine fighters were pouring cannon shells and rockets into the tree line.

Mortars were in action now, too, and the gray puffs of their shells could be seen behind the trees. From time to time, groups of a dozen or so troops would stand up, firing their automatic rifles and Tommy guns, and running forward a few feet. The enemy fire slacked off, but progress still was agonizingly slow.

By noon, the first troops were trickling into the tree line and the huts behind. The fighting had stopped, the enemy was gone, and the huts were nearly deserted. Here and there a mother nursed her baby, or a child peered from behind a bamboo curtain. But there were no men or older boys.

Earthworks littered with spent ammunition attested to an enemy who had been around very recently. Smears of blood on some of the fortifications were still wet. But there were no bodies, no wounded men.

Beyond the hamlet was a wide canal that could be forded only by sampan, and beyond it more trees. Presumably the enemy was there somewhere.

But it was noon, the blazing sun stood high in the sky, and the troops were hungry. Many of the soldiers already were stretched out on the big polished tables in the huts, or under the shady palm-frond awnings in front. Some had whacked the tops from coconuts, and were gulping down the sweet milk. A few had their pots boiling and were cooking rice. The order called for moving into this hamlet, and before anyone would go farther after the enemy, more orders from Saigon would be needed.

Some soldiers had found and raided a large supply of duck eggs in one hut, and were laughing as they carried them over to their field mess, under the hard eyes of an old woman who lived in the hut. An intelligence officer with a thin, scholarly face was making the rounds of the huts, asking how many Viet Cong there were and where they had gone. At each hut he was told, "I don't know, I didn't see them, I only heard a lot of shooting." Each time he would move on, sighing with resignation.

The operation would continue several days, covering more ground, exchanging a few shots with snipers, searching a few more huts. But for practical purposes, it was over already. If there were 200 Viet Cong around, they were gone now, and had had ample time to break up into small, innocent-looking groups, who could safely bide their time until the raiders had left.

In due course, the government would issue a communique: "Elements of the Seventh Division in helicopters of the U.S. Army's 57th Company attacked an estimated battalion of Viet Cong in Ap —— hamlet of Dinh Tuong Province. After a two-hour clash, the enemy was routed and the objective seized. The Viet Cong suffered an estimated fifty killed, carried off by the enemy, and friendly troops seized fifteen pounds of documents, two grenades, a French MAS-36 rifle with six rounds of ammunition, and captured five Viet Cong suspects. Friendly forces suffered twelve killed including two Americans, and twenty-three wounded, including four Americans."

That was fairly typical of thousands of helicopter operations in South Viet Nam for the first few years. Many operations, of course, produced no enemy contact at all, and others resulted in major fights with heavy casualties. But the pattern was usually the same.

There were refinements in tactics on both sides as the war went along, of course.

The U.S. Marine Corps, which had two companies (or rather, squadrons, as they call them) of troop-carrying helicopters almost from the beginning, worked along with the army groups. The marines use H34 helicopters, single-rotor aircraft that will carry the same number of troops or slightly more than the army H21. In 1964, some of the H34s were turned over to the Vietnamese Air Force, which began using them on helicopter operations of its own.

Helicopter warfare underwent a major innovation in late 1962 when the first of a new type of helicopter, the Bell UH1A, began arriving here. The UH1A, powered by a turbine engine, was much more powerful and faster than the obsolete H21s, although it would carry only seven or eight troops.

The first dozen or so of these machines, armed with four forward-firing machine guns and rocket pods, were organized into a unit called the Utility Tactical Transport Company. They were assigned the job of flying shotgun for the lumbering troop carriers, and in practice their mission was basically similar to fighter plane escorts.

This similarity led to an immediate controversy between the U.S. Army and the U.S. Air Force. At this writing, the Air Force still objects to the use the Army has made of the UH1A and the still more powerful UH1B, on grounds, essentially, that the Army has muscled in on Air Force territory.

In any case, it became clear to the Army that something would have to be done to replace the old H21s, which had not been manufactured since the late 1950s, and which were being rapidly worn out or shot to pieces in South Viet Nam. The last H21 flight in South Viet Nam was in the spring of 1964, and from that time on, all U.S. Army helicopter units in the country were equipped exclusively with the UH1A and UH1B, both for escort duty and for carrying troops.

Pilots were proud of their new "Hueys" ("huey" being the closest pronounceable approximation of the letter designation UH1A of the aircraft). Hueys were called "the Cadillacs of chopper warfare."

Army development centers quickly added fillips to the Hueys to give them as much firepower as World War II fighters. Four M60 machine guns outside the helicopter above the landing skids were mounted in electrically controlled, movable turrets. The copilot, in his left-hand seat, was given a highly accurate electronic sight suspended from the cockpit ceiling. Grasping the handle of the sight, the copilot could aim it at any target in front of him or off to the sides. In aiming the sight, electric servomotors in the gun mounts automatically aim the guns.

Also mounted over the skids were rocket pods containing eight (or in later modifications, six) rockets each. Each of the 2.75-inch rockets carries an explosive nose large enough to blow a hut to pieces. On the ground, these rockets make a horrifying roar as they speed toward their targets, which no doubt has a psychological effect. They are not always reliable. On one firing pass, the writer was sitting next to a rocket pod when it was torn to pieces by the folding fins of one of the rockets. The fins had protruded prematurely, before the missile had left its rack. The helicopter was jolted to a near stop in mid-air. In common with all bombs and shells, rockets can be set off if hit by tracer bullets, and mounted as they are outside the helicopters, they are highly exposed.

This fact probably accounted for the destruction of one Huey, in Kien Hoa Province near the mouth of the Mekong River. While making a strafing run on a powerfully armed Viet Cong defense perimeter, the Huey blew up in mid-air, and its fragments scattered over hundreds of square yards. All four crew members were killed.

Like human beings, helicopters can be killed by single bullets. At the same time, a hail of bullets may pass through them without happening to hit anything vital. I have seen many an H21 limp back to base with as many as thirty hits. But on one operation, in the Ca Mau Peninsula at the southern tip of Viet Nam, I happened to be in an H21 that was brought down by just one small-caliber carbine bullet. The bullet entered the helicopter's side two feet from where I was sitting, near the rear door. It tore through a pressure line and four engine control cables.

The pilot reacted swiftly, saving my life and those of his three crew mates. All helicopters are equipped with clutches which can be disengaged, throwing the rotors into free-wheeling "autorotation." If the helicopter is traveling forward fast enough, the rotors will continue to whirl, keeping the aircraft up enough so that it can glide in for a landing. Obviously, forward speed is essential to this maneuver, and if a helicopter is not flying fast enough, the pilot must make it dive to get up speed. He cannot do this if he is too near the ground. For this reason, slow-speed flight at an altitude lower than about two hundred feet can be fatal in the event of engine failure.

Our pilot was just barely within the minimum specifications for crash-landing, and we settled into a thicket of brambles, machine guns from our doors blasting in all directions. It happened that the Viet Cong—in this case, perhaps just one lucky sniper—failed to follow up his advantage, and eventually another helicopter came to pull us out.

There is an evacuation drill that all helicopter crews must go through if they are downed in Viet Nam. Besides getting themselves out of their aircraft, they must remove all the guns—four mounted guns and at least two machine guns hand-held by the door gunners. They must also take as much of the ammunition as possible. If it looks as though the Viet Cong is certain to capture the aircraft, it must be destroyed. The guerrillas love to capture guns and radios from downed helicopters.

The Viet Cong has never shown mercy to downed helicopter men, and has never taken one alive. In one downing, in mountains 250 miles north of Saigon, guerrillas moved in on the wreckage, where they found a wounded pilot strapped in his seat. Two other crew members were dead, and the fourth had escaped into the jungle without knowing there was another survivor. The wounded pilot was later found by rescue crews, shot through the head at point-blank range. This pilot, incidentally, was a colonel.

Communist North Viet Nam has issued a series of postage stamps in four colors, depicting the shooting down of helicopters by guerrillas.

On a statistical basis, helicopters have contributed more American casualties than any other aspect of the war in Viet Nam.

The experts have tried to make them safer. In some models, armor plate has been installed around the pilots' seats and around important transmission and control lines. In most cases, helicopter companies have removed all but the pilot armor, because they don't like the extra weight and consequent loss of speed and power. But the whole crew wears flak vests, and gunners usually sit on extra flak vests or steel plates.

Frayed engine cables have been replaced and improved (usually after fatal accidental crashes), rotor cotter pins have been strengthened, and other safety measures adopted.

But helicopters have often flown on little more than sheer on-the-spot ingenuity. I once saw a helicopter crew, whose craft had been downed by a bullet through a pressure line, fashion a plug from a wood stake they found in the field, ram it into the hole, and take off again.

On another operation, an H21 had just unloaded its troops in an assault zone and was taking off when one of the two rear wheels hit a paddy dyke concealed under water. The wheel broke off completely and the strut was rammed up into the fuselage, where it tore the main fuel tank. Viet Cong machine gunners were pouring fire at the helicopters, and an emergency landing was out of the question.

Under full power, the helicopter streaked for its base fifteen minutes away, a trail of high-octane gasoline gushing from its tail. The pilot signaled ahead for ground crews to quickly assemble sandbags into a cradle high enough for the H21 to land on without tipping over.

At the airstrip, the big H21 tried to settle down on the improvised cradle, only seconds of fuel remaining. A landing on flat ground would mean tipping over, and the rotors would break up, beating the helicopter to pieces and probably killing the crew. There were not enough sandbags, and the pilot had to think of something else fast. He spotted a water-filled ditch fifty yards away, picked up the helicopter, and slid it into the ditch at exactly the moment the engine quit. The crew got out without a scratch.

Others have not been so lucky. Helicopter crashes resulting purely from mechanical failures are common in Viet Nam, and have contributed heavily to the casualty rate.

Conditions for flying helicopters here are always terrible. For one thing, the war keeps them flying much longer hours than those for which they were designed, carrying staggering loads.

For another, it is usually hot in Viet Nam, and hot air lacks the density and lift of cooler air. This makes it harder for any flying machine to stay up, and engines must put out more power. The problem is more severe in the jungle-covered mountains of central Viet Nam, where high altitudes make the air even thinner.

During Viet Nam's monsoon season, helicopters must fly in

and out of rainstorms on most missions. Rain itself can be damaging to helicopter rotor blades, and they wear out often. The H21 had laminated wood rotors that were rapidly eroded by flailing against raindrops.

Viet Cong gunnery has improved markedly during the war, and with .50-caliber machine guns, the guerrillas can bring down helicopters easily, even when they are flying evasively at fairly high altitudes.

The philosophy behind the use of helicopters in Viet Nam is based on the idea of lightning assaults by large troop units in remote places.

In the early 1950s, when the U.S. Army began to experiment with helicopter tactics, the machines were used in much the same way landing craft are used against enemy beaches. Areas in which troops were landed by helicopter were called "airheads."

In Viet Nam, government troops outnumber Viet Cong guerrillas (although the ratio continues to shift in favor of the Viet Cong), but not nearly enough. During the long British campaign in Malaya against communist guerrillas, the experts concluded that it takes ten or twelve regular soldiers to neutralize one enemy guerrilla.

At best, government forces in Viet Nam never have enjoyed an edge of more than six or seven to one over the guerrillas, and in certain key districts the guerrillas actually outnumber the troops.

To offset this disadvantage, Saigon and its American ally decided on helicopters. Troops cannot be moved rapidly on land because there is only one railroad line (which is sabotaged almost daily), very few roads (also constantly sabotaged) and relatively few canals that are not blocked, sabotaged or ambushed by the Viet Cong. Even the job of clearing a road or canal is a major military operation, the fruits of which are generally undone within a few days by the enemy.

So when helicopters began arriving in Viet Nam, they were put to work ferrying whole regiments into virgin territory.

Vietnamese commanders were delighted with the new toys. Generals like Huynh Van Cao, whose territory included the

whole Mekong River Delta, spent days or weeks planning elaborate operations over huge areas. Plans always included huge
sector maps with plastic overlays, grease pencils in at least six different colors, and teams of staff officers to post the position of
blocking forces, artillery positions and so forth. Such maps always
exactly showed the Viet Cong positions, too, with the estimated
strength of the enemy in each place. They were nearly always
wrong.

But the cumbersome planning was always the subject of
much enthusiastic discussion. It was rare in those days that one
could not go to any downtown Saigon bar and learn in detail the
plans of an operation scheduled up to a week hence. The Viet
Cong probably also patronized the bars.

Viet Cong intelligence in Saigon was demonstrated in late
December, 1961, just after the USNS Core had brought the first
load of helicopters to Saigon. Within a few days, Radio Hanoi
broadcast not only the numbers and types of aircraft that had
been brought in, but their serial numbers as well.

For about a year and a half, the helicopters were used only
for massive and usually unsuccessful raids. Troops brought into
assault areas would move forward, rendezvous with other units,
occupy hamlets, and do all the things called for on the master
plan. Occasionally, by accident, government units stumbled into
enemy units, and there were sometimes bloody clashes.

But usually, mopping up an area merely meant marching
through it, picking up some suspects and raiding the henhouses,
and then waiting for the helicopters to take the troops back to
headquarters.

U.S. helicopter companies and American Army advisors generally had very little hand in the planning of these operations.
The Vietnamese commanders looked on the pilots as little more
than bus drivers. The only lever Americans could bring on the
Vietnamese was a negative one—threatening to recommend re-
moval of helicopters from a command to some other sector
where they could be more effectively used.

But fairly early in the game, the two U.S. Marine helicopter
squadrons, which at the time were stationed in the delta, began

evolving a new helicopter tactic they called "eagle flights."

Eagle flights rarely comprised more than five helicopters loaded with tough troops, often Vietnamese rangers or marines. They were not given specific objectives, but were told general areas where intelligence indicated Viet Cong strong points.

The eagle flights would cruise around looking for trouble. Vietnamese observers went along to spot enemy guerrillas, and the helicopters (powerful H34s) flew at altitudes inviting enemy ground fire. The first sign of enemy resistance would be met by an assault on the spot.

Eagle flights produced some results. Helicopters were often hit, but troops got into bloody fights with the enemy much more frequently than in the big, planned operations. Often, the eagle troops racked up excellent successes against enemy units, and brought back weapons and severed heads as trophies.

Some Vietnamese commanders objected strenuously, on grounds that the eagle flights were too dangerous and were piling up too many friendly casualties. It was reliably reported that Ngo Dinh Diem himself was unhappy with them.

After Diem's overthrow and death on November 2, 1963, the war in general almost stopped. Helicopter companies found themselves without missions day after day. Vietnamese commanders were shifted around or ousted, new tactics were discussed, confusion and apathy rose, and the Viet Cong politico-military war machine moved steadily ahead.

But emerging from the chaos was at least a government ready to work closely with American advisors, both in Saigon and in the field. As the war effort painfully got back into gear, the new emphasis was on small, fast-moving operations, leaving the big units on a semipermanent basis in the areas designated for "pacification."

Changes in helicopter tactics evolved. For one thing, all army units in Viet Nam were equipped with "hueys" by mid-1964, and hueys are not mere flying trucks, but have some of the characteristics of fighter planes as well.

Each of the new helicopters has a machine gunner in the open doors on each side. The escort helicopters also have the four electrically operated guns and rocket pods. Each troop-carrying company of twenty helicopters includes a platoon of five armed escorts. For most big missions, the Utility Tactical Transport Company, renamed the 68th Helicopter Company, adds its fire-power. The 68th helicopters generally go into an assault area first to soften it up with rockets and machine-gun fire, exactly the way fighter planes carry out similar missions. Sometimes they are accompanied by Air Force fighters, sometimes not.

Technically, the rules of this war do not permit Americans to shoot unless they feel they are in danger of being shot. This rule can be broadly interpreted. In any case, the helicopters and fighters invariably attack at the first indication of ground fire.

Then comes a column of troop-carrying helicopters, flying in tight formation with its platoon of heavily armed escorts weaving around on its flanks, looking for all the world like cavalrymen.

At the objective, only the troop-carrying helicopters land. All the escort machines continue flying circles over the area, firing at enemy resistance as it develops. The escorts generally leave with the troop carriers.

There are strong arguments both in favor of and against heli-copter warfare in Viet Nam. Those in favor already have been discussed.

But opponents of helicopters feel, in the first place, they are too easy to shoot down or trap. Well-trained paratroopers could be moved into assaults just as effectively using actual airdrops, they say.

But a more subtle argument against helicopters is that they tend to create a reliance on the part of Vietnamese troops and commanders on gadgetry. All troops tend to be lazy and generally prefer riding to walking. But the Vietnamese war tends to stalk along jungle trails, not in open fields or in strong points of the von Clausewitz type. Some of the most effective missions against communist units have been the work of patient, disciplined squads, willing to set up ambushes night after night along paths used by the Viet Cong.

"After all," a U.S. Army infantry advisor told me once, "the Viet Cong have no helicopters or airplanes. They didn't have any during the Indochina War either, but they still won. Helicopters are a partial substitute for infantry discipline, dedication and energy. They are useful in emergencies. But they are no substitute for first-class infantrymen willing to fight.

"After all, when you come to think of it, the use of helicopters is a tacit admission that we don't control the ground. And in the long run, it's control of the ground that wins or loses wars."

Of course, helicopters are used for many things besides carrying troops into assaults. One of their more important functions is ferrying Vietnamese provincial officials out to hamlets and district capitals to collect taxes, count noses and administer. In many areas, the only link between isolated islands of government control and the central government is the helicopter.

Helicopters are used constantly to bring ammunition, supplies and even food to beleaguered outposts. It has been effectively argued that there should be no isolated outposts in the first place, since they are too easy for the Viet Cong to overrun and sack for weapons. But the outposts still exist, and probably will continue to do so.

A detachment of helicopter ambulances (known by the code word "dustoff") also flies almost continuous missions, often under extremely hazardous conditions. At least one flight surgeon with the unit has been nominated for the Silver Star for his gallantry in picking up and treating wounded troops under heavy fire at night.

Night helicopter operations have become routine, and are primarily directed against Viet Cong onslaughts against outposts. The helicopters are guided to the outposts by "Paris Control," a radar navigation network operated from Saigon. Over the targets, post defenders mark the enemy with flares, lighted signals and their own tracer fire. Sometimes helicopter pilots can see the enemy's muzzle blasts. It is always a dangerous kind of mission, because the enemy is always very close to friendly troops.

Helicopter crews and the mechanics who keep the machines flying generally get home to soft beds, good meals and a beer or two at the local service club every night. But they lead lives that could scarcely be envied by infantrymen.

Casualty rates are very high, and crews must keep flying day after day on increasingly dangerous missions. Those who live at Saigon airport sleep in shacks little better than quonset huts, sweltering hot at night. They have good field messes, a PX, several service clubs, and get to see movies every night. But they rarely have time or energy to get downtown to Saigon.

At other helicopter bases, conditions are even less attractive. At Soc Trang in the Mekong River Delta, the monsoon season invariably inundates everything but the airstrip and hangars themselves, and the town of Soc Trang is usually off-limits to American servicemen. Up the coast in Central Viet Nam, the city of Da Nang has a good ocean beach and the most attractive night life outside Saigon. But there, again, helicopter crewmen are normally restricted to their base because of the pressure of their work. Very few of them are ever sorry to leave Viet Nam.

Pilots of the helicopters seem to keep getting younger each year, as the schools at Fort Rucker and other helicopter centers in the States churn out replacements for Viet Nam. There are eighteen- and nineteen-year-old warrant officers flying here at this writing, some of them already sporting the handle-bar mustaches that are almost traditional with helicopter men.

Helicopter traditions and even unit historians have begun to flourish. I once wrote a feature story on the 57th Helicopter Company, one of the first two companies to arrive in Viet Nam, in which I referred to the unit's men as "the deans of helicopter warfare." The name stuck, and men of the 57th and its successor company, the 120th, now wear the word "deans" on their uniforms. Among them are veterans of several wars, and beardless privates. There are outspoken publicity hunters, and there are modest, quiet men who just work. There are helicopter men who earned the title "soldier of the month" in army competitions, and there are helicopter men continually in trouble with the MPs.

But as a subjective judgment, it seems to me that the American helicopter men in Viet Nam are as efficient, hard-working, dedicated and courageous a group of U.S. servicemen as I have ever run across. Like all Americans, some of them are brilliant, some of them are stupid, and most are somewhere in between. Their missions are often frustrating and unsuccessful, and when they are shot up day after day by enemy forces, their morale is sometimes low. In 1963 after an engagement at the hamlet of Ap Bac, in which fourteen out of fifteen helicopters were hit and several downed, some helicopter man wrote about fifteen verses of a song called "On Top of Old Ap Bac, All Covered With Blood." The lyrics were clever, cynical, and highly derogatory to Vietnamese troops, the Saigon and Washington governments, the commanding general, Paul D. Harkins, and everyone else involved in the fight. But the helicopter men went right on working and fighting as they sang "On Top of Old Ap Bac."

The lyricist (whose name I will not mention, since he is still in the Army) was badly wounded not long after writing his verses, while firing his door gun with devastating results into a Viet Cong bunker.

It is almost axiomatic that a soldier fights because he wants to preserve the good opinion of his buddies. He very often fights because his buddies have been killed, and he has come to hate the enemy.

Oddly enough, I have yet to hear an American helicopter pilot say he hates the Viet Cong. Pilots and gunners have not run wild with the relaxation of orders that they must shoot only in self-defense. Pilots and gunners generally hold their fire until they are sure their targets are enemies. Many a gunner has been too softhearted to kill single Viet Cong guerrillas running in panic across open fields, even when rifles were visible.

Viet Cong military prowess has impressed many Americans in Viet Nam, and some helicopter men frankly respect their enemy.

I returned from an operation once in a Huey that also was carrying a wounded Viet Cong prisoner, his arms bound behind him, and a Vietnamese Army lieutenant. The lieutenant was on a seat between the two American door gunners, and the prisoner was on the floor in front of the officer. As the helicopter took off, the prisoner groaned slightly, and the officer gave him a sharp kick. One of the American gunners lost his temper and did something that could have (but did not) get him court-martialed.

Yanking the Vietnamese officer roughly by the shoulder, the gunner yelled, "Knock it off, you! The Viet Cong are better soldiers than you'll ever be, and this man deserves at least the proper treatment of a prisoner of war."

Many helicopter men, in common with Americans in Viet Nam in general, are puzzled and worried about the political implications of this strange war.

It strikes me as a testament to American fighting efficiency that helicopter men go on doing as good a job as ever in the face of potential sudden death, despite all the uncertainties. They are good soldiers.

Chapter 6

Ambush

Ambushes continue to take place. When you analyze an ambush you can always tell in retrospect what was done wrong. Many of them take place at the end of the day when people are tired and they assume the day's work has been done, and they're simply returning home.

Everybody, I'm sure, from [South Vietnamese Premier] General Khanh on down on that side, and General [William C.] Westmoreland [commander of U.S. forces in Viet Nam] down on our side is unhappy about ambushes. General Westmoreland has spent a lot of time thinking about this and consulting with his advisors, studying the ambushes, recommending the use of aircraft overhead, asking advisors to recommend [to the Vietnamese] improved tactical security—people out front, people on the flanks, people in plain clothes. Whether or not this has had any effect at the present moment, I just don't know. . . .

Ambushes are placed where no American soldier would expect one. For example, we've been trained to expect an ambush where the road goes through a tree line or through a defile—in other words, where we would put an ambush. And yet, we have all seen ambushes that have been put along roads right out in the open, against all the tactical principles that one has ever been taught. As a matter of fact, if I were commanding a rifle company and I were moving across a wide-open space with a road entering a woods, in accordance with my training, I would be concerned about an ambush at the wood line. But I wouldn't, until I came over here [Viet Nam], have been concerned about an ambush out in the middle of an open field. And yet, we're finding them. . . .

Our fervent hope is that they'll [the Viet Cong will] stick their neck out with about six battalions around here some day and try to hold something, because as of that time, they've had it. We can move more battalions to any point in Viet Nam faster than they can and keep feeding them in, and the Vietnamese Army can beat the Viet Cong in a stand-up fight any day of the week, and the best thing that could happen to defeat the VC would be to have them come out in the open and fight. . . .

In due course, this [ambush] challenge has got to be met, and it can't be met by putting troops up and down the highway in a defensive position. It eventually has to be met by offensive operations against the VC units that are operating in the general area.

You can't defend a road effectively against ambush. The road's too long, unless you put twenty battalions along the road, which aren't available. But if you strung out six or seven battalions along the road, even then, at night, at any one point on the road, the density of troops would be less than what you could bring in against it, so that is a forlorn strategy, to try to hold the road defensively. The only way to keep the road open is to attack the VC units, which in turn have been attacking the road. . . .

The VC are excellent at ambushes, but that's kind of a coward's way of fighting the war, and almost anybody, if you can open fire with an overwhelming volume of fire at the beginning and get the psychological advantage, anybody's army would have a hard time withstanding it, and anybody else's army would have a good chance of success.

But if you catch them out in the open, where they've got to maneuver and move and react to new situations, I don't think the VC are ten feet high.[1]

A few days before Christmas, 1961, a young American soldier, Sp4 James T. Davis of Livingston, Tennessee, was riding with ten Vietnamese soldiers in a big "deuce and a half" truck a dozen or so miles from Saigon. It was to have been Davis's first Christmas away from home, and his thoughts may have been straying back to Tennessee. The road was good, and there was no reason to worry about anything in particular.

Without warning, a huge blast erupted from a mound of earth at the side of the road, smashing the truck like a toy, and spewing bloody troops in all directions.

Davis was alive and mad, and his carbine had been loaded.

[1] Excerpts from the transcript of a press conference given October 6, 1964, in Saigon by Brigadier General William E. DePuy, operations officer of the U.S. Military Assistance Command for Viet Nam, following a month of particularly bloody Viet Cong ambushes against Saigon units.

He managed to empty two magazines of cartridges at the attackers. But the men in the bushes had machine guns. And so, on December 22, 1961, Specialist Davis became the first American serviceman to die in combat with the Viet Cong. It is in keeping with the character of this war that Davis died in an ambush.

At this writing, more than two hundred other Americans have died fighting in Viet Nam. The majority of them have died in airplanes or helicopters, but the major share of the rest have died in ambushes. A general's son was among them. Some have known they would be ambushed, but were powerless to prevent it. They just couldn't persuade the Vietnamese officers they were assigned to advise to take the security measures they felt were essential.

The people who fall prey to ambushes may be petty officials riding in lone vehicles, or generals riding in armored convoys. Ambushes may happen in the dead of night or at high noon; in the depths of the jungle or in open fields; in relatively secure areas or in Viet Cong base areas. The one thing they all have in common is that the Viet Cong is almost always in the superior position, both in terms of numbers and firepower, and in terms of the element of surprise.

I once visited a place called Dong Xoai on National Route 14 a few hours after one of the typical big ambushes. It happened this way:

The rich, alluvial flatlands of the Mekong River Delta extend north to Saigon. But north of Saigon, the verdant rice fields trail off into uncultivated jungle, dotted here and there with enormous rubber plantations. The rubber trees and scrub growth of the jungle look from the air like a continuous, green canopy, slashed in places by narrow roads. For more than fifty miles north of Saigon, this flat jungle extends to the foothills of the foreboding and remote central Vietnamese mountains, where the real rain forest begins.

From Saigon, there are three main roads heading north.

The first is National Route 1, which goes fifteen miles north of Saigon to Bien Hoa, then cuts due east across the great flat jungle to the South China Sea coast, and then 400 miles north, right along the coastline, to the border of communist North Viet Nam. South Viet Nam's only railroad line runs parallel to this road.

The second road, National Route 14, slices north-northeast of Saigon, up through the flat jungle, to the highlands capital of Ban Me Thuot 160 miles away.

The third road, National Route 13, goes due north of Saigon, through the flat jungle and many rubber plantations, to a place called Loc Ninh, which is almost on the Cambodian border. The road ends at Loc Ninh, sixty miles north of the capital. There used to be a railroad spur paralleling this road, but the Viet Cong mutilated it so badly it has not been used in years.

Along all of these roads are hamlets and towns, with military posts and headquarters. Hamlets are concentrated along these three main roads because the rest of the countryside is so isolated from communication with the outer world. Hamlets mean tax collection and administration, and therefore are guarded by military posts. These posts, in turn, have to be supplied with ammunition and equipment, and their troops must be paid.

Resupplying posts on any of these three roads is a risky business. The things carried by truck to military posts are the very things the Viet Cong needs most and will try to get at all cost. For this reason, supply runs are always escorted by troops and sometimes with armor.

This convoy was a routine, monthly supply run from the province capital, along Route 14 about thirty miles northeast, to a post a few miles beyond the hamlet of Dong Xoai. Troops along the way would receive drums of gasoline for their vehicles, rice and other provisions, replacement weapons and fresh stocks of ammunition, some new field radios, and a payroll of two million piastres (about $20,000).

The guerrillas had been active lately, and it would be better not to take chances. So the province chief made up the convoy this way:

The first vehicle and the last vehicle would be "Ferret" armored cars, with 37-millimeter cannons in their turrets. The second and third vehicles would be jeeps for use by the convoy commander and his aides. The next seven vehicles would be two-and-a-half-ton trucks, loaded with the supplies and escort troops.

Each truck was open, giving troops riding in the back clear fields of fire. Behind the cab of each truck a ring-mounted heavy machine gun would add more firepower.

In short, this was to be a "heavy" convoy, protected by armor, two antitank cannons, seven heavy machine guns and about fifty soldiers, many of them carrying Tommy guns or other automatic weapons.

The convoy commander, a major named La, had a leisurely breakfast at an open-air coffee shop in town near province headquarters. He told officers with him he hoped to finish the day (a Friday) early, because he was planning to go down to Saigon over the weekend to see his family.

The officers, all in battle gear and carrying weapons, were relaxed and cheerful as they sipped glasses of coffee made sticky sweet with condensed milk. This resupply job had been planned many days in advance, right down to the last detail, and nothing could go wrong. Some civilians drinking coffee at other tables listened quietly as the officers talked.

An hour later, at about 9 A.M., the convoy rolled boisterously out of the barbed wire barricades of the province headquarters compound, dogs yapping at the wheels of the armored cars. It was a sunny, cool morning, and the soldiers were looking forward to the ride.

The cars and trucks roared through the market place, taking street corners so sharply that bicycles and pedestrians ran up on the sidewalks for cover.

The main street narrowed to a smooth, blacktop road, and the houses, shops and junk yards gave way to jungle. This was Route 14 proper.

The jungle was dense, but not quite so dense as in parts of the delta, where trees and vines grow right at the edge of the pavement, hiding anything more than ten feet from the road. Here, the trees were taller and the scrub growth more spread out. The flanks of the road had been cleared fifty yards or so on each side of the pavement. The road itself was level, and ran straight as an arrow for miles, with only slight curves at a few points. The pavement was in good condition, and the convoy sped along at fifty miles an hour, the vehicles spaced about fifty yards apart.

Here and there, the road passed mountain tribesmen's small settlements, surrounded by sharpened picket fences.

The huge tribal "long houses," on stilts and with towering eaves, contrasted sharply with the small, ground-level Vietnamese huts.

Major La, sitting in the front of his jeep next to his driver, yawned with boredom and peeled a banana he had brought along. It would be only a matter of four miles before the first stop, where the hardest part of the trip would be over.

Hidden in camouflaged foxholes and under bushes on the right side of the road 100 yards ahead were more than 1,000 Viet Cong guerrillas, but nothing showed.

The first thing Major La saw was a geyser of orange flame and debris crunching against the armored car just ahead. The next thing was the blast of a recoilless cannon somewhere off in the bushes, and the almost instantaneous impact of an armor-piercing shell on the armored car. The third and last thing was the simultaneous roar of twenty-five mines exploding all along the convoy, the shattering crack of more recoilless cannon fire, and the roar of such concentrated machine-gun fire that the sound of one shot could not be distinguished from another.

The entire convoy was stopped, burning and bleeding, in the space of ten seconds. A huge fireball had burst from one of the trucks loaded with gasoline drums. The leading armored car was burning fiercely, its ammunition exploding inside the red-hot hull. The stricken machine heaved with each blast in its innards, like a dying beetle.

Most, but not all of the troops were dead or dying. Some were still fighting.

The entire convoy was stopped, and burning vehicles blocked the road, both fore and aft. The only hope of survival was to fight. Three of the heavy machine guns were in action, firing continuously into the bushes.

But after the first volleys of mines, recoilless cannon and

machine guns, the Viet Cong had left their holes and were now swarming over the convoy. They were sturdy young men, dressed in baggy black trousers and blouses, and armed to the teeth. They moved like lightning, darting in and out of exposed areas, and up on the trucks themselves. From time to time, one of the convoy machine guns would catch a cluster of them in the open and cut them to pieces.

Major La's jeep had rolled over on its side after swerving off the road. He was wounded but still alive when they found him. A guerrilla yanked La's pistol from his hand, laughed, and shot the officer through the eye. In the back of the jeep, the intruder found a cloth sack containing the payroll. He grabbed it and ran back to the bushes.

The guerrillas clawed their way up even on the burning vehicles, shooting and knifing the defenders, and stripping off radios and machine guns with the speed of skilled mechanics. Hordes of unarmed guerrilla bearers had now joined the assault force, carrying and dragging bags and crates off into the jungle. Some of them were picking up the bodies of guerrillas killed in the fighting, and lugging them off, too.

Fifteen minutes after the first explosion, some of the convoy guns were still firing, but it was all over. One of the guerrillas blew a few shrill blasts from a police whistle, and the whole mass of black-clad men fell back as fast as it had attacked.

One of the radios in the convoy had had time to send out a distress signal before the end came, and a relief column was being slapped together. The relief column, which consisted of four truckloads of troops and four more armored cars, arrived two hours later, at about noon. I came along with it.

The ambush site was eerie. Jungle life had nearly returned to normal, and all was deadly quiet except for the chirping of a few birds and the hissing crackle of brush fires and burning vehicle tires. Every few minutes a shot would ring out and troops would jump for cover. But each time it was only a cartridge exploding from the heat of flames.

The trucks and armored cars were slewed around at odd angles, one of them turned completely around. For a half mile around, the jungle stank of cordite smoke, gasoline fumes and roasted flesh. The pavement was bloody, and the moaning wounded lay jumbled together with the dead.

All but two of the heavy machine guns had been carried off by the guerrillas, along with about forty rifles and submachine guns, five field radios, ammunition, two heavy mortars and a lot of other things. Nearly every dead soldier had been stripped of his watch and his wallet. Out of the whole convoy, fewer than one third of the men were still alive, and only a half dozen, who had taken cover in bushes on the other side of the road, were without wounds.

But the right side of the road showed that the guerrillas had not emerged unscathed. Shreds of black clothing and odds and ends of field gear clung to the bushes, all of which were spattered with blood. Twenty-seven guerrilla bodies were strewn around in the bush, some of them curled up like embryos in the holes where they died.

Some had been literally chopped to pieces by .50-caliber machine-gun fire. At one spot, I found an arm and shoulder around which still hung a canteen made from a bamboo log and filled with coconut milk. The rest of the body was nearly ten feet away. There was moot evidence that many of the dead guerrillas had been carried off by their comrades. Under a bush about fifty yards from the road I found a human brain so completely intact that it looked like the result of a surgical dissection. Next to it was a chunk of skull about five inches square, with fragments of scalp and hair still attached. But there was no body within thirty yards of the place, only a trail of blood on the bushes leading back into the high jungle.

The guerrillas plainly had taken losses, although it was impossible to estimate how many. But by their own standards, the ambush had been a brilliant success. Enough arms and ammunition had been looted from the convoy to equip an entire guerrilla heavy weapons company, along with a payroll that would make the political commissars back in the jungle happy for weeks.

The backbone of the ambush had been mines and recoilless

cannon. We found later that forty mines had been planted along the road, only twenty-five of which had exploded. Demolition crews dug up the others, and found that they all had been made from captured American 105-millimeter howitzer shells. The nose fuse had been unscrewed from each shell and an electric primer cap inserted into the well instead. Wires from each mine led back to a place about a hundred yards from the road, where the guerrillas apparently had used some kind of electric generator. We also found a number of cartridge casings from the recoilless cannon shells they had used.

The perforated brass cases appeared to be the standard American 57-millimeter variety, but weapons experts said later there were marks on the bases of these shell cases that identified them as Chinese communist.

I have described the Dong Xoai ambush in some detail, not because there is anything extraordinary about it, but because it was so typical of hundreds and perhaps thousands of similar minor disasters for the Free World.

The guerrillas outmaneuvered government forces from start to finish, for the following reasons:

Viet Cong tactical intelligence was excellent. The guerrillas knew exactly when and where the convoy was to go, and they must have known that it would be carrying supplies they wanted, or they would not have mounted such a heavy attack.

Government intelligence was wholly inoperative. Despite the fact that more than a thousand guerrillas and bearers had moved through fairly populous areas near the road, had dug up road shoulders for a half mile to place their mines, and had lain in wait for several hours at least, no word of warning ever reached government authorities. Many peasants and children must have wandered right through the ambush and must have known what was planned, but nothing was said.

There is a standing rule with the Viet Cong that battle must never be given unless guerrilla forces outnumber the enemy in men and weapons by overwhelming odds. Therefore, the guerrillas had to know in advance fairly exactly how strong convoy defenses would be, and they did know.

Finally, the guerrillas had psychology on their side. They

picked a harmless-looking spot for their ambush, nowhere near a turn in the road or a hill or a tree line, or any other obvious route, knowing that the troops would be relaxed and off guard as they neared their destination.

As the convoy moved through the fatal spot, it had fairly dense foliage on its left but fairly open scrub growth on its right. A West Point-trained officer would expect, if there was an ambush at this point, that the guerrillas would hide themselves in the cover offered by the left side of the road, which would give them a clear field of fire through the convoy and into the open side. Instead, the guerrillas did exactly the reverse. Furthermore, they had studded the bushes and reeds on the left side of the road with barbed steel nails and sharpened bamboo foot traps, on which a few of the convoy soldiers who had tried to fall back were wounded.

According to later intelligence, only about two hundred of the guerrillas were armed, regular Viet Cong troops. The rest were peasant youths living in the area, pressed into service by the fighters to serve as coolies in digging foxholes and mine emplacements, and to carry off equipment and bodies. But none of these "extras" turned traitor to their bosses, and all of them worked with the same courage and discipline as the regulars.

No matter how you look at it, this kind of thing is depressing. A really successful ambush is always a morale booster for the Viet Cong. Normally, the guerrillas pull out fast when they have completed the job. But sometimes they stick around long enough for their field photographers to do some work.

Many a captured or dead Viet Cong is found carrying war photographs pasted into his field manual. Such pictures most often show a guerrilla holding a Tommy gun or rifle, his bush hat cocked at a rakish angle, standing with one foot on the neck of a government soldier, with a burning truck or jeep in the background. Sometimes the guerrillas ham it up for the photographers, and even carry bugles hung with Viet Cong pennants. One of their proudest pictures showed a trio of guerrillas standing atop the wreckage of a U.S. Army H21 helicopter, grinning and with their arms akimbo.

Not all ambushes are successful, of course. Sometimes an

ambush may consist only of one mine in the road and ten or twelve guerrillas ready to open fire on the hapless vehicle it disables. My own life has been saved more than once by drivers with quick reflexes, who stamp on the gas when the mine goes off. The mines nearly always are planted at the side of the road, not directly under the vehicle, and there is usually a fair chance of getting away, even if it means driving at seventy miles an hour on flat tires.

It is possible to drive through even Viet Cong base areas without incident, if you are lucky and you don't look military. Because of an emergency (an attempted coup in Saigon and the consequent grounding of all airplanes), I once had to drive all the way from Ca Mau at the southern tip of Viet Nam to Saigon, through 160 miles of the most dangerous terrain in the country. I rented a rusty and badly dented 1938 Chevrolet sedan for the drive, and the local province chief insisted on assigning me a troop escort for the first ten miles out of his headquarters. There were sixty soldiers concealed in two gaily painted produce trucks, which followed me at a very discreet distance.

Soon after the trucks turned back, in a desolate stretch of woodland, two men in black on bicycles darted from the foliage into the middle of the road, forcing me to stop short. They pedaled slowly past the car window, looking me over closely, and then past the car and back into the forest. Apparently I passed inspection, and nothing further happened.

Single vehicles often are checked at Viet Cong roadblocks. On the highway leading fifty miles from Saigon to the picturesque seaside resort of Cap St. Jacques, thirty or forty cars and buses sometimes are halted at a time by a Viet Cong agitprop (agitation and propaganda) block. Traffic on the highway is especially heavy on weekends, and a good share of it is diplomatic— especially French and English officials off for a day of sunshine and lobster dinners. In keeping with the social caliber of this traffic, the Viet Cong who man the blocks along this road generally are polite and avoid violence.

Typically, the Viet Cong guard, dressed in a crisp khaki uniform without insignia, walks up to the car driver, salutes, and says (in French): "Good afternoon sir, I hope you have a pleasant day at the beach. The National Liberation Front would appreciate it if you would take these brochures along to read at your convenience. You may proceed, but I would advise you to return to Saigon before dark, or else stay over at Cap St. Jacques until tomorrow. Thank you."

The brochures, neatly mimeographed leaflets in French, always begin "Dear foreign friend," and are signed "The Phuoc Tuy Provincial Central Committee of the Front for the Liberation of South Viet Nam."

A few miles farther down the road, the driver comes to a government check point, where police salute smartly, wish the driver a pleasant day at the beach, and collect a ten-cent tourist toll, if the car happens not to have diplomatic license plates. The whole thing is very correct and proper. Even Americans normally go through the check points with no trouble, since identification papers and nationalities are not checked, this being a Viet Cong "showcase road." French drivers take no chances, and their cars always have little tricolor flag decals stuck to their windshields and rear bumpers.

Only an occasional eyesore mars the road. In a few places, the holiday driver can see the burned-out wreckage of military trucks. At one point, a simple concrete monument erected by Madame Ngo Dinh Nhu, former Vietnamese first lady, marks the place where two girls from Madame Nhu's paramilitary women's corps were butchered by the Viet Cong.

On other roads, the Viet Cong is a little rougher on passers-by. Buses are often stopped and searched. If any passengers turn out to be soldiers, in or out of uniform, they invariably are taken off in the woods. The rest of the passengers normally pay a tax (whatever jewelry they have, and most of their money) to the Liberation Front men, and then attend a mandatory lecture in the woods. After a few hours' delay, the buses generally are allowed to pass.

Recently, incidentally, the government put a new bus into service, in the hope of giving some guerrillas an ugly surprise. The bus is one of the usual, rickety provincial varieties, with cramped little seats, a smoky, noisy engine, and sides gaily painted with green, yellow, red and pink dragons.

But inside this particular bus, the sides are lined with steel armor plate against which sandbags have been stacked. A layer of sandbags also covers the floor, as protection against mines, and the engine has been replaced with a powerful diesel truck motor. Concealed around the front and rear bumpers are launching tubes capable of hurling shells in all directions in a pattern 100 yards out from the bus. And the passengers all are heavily armed Vietnamese special forces troops, whose machine guns bristle from concealed ports in the sides of the bus. At this writing, the Viet Cong has not yet tried picking on this bus.

Theoretically, trucks used in road convoys in Viet Nam are supposed to have been modified so that their seats for the soldiers are removed from the sides—in which position the soldiers must sit facing in—and replaced by seats in the middle, on which the soldiers face out. Actually, there are almost none of these modified trucks, and troops still ride along with their backs exposed to the sides of roads. A few trucks also are supposed to have been fitted with armor around the troops, but I have yet to see one.

Somehow, the monotonous horror of convoy ambushes never abates, and increasing numbers of Americans are dying in these slaughters. The death toll along Route 13 in particular has earned that awful road the name "Bloody Route 13."

The particular aspect of both Routes 13 and 14 is that they very nearly bisect the huge, flat jungle zone owned by the Viet Cong just north of Saigon. To the north and northeast of Saigon is a 2,000-square-mile stretch of jungle known as "D Zone."

Since French colonial days, D Zone has been a primary base area for the guerrillas, and they still operate in enormous strength under its protective green shroud. Because of the huge trees that blanket the whole area, helicopter landings are impossible, and parachute drops are extremely risky. D Zone is a bad place for a paratrooper to get hung up in a 200-foot tree. There are virtually no roads in the area, and movement of ground troops over this vast pocket of wilderness is agonizingly slow. From the air, only an occasional rivulet or stream bed breaks the terrain, and fighter planes practice their strafing and rocket runs here. The trees are so high the tracers and rockets just disappear into the green carpet below, with no sign of explosions or impacts.

To the west of D Zone and more or less contiguous with it is another vast wilderness sometimes called "C Zone," which stretches all the way to the unmarked frontier between Tay Ninh Province and Cambodia. The same jungle extends many miles over into the Cambodian side, and it is impossible to tell without maps where the border lies. The supreme headquarters of the National Liberation Front operates somewhere within this huge C Zone. So does a powerful Viet Cong propaganda transmitter called "Liberation Radio," which Saigon forces never have been able to fix and destroy.

The guerrillas, obviously, have a free hand in both D Zone and C Zone. The latter can easily be reached from the jungles of Cambodia, which extend up through increasingly high and remote mountains to the Laos frontier. The part of Laos where the South Vietnamese and Cambodia borders meet, incidentally, has been controlled for years by the communist-led Pathet Lao, the Viet Cong's sister organization.

Combined Pathet Lao and Viet Cong territory from there on runs all the way up through North Viet Nam to the frontier of communist China. Travel through this rain-soaked, jungle-choked part of the world, where food is always scarce and tigers are plentiful, is arduous and unpleasant. But the Viet Cong has had decades to learn how to do it.

To return to my subject, Routes 13 and 14 lie crimped between C Zone and D Zone, and their strategic importance is obvious. For the Saigon government, they are the sole overland communications link to the north central highlands, and the various hamlets and posts along the way. They also serve some very large French-owned rubber plantations that continue somehow to operate profitably, right in the Viet Cong's back yard.

For the Viet Cong, neither of these two roads provides any difficulty in communication between C Zone and D Zone, since neither road can be guarded adequately without deploying every soldier in South Viet Nam along it. But they are useful arteries from which to suck government blood and materiel. The government is forced to continue using them, if only for the reason that to abandon these two deathtraps would mean virtually surrendering a sizable hunk of Viet Nam to the enemy altogether. Posts can always be resupplied by air, but this does nothing to solve the ultimate problem of regaining control of the countryside.

On the other hand, no measures aimed at securing Routes 13 and 14 ever can be effective until Viet Cong strength is broken in the huge zones flanking them. These two roads thus pose a dilemma to the Saigon government that has all the marks of a vicious circle.

Nor is this situation static. C Zone has been expanding almost continuously, and now bulges south over some other key roads. The most important of these is the main highway from Saigon to the city of Tay Ninh sixty miles to the northwest. One year ago, this road was fairly safe throughout its entire length, except for a risky ten-mile stretch around the town of Trang Bang. At this writing, however, the road has become as bad as either Routes 13 or 14 starting from the town of Cu Chi, only seventeen miles from downtown Saigon. East of Cu Chi is a stretch of rubber plantation country near Ben Cat that extends as a salient of Viet Cong strength aimed right at Saigon. This zone, honeycombed with Viet Cong fortifications and jungle bases, has come to be known as the "Iron Triangle," because of the poor results government forces have had in trying to dislodge the guerrillas.

The kind of terrain I have been describing is next to useless for fighting big battles. Air cover is extremely handicapped. Artillery must fire blindly. Ground troops get lost in the maze of trees. The enemy has the advantage of prepared positions and mastery of the terrain. A division of regular troops can get mired in such a maze without finding anything more than a few snipers. But this is ideal country for ambushes.

The Dong Xoai ambush was a fairly simple, straightforward operation compared with many the Viet Cong has mounted.

In February, 1964, for instance, the Vietnamese decided to jump three battalions of paratroopers on a field operation—a venture requiring extremes of courage and tactical shrewdness.

This particular operation (near the edge of C Zone) was under the command of Colonel Cao Van Vien himself, the top government paratroop officer, and was supported by M113 amphibious armored personnel carriers.

As usual, Viet Cong intelligence was excellent and their planning nearly perfect. Fifteen hundred crack government troops with armor comprises too much of a bite for most Viet Cong units to chew, so the Viet Cong decided to try to knock off just the headquarters company and Vien himself.

Vien's force had been moving eastward along the Cambodian frontier in fairly open country. His battalions were strung out more or less in column, although the troops were not moving by road. With them were several American advisors. Vien's headquarters company was toward the rear of the line of march at the time. This company was just passing about a hundred yards south of a deserted-looking hamlet when the Viet Cong in the hamlet opened up. With Vien were fewer than 200 men, all out in an open field, and right under the guns of the concealed Viet Cong emplacements. The guerrillas had many 57-millimeter recoilless cannon and a solid wall of machine guns, all dug in at ground level to produce grazing fire, the most dangerous kind.

Vien's men were dying like flies all around him. Several of the armored personnel carriers had been disabled or forced back by cannon shells. A Vietnamese brigadier general who happened to have accompanied the operation was driving one of the M113s, desperately trying to rally the other vehicles.

Vien saw only one chance: An old-fashioned frontal charge right into the Viet Cong lines. He yelled to his men, and got up and ran. Many of the little unit were cut down, and Vien was shot through the shoulder. An American advisor with Vien found himself at one point staring into the muzzle of a Viet Cong recoilless cannon, and felt sure he was about to be blown to fragments.

The enemy gunner tried to fire, but the cartridge was a dud, and the American shot him as he started to run.

From there on, it was a bitter trench fight. Vien's unit found that it had fought its way only into the first of five lines of Viet Cong fortifications concealed in the hamlet. But by now, relief forces had got themselves turned around and were moving in to help Vien. Eventually, the bulk of the Viet Cong forces slipped out of the rear of the hamlet into the marshy fields beyond, and escaped.

Vien's forces had suffered heavy casualties, but at least this time the enemy had left behind a satisfactory pile of bodies. Vien was shipped to a hospital in Saigon. A few days later, the Premier himself, Major General Nguyen Khanh, stopped around to pin the Cross of Gallantry and brigadier general's stars on Vien's pajamas.

Increasingly, the Viet Cong have been learning how to set up decoys in planning their ambushes. The usual way is to send a company or two of guerrillas to attack some government post, which can normally be approached along only one route. The guerrillas lob mortar and cannon shells into the post and cut it up with machine guns, but make no effort to overrun it. This normally at least frightens the post defenders enough that they call for help by radio. The Viet Cong, incidentally, also have radios tuned to the same frequencies as the post defenders, and eavesdrop with interest on such conversations.

Meanwhile, a much larger Viet Cong force sets itself up in ambush a few miles away from the post, and waits for its inevitable quarry.

This technique has been sophisticated to such a degree that sometimes the primary ambush is not the main objective, but itself becomes the bait for a second and much larger ambush, as a relief force is sent to relieve the relief force. When the Viet Cong feels it has hooked a fish of regulation size, it then chews fast and moves out before the thing starts turning into a conventional battle.

While the conventional military ambush makes use of existing cover and terrain features, the Viet Cong uses some fiendish tactics that have something in common with judo. There is, for example, an oblique crossfire gambit that has cost many a government unit in the flat rice country of the delta dearly. It works like this:

A small government unit, say 100 men, is moving across

a long stretch of flooded rice paddies. The only high ground on which to walk is a straight, narrow path or road atop a wide paddy dyke. It is a strong temptation for any unit to move in a column along one of these little roads. It is exhausting to go for mile after mile in the paddies themselves, pulling one leg after the other out of the knee-deep muck. Especially when an operation has had no contact all day long, the quick, easy way of covering ground is almost always the method of choice.

Now our column is out in the middle of an ocean of these fields, the nearest tree line a mile or more away. Suddenly, heavy machine-gun fire starts coming in from the right side, 400 or 500 yards away.

The enemy machine gun is too far away to destroy the column, especially since it is firing at a long column facing it sideways. All the troops are in position to fire at the lone enemy gun, and the advantage is clearly on the government side. But still, the gun is not far enough away that it can be ignored. Slugs are snapping just overhead or thumping into the right bank of the dyke, and perhaps several of the men have been hit. So the main force does the instinctively correct thing: it jumps off the left side of the dyke into the paddy, so as to get maximum cover from the enemy gun and to use the road as a firing parapet.

But as in so many aspects of this war, the instinctively right thing is the wrong thing in practice. The left side of the dyke turns out to be studded with spiked foot traps, booby traps and mines. And another enemy machine gun, only 100 yards ahead and almost up against the left bank of the dyke, opens fire. This gun has the government troops in what is known as enfilade, which is the worst way to be. It means that only the few troops at the head of the line can fire on the enemy to defend themselves, while the enemy can cover the entire friendly group without having to change his aim at all. If he's lucky, one of his bullets may go through two or three of the defending soldiers.

This is a type of ambush in which the Viet Cong does not need overwhelming superiority of numbers to win. In fact, twenty-five guerrillas stand a reasonable chance of wiping out 100 government troops with minimal losses to themselves. The

keys to success are exact planning and perfect camouflage.
Camouflage is afforded easily, even in open fields, by such
devices as lying under water with one's head protruding under a
pile of straw.

On a somewhat larger scale, a government battalion of 400
men set out recently on a "search and destroy" operation within
the Viet Cong stronghold known as the "Iron Triangle." There
had been intelligence reports that a couple of reinforced Viet
Cong companies were camped dead ahead of the government
battalion's line of march, and the object was to make contact.

The jungle was dense and movement was slow. At nightfall,
the government force reached a deep stream and decided to defer
crossing until morning. Scouts were sent out during the night to
pick a line of march for the following day. They discovered a
bridge made of two logs flung across the stream, and decided
the main body would start here in the morning. American advisors said later they felt pretty sure the Viet Cong had put down
those two logs to smooth the path into the trap.

So the following morning, 400 troops moved across the makeshift bridge, and found themselves on a faint trail. To the left of
the trail was dense jungle clogged with vines, and to the right
was underbrush which looked a little more open. The troops
started cautiously down the trail, alert for ambush.

After a quarter of a mile, fairly heavy small arms fire opened
up on them from dead ahead. By the sounds, at least a platoon
and possibly a company was firing. The bullets ticked through
the tree branches, but the fire was spotty and inaccurate.

"Aha," the battalion commander told an aide, "they think
they've caught us, but they opened fire too soon. We'll turn the
tables on them and flank their ambush."

With that, the commander assigned a platoon to stay in the
path to continue fire at the Viet Cong up ahead, while the commander and the rest of the battalion moved off to the right into
the scrub. Making a wide arc, the whole government force
threaded itself through the underbrush until it had come up
abreast of the sound of the enemy firing and about 500 yards to
the right of the presumed Viet Cong ambush. Then the roof
fell in.

Concentrated machine-gun fire from three sides swept over the battalion, and it was immediately apparent the unit had walked into the open end of a horseshoe-shaped trap. But the worst was yet to come. A few seconds after the new firing began, the first of a series of heavy mortar shells landed right in the middle of the loose battalion formation, killing a dozen men. A hideous barrage of 81-millimeter mortar shells hissed down through the treetops, and each shell had fatal results. There were no marking rounds or "walking in" to bracket the target; the first shell was right on target.

The battalion lost more than one third of its men in the first ten minutes of the barrage. There is no apparent reason why the Viet Cong could not have gone on to annihilate the whole unit, but for some reason the guerrillas decided not to. They broke contact as abruptly as they had begun, and faded away into the jungle, probably without a single casualty.

A relief force and the remnants of the battalion later inspected the deserted Viet Cong positions. The Viet Cong had so precisely pinpointed the spot where they would nail the government battalion that their mortars had been zeroed in in advance. And to make sure nothing went wrong with the mortar shells, the guerrillas had even chopped away foliage over their mortar tubes to coincide exactly with the trajectories they planned to use.

That operation was an unpleasant demonstration not only of the sophistication with which the Viet Cong has learned to operate ambushes, but of the real insight of Viet Cong commanders into the military psychology of their Western-trained opposite numbers. More than anywhere else, the doctrines of St. Cyr and West Point led that ill-fated battalion to its undoing.

Part of the effectiveness of Viet Cong ambush tactics depends on lightning speed in engaging convoys in hand-to-hand combat.

Not long ago, the American pilot of an L19 spotter plane was cruising over the Mekong Delta, directly over a marching column of Vietnamese troops. He happened to be watching this column move across a field when suddenly the unit was taken under fire. Men were running and falling, and at 1,000 feet, the pilot said he could clearly hear shooting, but the source of the shots could not be discerned. All at once, a second column of men, clad in black, materialized alongside the government group. The Viet Cong had been so perfectly camouflaged that when they stood up it seemed as if the roadside was turning into men by magic.

The pilot swooped down as he called by radio for help for the stricken unit. He thought of firing his automatic rifle at the attackers from the window of his plane, but by this time the Viet Cong were completely mixed in with the defenders, hacking them to pieces, man by man. Some of the Viet Cong were aiming automatic rifle fire at him, and he was forced to climb to avoid being hit.

Ambushes are not all on roads. Throughout the delta, a vast labyrinth of communications canals actually forms the primary means of travel, both for civilians and soldiers.

Some of these canals, especially the ones deep enough to accommodate gunboats, are kept closed down by the Viet Cong. The guerrillas, using armies of forced laborers, simply dam up the canals with a lattice of logs overlaid with mud. To make sure the dams stay in place they are usually mined. It takes a team of government frogmen more than a day to demolish one of these dams with underwater charges. And then they are usually rebuilt in a matter of weeks.

But on other canals, the Viet Cong rely on ambush to keep out intruders. Many canals are not much wider than roads, and afford exactly the same ambush potential. Convoys of government boats generally travel with light landing craft or French FOM gunboats, serving exactly the same purpose as armored cars in a road convoy. The gunboats generally are armed with .50-caliber machine guns or 20-millimeter cannon, with which they can sweep fields beyond the canal banks. But they are just as susceptible as armored cars to ambush.

In the early years of the war, the Viet Cong invented a gadget they called the "lance bomb," which is just about as destructive as a 3.5-inch rocket. The lance bomb, entirely homemade, has a high-explosive warhead made of scrap iron. Behind the head are four small fins, and trailing back behind is a tube that looks like a stovepipe. This tube contains a propellant charge that is set off electrically. To fire a lance bomb, a stake with a short yardarm is needed. The yardarm is shaped so as to fit snugly inside the end of the rocket tube of the lance bomb. The stake is driven into the ground just before firing, with the yardarm and bomb precisely aimed at the target. The guerrilla then runs his wires back to a safe distance and cranks his magneto.

A lance bomb will demolish a brick watchtower or stop a light tank. It will also pierce an armored gunboat. Lance bombs are often mounted in trees overlooking canals, pre-aimed at just the place where the hull of a passing gunboat would meet the water. A guerrilla hundreds of feet away has only to watch the boat come, wait for it to come exactly abreast of some landmark, and then crank his magneto. Many a landing craft and gunboat are now rusting at the bottom of canals as the result of lance bombs.

Railroad ambushes deserve special mention. The national railroad, which, as I mentioned earlier, runs all the way up the coast of South Viet Nam from Saigon, has been sabotaged at one point or another several times a day for the past two years. It is a marvel to me that it continues to run at all. Big steel bridges are regularly blown up, long trains are derailed by running over torn up track, and a tattoo of sniper fire rolls down at trains from a hundred spots. Occasionally the Viet Cong stops a train, detaches the locomotive, and sends it hurtling driverless down the track at full speed. The locomotive invariably smashes into something, usually another train stopped at a station. But while these incidents make for spectacular destruction and sometimes heavy loss of life, they are not quite the same thing as ambushes. The true ambush involves shooting up and halting a train defended by troops, and then looting it for supplies and equipment.

In any case, train rides in South Viet Nam are not particularly pleasant, even though the passenger coaches are comfortable and good dining cars are usually taken along.

I made one trip from the central Vietnamese city of Quang Ngai to Saigon at a time near an important Vietnamese holiday, and many of my fellow passengers were troops on pass going home to their families. None of them was in uniform, and each was trying to look as much as possible like a harmless civilian.

I noticed that when the train slowed down to five miles an hour or so (which it always did over stretches where derailment could mean a plunge over a cliff) the soldiers would take out their military identification cards and hold them out the open windows of the train. I asked one why.

"If the Viet Cong board the train, we don't want to be found carrying these cards. They would take us away for good," he said.

At one place, near the town of Tuy Hoa, nine soldiers locked themselves in a tiny lavatory for a solid hour while a trackman checked conditions up ahead of the stopped train. Passengers have grounds for fear.

After leaving Saigon, the railroad goes fifteen miles north to Bien Hoa, and then, paralleling Route 1 all the way, strikes east through part of the jungles of D Zone on its way to the sea. The track then arcs north, and gradually reaches the coastline itself. This stretch of track is where a lot of the worst ambushes occur.

One night, some American advisors were enjoying martinis on the roof of their hotel in Phan Thiet, a small coastal town 100 miles east of Saigon, near which the rail line passes. As the advisors stood chatting about their day's work, a glaring, orange fireball billowed up from the distant jungle, followed a few seconds later by a dull boom. The Viet Cong had attacked a large supply train moving north, and a cannon shell had ignited the train's supply of diesel fuel. It proved impossible to send a relief force out to the stricken train that night, but about dawn a relief train loaded with troops moved into the area and was promptly ambushed. The relief train was badly mauled, but most of its troops survived and fought their way to the first train, where guerrillas were still carting off huge stocks of rice and other provisions. It was estimated later that more than 2,000 Viet Cong must have worked on that train all night long, unloading its cargo and padding off into the jungle.

One of the things the Viet Cong found aboard the train was half a boxcar of bottled beer—tens of thousands of bottles. There was an amusing aftermath to the big beer haul.

Phan Thiet itself is more or less under government control, but everything immediately outside the town is in Viet Cong hands. Even the airstrip one mile away is sometimes under mortar fire. One end of the strip is almost in the jungle, and it is dangerous to park planes there. The other end of the strip is at the top of a cliff of red earth that drops several hundred feet to the ocean. Because low approaches over the jungle end of the strip draw dangerous ground fire, planes must land coming in from the sea, something like landing on an aircraft carrier. And they generally take off in the opposite direction, regardless of the wind.

But 500 feet from the end of this runway is a hamlet, which at least part of the time is fairly friendly to government authorities. From one side of the hamlet is a gently sloping field that ends in a cliff over the ocean. This field is full of small game, and several American enlisted men from the Phan Thiet detachment used to like to hunt there.

One of these Sunday afternoon hunters was a sturdy little sergeant first class named Roque Matagulay, who had been born and raised on Guam, and who knew a lot about guerrilla warfare from Japanese occupation days on his home island. But one afternoon, a Viet Cong squad was out waiting for Matagulay in his hunting preserve, and they jumped him. He held off the guerrillas until his ammunition ran out, and then had to surrender.

Matagulay was in Viet Cong hands about six months, and conditions in the jungle were very bad. A political re-education officer assigned to him worked him over for long hours each day.

"As a Negro, you should understand as well as we the nature of American racist imperialism," the commissar told Matagulay one day.

"But I'm not a Negro, I'm a Guamanian."

"What's that?"

Matagulay patiently sketched a map of the United States on the ground, and another map of the coast of Asia, and in the Pacific Ocean space in between he marked with a dot the island of Guam.

"Ah, then you are an Asian and one of the peoples oppressed by the Americans," the commissar said.

"No. I'm a Guamanian and an American," Matagulay answered.

This kind of thing went on for a long time. Matugulay was

fed no worse than his Viet Cong captors, but no better, and they were living on rice and rat soup. He contracted malaria and, later, dysentery. Matagulay held out better than most American prisoners, but his health was dangerously bad. The Viet Cong knew they would have to improve his diet if they wanted him to live, and they already had decided on sending him back to his detachment, so they wanted him to look as good as possible.

One day, Matagulay awoke from a fevered nap to find one of his guards offering him the best dinner he had seen since being captured. There were salted meat, some canned vegetables, canned fruit, and even a nice bottle of beer.

"Where in hell did all this come from?" he asked the commissar. The Viet Cong smiled, and said: "By good fortune, it happens that last night the people's forces blew up an imperialist train near here. All this, including the beer, comes from the train."

The Viet Cong have even tried to ambush helicopters by tempting them to land in traps.

Viet Cong radio communications are so good that the guerrillas can very often monitor helicopter frequencies and make effective use of the conversations they hear. On many missions, helicopter pilots ask ground troops to mark safe landing spots with smoke grenades. These grenades produce different colors of smoke used to signify different things. Not long ago a helicopter ambulance was called into a battle area north of Saigon to pick up some casualties. The area was mostly covered with jungle, but there were a few clear patches apparently safe for landing. The pilot radioed to the ground: "I can't see you. Give me some brown smoke."

Almost instantly, a puff of brown smoke rose from one of the patches, and the helicopter settled down into it. The machine was within ten feet of the ground when a fusillade of tracer bullets came spraying out of the woods at it. The pilot glanced around, saw no troops of any kind, and hastily pulled full pitch, rocketing out of the clearing. At a little higher altitude, he spotted another column of brown smoke rising from a patch nearly a mile away. The second patch turned out to be the right one.

Many of the clear fields around hamlets in the Mekong Delta appear from the air to be perfectly safe landing spots, but actually are studded with long wooden spikes that would tear a helicopter fuselage to shreds. Viet Cong units sometimes try to lure "eagle flights" of helicopters into landing in such places.

In summary, it is probably safe to say that the primary distinguishing military feature of the Vietnamese war is the ambush.

Americans tend to despise the ambush as an inferior form of warfare employed by cowards and thieves in the night. It may be both of these things, but it is as effective now as when the American Continental Army used it against the British redcoats. It is a tactic that enables the weak to attack and destroy the strong, particularly when used by highly skilled military tacticians.

Various defenses against ambushes have been developed. Armored railroad coaches called Wickham trolleys now travel with many Vietnamese trains. The Wickham trolleys, used by the British in the Malayan guerrilla campaign, have gun turrets, and actually are tanks on rails. And they are often derailed.

To deprive guerrillas along roads and canals of natural cover, the U.S. Air Force put into effect a huge program to spray the jungles along communications arteries with a herbicide spray. After nearly a year of experiments, the Air Force finally got the defoliation program to work, and now broad strips along roads and canals have been cleared of foliage. But the ambushes continue. Unfortunately, skillful Viet Cong guerrillas can mount successful ambushes just as well in open fields as in jungle growth.

Trucks have been armed with all kinds of antiambush gadgets, including one that spews bombs in all directions at the touch of a button in the driver's cab. About thirty trainees were killed by accident in a demonstration of one of these things at a camp near Saigon once, but I know of no instance in which the device was used successfully against a real ambush.

The biggest reason for ambushes is that the Vietnamese Army is a conventional army trained in conventional tactics, and it depends primarily on roads, railroads and canals for transportation. All these things can be ambushed, even when convoys observe all the safety rules. An army that travels mostly in twos and threes, making rendezvous only at the precise moment of battle, cannot be ambushed. That is the way the Viet Cong usually travels.

Of course, the Viet Cong slips up on the rules of guerrilla warfare too, especially when things have been going well. Government ambushes sometimes have turned the tables on the guerrillas, who have been badly mauled by their own techniques. But this is unfortunately rare.

Many ranking American officers believe the dangers of ambush can be materially blunted by air cover over all important convoys. The U.S. Army has a two-engine plane called the Mohawk, a powerful plane armed with rockets and heavy machine guns, that can fly slowly enough to keep pace with convoys. A half dozen of these have been in service in Viet Nam for some time. Helicopters also sometimes fly antiambush missions. Several American tacticians say they are certain many ambushes have been prevented just by the presence of planes overhead.

This may be. But air cover is obviously not foolproof, as demonstrated by the presence of the spotter plane over the convoy I described earlier. The Viet Cong may have known the L19 was not armed. But even if it had been, it could not have done much to help, since the guerrillas were on top of the convoy so fast. To have strafed the guerrillas would have meant strafing the convoy along with them.

The history of the Indochina War shows the French never found an adequate solution to the ambush problem. Even after the Viet Minh shifted gears from guerrilla warfare to full-scale mobile warfare, their basic operating pattern remained the ambush, on a huge scale. One after another, French regimental combat teams were hacked to pieces simply moving from one place to another, and this kind of thing continued right up to the end of the war.

The ambush appears to me to be a key element in the new face of war. I think the Free World faces the choice of living with this fact, or dying with it.

Chapter **7**

Terror and
Counterterror

The agony of Dam Doi began many years ago and it is not over.
The little hamlet of a few thousand souls has bled and bled and
bled, to the point at which it is hard to understand why anyone
still lives there. The ties of ancestral bones buried in the alluvial
mud nearby must be strong indeed.

I first visited Dam Doi in February, 1962, and have been there
often since then, always on grim business.

At the southernmost part of Viet Nam is a large tongue of
land called the Ca Mau Peninsula, which juts down from Indochina, dividing the South China Sea from the Gulf of Siam. Ca
Mau, the capital of this region, is the southernmost town in Viet
Nam of any substance. There is more land below Ca Mau, much
of which is trackless mangrove swamp and practically all of
which belongs to the Viet Cong, except for a few pinpoints on
the map like Dam Doi (pronounced in Vietnamese as "dom
yoy").

To the west of Dam Doi is a forest about forty miles long,
running along the coast of the Gulf of Siam. This forest is the
base of the Viet Cong's notorious U Minh Battalion, one of the
most feared units in the nation. To the east and south of Dam
Doi are other important Viet Cong base areas, most of which are
openly administered by the Viet Cong as "liberated zones."

There is no road connecting Dam Doi with the provincial
capital of Ca Mau—only a footpath and a network of canals.

It was a scorching hot February morning when I first arrived
in Ca Mau in a light plane that slid into the landing strip right

in the center of town. A little river, thick with sampans, house-boats and fishing nets curves through the center of town, and the part of the city inside the curve is a thriving market place. Cool, maritime winds blow over Ca Mau in the monsoon season, but in February there is no relief from the merciless heat. No one works any harder than necessary.

Ca Mau is the capital of An Xuyen Province, one of forty-five provinces making up South Viet Nam. Each province is divided into districts, and each district is divided at progressively lower levels into cantons, villages (which are not actual towns but geographical subdivisions), and, finally, hamlets.

Dam Doi, despite its tiny population, is the capital of Dam Doi District.

I mention these trivial, administrative matters only because they have a bearing on the horror of life in places like Dam Doi. Each time an urgent plea for help passes from one level to a higher one, it must be processed through the red tape mill at each level. Really important things often have to go all the way to Saigon (which does not work nights or on weekends).

Let me set the stage a little more. At the time I arrived in Ca Mau, it happened that two battalions of Vietnamese marines, that is to say about nine hundred officers and men, were temporarily assigned to the province, to guard work crews repairing a road in the northwest part of the province. It takes that many troops to prevent a road crew from being wiped out by the guerrillas.

Of course, as soon as the road crew and the marines leave, the road is invariably ripped up and planted with mines and bamboo groves, but the exercise is presumably good training for all concerned.

An Xuyen Province is too poor and too low on the priority list to rate any regularly assigned government troops. But besides its regular army, South Viet Nam has two paramilitary forces, which do more fighting and take more casualties than the regular army. These are called the Bao An (Civil Guard) and the Dan Ve, translated either as People's Militia or Self-Defense Corps.

The Civil Guard is supposedly a provincial force. This means that if a man joins the Civil Guard, he is not as well paid as a regular soldier, but he is reasonably assured that he will always be stationed in his home province. At a lower level, membership in the Self-Defense Corps means even lower wages and fewer benefits, but it theoretically means that a man never need serve outside his home district. Often he actually lives at home, or in a compound right next to it. This system of military organization is exactly duplicated by the Viet Cong, incidentally.

In rural administrative centers, civilian government officials also are trained to fight in case of emergency. Under the defunct Diem regime, they dressed in blue uniforms and were called the Republican Youth Corps. The old name and the blue uniforms have been dropped, and they now are called the Combatant Youth.

So An Xuyen had a share of Civil Guards (dressed in uniforms almost identical to the regular army), Militiamen (dressed in black uniforms), and Youth Corpsmen.

The city of Ca Mau had (and still has) a few 105-millimeter howitzers that are fired nearly every night, supposedly to destroy Viet Cong as they attack outlying hamlets. But these howitzers rarely hit anything except an occasional hut, and their range is not great enough to do anything for places like Dam Doi.

In addition to these forces, a Roman Catholic priest of Chinese origin, the Reverend Nguyen Lac Hoa, has for years maintained his own private army of irregulars at a hamlet called Binh Hung south of Ca Mau. Father Hoa, a refugee from China and a former colonel in the Nationalist Chinese Army, settled his little band of Chinese refugees in about the most desolate and unpleasant bit of land anywhere in South Viet Nam. Almost completely cut off from the rest of the world and surrounded by large and extremely hostile Viet Cong units, Binh Hung nevertheless survived and grew.

Some Vietnamese from the province went to live in muddy Binh Hung, and Father Hoa recruited and trained his own irregular defense force, which he named the "Sea Swallows." More than one thousand men strong, this little fighting unit began to establish a reputation for disciplined and courageous fighting, and its reputation as a thorn in the very intestines of the Viet Cong began to spread.

The American Central Intelligence Agency took a keen interest in Binh Hung, and through its Combined Studies Group in Saigon and the U.S. Army Special Forces, regular airdrops of supplies began to pour into Binh Hung.

Binh Hung actually got some of these supplies before they were issued to anyone else—even the U.S. armed forces. Supplies included the new ultralight AR-15 Armalite automatic rifle—a weapon weighing only about seven pounds, capable of throwing out super-high-velocity slugs faster than a conventional machine gun. Binh Hung also was the first to get the new unsinkable Fiberglas assault boats equipped with outboard motors. U.S. planes flew down to Binh Hung at night whenever the Viet Cong mounted a large attack, dropping flares to help the defenders. An aging Chinese wearing a priest's robes and a steel helmet and pistol belt is a strange study in contrasts, but the combination worked. Since those early days, Father Hoa has given up his military command and the Sea Swallows have been incorporated into the regular national armed forces, but Binh Hung is still fighting.

At any rate, the Sea Swallows in 1962 were a valuable addition to the normal forces of An Xuyen Province. Father Hoa felt secure enough that he would even loan neighboring district chiefs a platoon or two of Sea Swallows, at times when they felt extra shotguns were needed.

In February, 1962, a thirty-one-year-old Vietnamese army captain named Tran Van Kha was the chief of Dam Doi District. They say he had a wife in Saigon with whom he didn't get along, and this was one of the reasons he welcomed his assignment to Dam Doi. He had been there about three months.

Kha was an ambitious young officer, spoiling for a fight with the guerrillas who ruled the murky jungle. He was also worried about Dam Doi's defenses.

Counting all his Civil Guards and Militiamen, he had only about a score of able-bodied men to hold the hamlet itself. Every night the guerrillas did a little sniping and probing, and you never know what may come next. So Kha sent word to Father Hoa that he would appreciate some extra men. Father Hoa obligingly sent a platoon of Sea Swallows over to Dam Doi, giving Kha a complement of sixty-four men, counting himself. That was how things stood when I arrived in Ca Mau.

It was long before dawn on a Saturday morning when Kha decided to lead his men out for a foray against the enemy. Two things probably led him to do it. One was his boredom with always sitting behind the barricades of Dam Doi, the initiative always on the side of the unseen but lethal enemy outside. The other was Kha's mistress, a girl of about twenty, in her seventh month of pregnancy. Through "contacts" of her own, the girl had told Kha, she had learned that a squad of Viet Cong propagandists was operating in a cluster of huts about three miles south of Dam Doi, and could easily be caught red-handed by such strong forces as Kha commanded. It has never been established whether or not Kha's mistress actually was a Viet Cong agent. But there is no question that this bit of intelligence she gave him led directly to his death.

By Saturday evening, Kha and his men had still not returned. A village official—a man too old to fight—was worried. He managed to raise Ca Mau by radio.

"The chief and his men have not returned after all this time. The sun is setting, and there are signs the Viet Cong may be planning an attack. Please send help. Please, please, send help," the old man said.

A radio operator in Ca Mau dutifully took down the message, and carried it to the duty officer. The duty officer asked for confirmation of the time Kha had left. Confirmation came back. The duty officer was stuck with a hot potato, and he knew it. But he manfully swung into action to pass the word to higher command.

I was having a flyspecked dinner with a major named Hoang at the time. Two listless sentries with the dark, round faces of Cambodians stood at the gate outside. A few schoolgirls in their ankle length *ao-dais*—graceful, high-necked dresses slit to the waist, and worn over loose, white silk trousers—still stood chatting in the dusk, twirling their conical hats, fluffing their long black hair, and giggling. A steady stream of bicycles hurried people home to their dinners. Somewhere in the distance, a street vendor was yelling for customers for *pho*, a savory noodle soup favored by South Vietnamese.

The house was not the best in town, but neither was it the worst. It was a simple, stucco house fit for a deputy province chief, which was the office Hoang held.

On the front porch, a squad of tough Civil Guards, their skin tanned almost black and all carrying Tommy guns, was settling down for the night, stringing mosquito nets from the railing. But apart from these cutthroats, the scene was one of complete peace.

The dinner was tough chicken chopped in small pieces without regard to the pattern of bones, cold rice, some watery soup and an aging, flyspecked salad. But the major had some good Algerian wine, and we shared it.

There were no cigars or cognac, but there was more wine after dinner. Hoang spoke fluent French, and felt disposed to talk.

"You know, the province chief, Colonel Ut, and I were in the same class together at the military academy," he began.

"As a matter of fact, I usually got higher marks than he did. Fate plays peculiar tricks. Here am I in this miserable job in this wretched house, away from my wife and children, and there is he, in that palace of a house, a full colonel, and enjoying a full and happy life. Tonight he is holding a dinner party for some people down from the Interior Ministry. You can be sure it will be a good party! Why don't you go over?"

I said I was tired.

"Well, then. Have some more wine. Perhaps later I can escort you for some sight-seeing around Ca Mau? There's not much to see, but you shall see Ca Mau by night—the pearl of Viet Nam's buttocks."

But Major Hoang did not have an opportunity to show me around Ca Mau. (He was right. There is not much to see at night, although market stalls lighted by little acetylene lamps and fragrant with the smell of tasty soups are attractive places. Most

Vietnamese provincial towns are on or near waterways, and it is always pleasant to stroll around them in the evening.)

Major Hoang was interrupted when a jeep roared through the gate, throwing gravel as it braked. The sleepy sentries snapped to attention, and the duty officer strode up to the stone bench in front of the house door where Hoang and I were sitting. He glanced at me suspiciously, saluted Hoang, and handed him a note.

Hoang frowned as he read, and then excused himself without explanation. He was locked in his combination office and bedroom the rest of the evening, and I didn't see him again until morning.

I learned the next day that Hoang had not been able to reach Province Chief Ut during the night, either because Ut was unavailable or Hoang was unwilling to break up Ut's party with bad news. In any case, Ut didn't hear about Dam Doi until more than twenty-four hours had passed since its district chief had set forth into the jungle.

It was a pleasant Sunday morning in Ca Mau. Children were strolling and laughing in the streets, and the sun was not high enough yet to make things oppressively hot. But an odd, mixed convoy of army trucks, ornately painted but rickety civilian buses, and a handful of prewar automobiles, was rolling into town—loaded to the roofs with marines in battle gear. I asked one of the marine officers what was going on, and he said he had no idea.

"We were out guarding that cotton-pickin' road project," he said, "and nothing's happened all week long. Now, all of a sudden, along comes this convoy of buses and trucks, and we're ordered back to Ca Mau. You never know what to expect in this country."

"Where'd you learn English like that?" I asked.

"Quantico," the officer snapped back. "A marine's not a leatherneck if he hasn't been there, regardless of his nationality."

I went to the province chief's house to find out what was going on.

Ut, looking dapper in camouflaged fatigue uniform with razor-sharp creases, did live in a fine house. A long driveway led to the magnificent portico of the big, yellow stucco house. The wide doorway entered on a very large reception room with black and yellow tiled floor, comfortable and fairly modern furniture, an electric overhead fan and a tray of beer and cold soda ready for all comers. On the far wall, a portrait fully eight feet high of President Diem dominated the room, flanked by yellow and red national flags and bunting.

"There may have been some trouble down in Dam Doi, a town about thirty miles southeast of here," Ut said. "We've—well, it seems we've lost contact with the district chief there. We're going to have to have a look, so I pulled back those marines for a look at the area. They'll be leaving in a few hours. Want to go along?"

I did. I loaded my few belongings into my field pack and rejoined the marines, who were resting under the trees of one of the streets.

About 11 A.M., we marched through the streets to the river front, where Colonel Ut had assembled the most incredible armada of boats I had ever seen.

The backbone of our river task force was made up of three or four salvaged and reconditioned French gunboats called FOMs. The FOM is a steel boat about forty feet long. Its armored sides are pierced at regular intervals with gun ports. On the top is perched a slab-sided little machine-gun turret. The ship is painted black, and is altogether one of the most ugly vessels I have ever seen.

Tied up alongside the FOMs were about twenty commercial river boats about the same length. But they were made of wood with high, curving bowsprits. They were painted yellow with red trim, and each had painted eyes just at the bow, staring forward, to bring good luck to river navigators. The squat diesel engines inside their cabins were already belching smoke. Each of the boats in our fleet carried a large national flag—yellow, with three horizontal red stripes—at the stern. It looked like the beginning of some odd regatta.

The marines bundled their packs, rifles, machine guns and

mortars aboard the boats, and we chugged off down the river, in single file, fifty yards or so apart. The market place, jetties and riverside huts slipped away and were replaced by a dense, green wall of palms and bamboo on both sides of the narrow river.

We all knew that the Viet Cong had sunk many a boat—even armored boats—along here, using homemade rocket launchers mounted in trees along the banks. But the marines accepted this knowledge philosophically. Rather than crouch tensely behind their rifle sights, most of them went to sleep.

The convoy threaded its way through progressively more narrow tributaries and canals, passing an occasional outpost, the defenders of which just stared listlessly at us.

It was about 2 P.M. when the convoy reached a fork in the stream along which it had been traveling. The banks at this point were so close together the long palm fronds spreading from opposite banks almost touched overhead. The fork was sharp, and the banks on each side of it were steep. They were also studded with dagger-sharp bamboo foot spikes hardened by fire.

The fork formed the apex of a little, triangular outpost defended by a dozen Civil Guards, who had used their pitiful means for fortifying the place the best they could. A big national flag was perched bravely in the middle of the jungle enclave.

"From here on we have to walk," the English-speaking marine officer grumbled to me. By now, the bows of all our ships were jammed into the muddy bank, and the marines filed ashore, many of them muttering "*troi oi*"—a mild oath ("my God") that Vietnamese troops invariably use when strenuous physical exertion appears imminent.

We moved away from the outpost along a path hemmed in by jungle and still as death in the shimmering heat. The whole column was moving single file and fairly rapidly, with no flank scouts or any other precautions against ambush. The idea now was to get to the relative safety of Dam Doi before sunset. The night belongs to the enemy, Quantico training notwithstanding.

The path ran more or less parallel to a small canal occasionally visible off to our left. Smaller canals and ditches cut across the path every few hundred yards. Some were spanned by single logs. Poles jammed into the mud bottoms of the ditches afforded hand holds on which to balance across, but the logs were slippery, and falls were frequent. Progress was painfully slow.

Every once in a while we passed a lone hut, generally neat, with a large pile of threshed rice in front of the door, a few flowers, and a water buffalo or two tethered in an adjacent shed. But no sign of human life.

It is not healthy to be in an isolated hut when either the Viet Cong or government forces come through, and it's generally safer to go off into the jungle and hide for a few hours.

There was not a trace of the enemy, either. No barricades or foot traps across the path at all, for a change.

I should note at this point that I am writing about an incident in 1962. It is more than two years later at this writing, and one aspect of operations of this kind has changed. The Viet Cong is strong enough now that it almost invariably ambushes a relief column, and does so with such strength of numbers and firepower that these ambushes are nothing short of slaughter.

The shadows grew longer, and the faint stirring of air in the treetops that comes with dusk began. Sunrises and sunsets are short in the tropics, and night quickly follows dusk. By seven every night of the year in South Viet Nam it is dark.

All at once, we began moving past huts in groups, and the path widened. Before us was a fairly wide, wooden footbridge. Beyond the bridge was Dam Doi, and we could see even at this distance that a national flag was flying.

Dam Doi, which is on the right side of the canal we had been paralleling, is bisected by a smaller canal that runs at right angles to the main one. The side of the town we were entering included a fairly large, circular market place flanked by a few fairly large, wooden buildings. Streets, actually paths of well-trampled mud, radiated from this to form the residential district of town. On the other side of the bisecting canal, crossed by another fairly good footbridge, was the military part of the town, including the district headquarters compound.

There were several hundred people milling around the market place, where acetylene lamps were already beginning to cast their harsh, white light. The people had clearly heard our approach, and had turned out for a look at their visitors. But they stared incuriously, with no noticeable expression. Most were women and children. None waved or called out. Their welcome didn't seem actively hostile, but they certainly didn't greet us like liberators, either.

The long column moved silently through the heart of downtown Dam Doi, weapons clanking, then over the footbridge, a dozen at a time. Here the main "street" ran right next to the main parallel canal. And facing the canal was the compound where we would spend the night.

District headquarters was a building with, inevitably, yellow stucco walls, black and yellow tiled floors, a small yard in front facing the canal, a flagpole in the center of the yard, and a wooden watchtower about thirty feet high in the back. A smaller building facing the courtyard, a kind of shed, was festooned with gaudy paper stars and bunting left over from an observance of *Tet*, the lunar New Year that had passed a few weeks earlier. *Tet* is by far the most important holiday in Viet Nam, and even the Viet Cong quits fighting during the four-day holiday.

But the holiday decorations looked wrong. Inside the shed, men were hammering planks together into what were obviously coffins, and the smell of death was heavy all around. A handful of women wearing white bands of mourning around their heads were wailing in front of the main building; all of them had babies in their arms.

The smell of death was coming from the canal, where an FOM gunboat was tied up. In a small sampan the FOM had towed in were two bodies, in a ghastly state of mutilation and decomposition. They were so bad that the FOM crew had not been willing to take them aboard the big boat itself, but insisted on towing them back. Two families in Dam Doi had recognized what remained of the faces as their own. These two had gone out with Captain Kha that black Saturday morning forty hours ago.

Inside the barbed wire of the headquarters compound, marines everywhere were setting up their mosquito nets and boiling rice in the pots they always carry with them. Captain

Kha's dry-eyed mistress was pouring tea for the officers inside the headquarters building.

If I said that Dam Doi was completely isolated from Saigon, this was not quite accurate. Saigon's government radio station has repeater stations all around the country, so that it is possible to receive the station any place. Very few peasants own radios of their own, but every hamlet of any consequence has a radio (from the U.S. Aid Mission) hooked up to a large loudspeaker which blares away all day long. Dam Doi's loudspeaker was mounted in the watchtower. I remember that it was playing an old recording of "In the Blue of Evening" that evening. The mourners went right on wailing.

Kha's mistress gave orders for dinner to be served to all the officers (and to me), and had cots set up indoors for all of them. This was a bit of unexpected luxury, but the word had already got around that this girl might have had something to do with Kha's disappearance. Every man slept with his service automatic in reach, and took turns posting guard.

There was no idea of going out to look for Kha and his men at night, who, by this time, had been missing about forty hours. For one thing, the night is risky even for large units, and for another, Dam Doi itself had to be protected.

Kha's girl friend showed us pictures of her man, and her eyes finally began to show signs of misery. He was young and strong and ambitious, she said, and had been terribly anxious to be able to report a victory. If only he had not been so headstrong. One of the pictures showed Kha talking into a microphone in front of the big picture of Diem over the front door of the headquarters building. It was probably a rally of some kind given for some visitors from Saigon.

All through the sweltering night, the geckos (lizard-like creatures that eat bugs) trumpeted their love songs, but otherwise the night was still. Apparently the Viet Cong had no appetite for a fight with a force of marines this large.

By sunrise we had all gulped down some cold rice and were ready to move again. The direction was the same, farther down the parallel canal. It would only be a matter of three miles or so before we would reach the place where Kha had gone.

Crowds of women chattering excitedly and looking worried now crowded the compound courtyard. They were waiting for word about their husbands, sons and fathers who had gone with Kha. Outside the barbed wire, children trudged along with the marines for a few hundred yards before turning back.

The jungle was very thick again, and the path narrower than ever. We slogged along about two miles, and then sent out some scouts to the right.

The scouts moved a few hundred yards through the trees, their rifles and Tommy guns at the ready. Then they stopped. They had smelled something that could only mean we were headed in the right direction.

The whole column turned right to follow the scouts. We were soon on another path, very muddy, and heavily tracked and rutted. The smell of rotting human beings was almost overpowering, as we moved along, and a few marines tied pocket handkerchiefs over their noses. This does no good whatever, by the way.

The jungle thinned out a little, and we came to some huts— the hamlet. All of them were deserted completely; there weren't even any chickens or buffalo. Behind the huts was a water hole about thirty feet in diameter with mud sides that sloped down to the filthy water. Neatly ranged around these sides, like spokes in a wheel, were thirty bloated corpses, all in the uniform of government troops. The hot sun had hastened the decomposition of two days, and intestines had forced their way out of gaping belly wounds, making yellowish piles atop each body. Tracks showed that the bodies all had been towed to the place by ropes tied to buffalo.

From a small, bamboo flagpole a few feet away fluttered a large Viet Cong flag—red on top, blue on the bottom, with a large yellow star in the middle. The enemy had left a display for us.

Someone found a rope, and all of us got out of the way while the flagpole was pulled down. The precaution proved to have been wise. The flagpole disappeared in a geyser of mud, and grenade fragments snapped through the trees. Booby trap.

The Viet Cong no doubt held a fine victory celebration before we arrived, with drill formation, salute to the colors, photographs of the war booty, and all the rest. But now they were gone.

Under trees and in clumps of weeds we found more bodies. Among them was the body of Kha. But we could not find Kha's head, which apparently had been hacked off with a machete. Perhaps the Viet Cong stuck it on the end of a pole and took it parading around some other hamlets, as they sometimes do.

Beheading is a terrible thing to do to a man in Viet Nam. Most people believe that the loss of the head damns the spirit to an eternity of restless wandering. It is the worst way to die.

We found a little store in the hamlet, boarded up with folding, louvred wooden doors. The marines ripped the doors off, and found a large stock of joss sticks—the long, tan sticks that burn like incense, and are said to please the spirit world. The whole stock, several thousand sticks, was stuffed into jars and lighted. The burning joss didn't improve the odor of things much, but perhaps it made things better for the spirits that had left the carnage at the water hole.

We ripped the door sections from their hinges to make litters, and began the revolting job of picking up the bodies. A half-dozen marines were retching as they worked. A large sampan had pulled up to the hamlet along a creek, and the bodies were heaved aboard like sides of beef. I noticed that some of them wore the shoulder insignia of Father Hoa's Sea Swallows.

The sampan, water almost up to its gunwales, moved off, and we started probing the jungle around the hamlet in a futile quest for the enemy. Someone spotted a lone figure in black, running through the trees a few hundred feet away. The marine snapped up his BAR and emptied a whole magazine at the figure, but I don't think he hit him.

Nothing much happened from then on, and eventually we marched back to Dam Doi. The corpse boat had preceded us there, and the bodies were now all laid out on the ground in front of the administration building, wrapped in the mats that are used in Viet Nam both as mattresses and shrouds. Scores of women, all in the white dress of mourning, were wailing and prostrating themselves before the bodies of their dead men. The coffin factory was going full tilt, with old men and boys filling the little building with lumber and hammering away. Some coffins were finished and mounted on sawhorses, a candle or two on their lids.

The sun was setting again and Pat Boone was singing something or other from the tower loudspeaker. I asked an officer if he couldn't turn the damned thing off.

"Sure, but it's better not to. Our people here don't care. And for the Viet Cong out there, it's a sign we're still alive and still able to resist. With that thing playing and the flag flying, we still have something."

I left Dam Doi, but somehow every few months I found myself back there. Each time it was somewhat the worse for wear. American advisors and helicopters began to arrive in Viet Nam, and at least it was easier to get to Dam Doi each time it was hit.

The low earth fighting walls around the district headquarters compound were scarred with countless bullets and the courtyard was pocked with scores of mortar shell craters. None of the shells and bullets seemed to have gone into the residential side of town across the little canal, though.

But the last time I went to Dam Doi, more than two years after my first visit, the place was almost unrecognizable. In the administrative compound, all the smaller buildings were flattened in a tangle of bamboo. The administration building was wrecked, its walls blasted with huge holes by 57-millimeter recoilless cannon shells. The watchtower was destroyed, and for the first time, the loudspeaker was silent. I almost missed it. The flagpole was gone.

Twenty or thirty huts built behind the administration building for the wives and children of the defense force were burned to the ground. I nearly stumbled over the charred bodies of four pregnant women as I walked through the embers. The bodies were so badly disfigured that no one had claimed them and picked them up. On the tiled floors of the building, dozens of corpses were lined up, a few propped in seated positions around the walls. More bodies were laid out in front, most of them on litters made from sections of corrugated iron blasted from roofs. They were covered with rattan mats and tagged. A lot of them were small—the bodies of children. One live child of about five clung to one of the large bundles, screaming uncontrollably. It was his mother.

The National Liberation Front had come steathily in sampans at about two in the morning. They had cut some of the barbed wire, and were inside one corner of the compound before anyone knew what was happening. The fight had lasted several hours before the little garrison was finally wiped out. Brass cartridge cases were scattered everywhere, and some of them were Russian or Czechoslovak submachine-gun ammunition. Their bases were dated 1962.

Among those who had died was the district chief—the third in a row to die at his job in Dam Doi. He, too, had lost his head. Some Viet Cong unit must have quite a collection of heads.

Tile was blasted from some of the roofs of the houses in the residential section across the canal, although most of that part of town, as usual, showed little damage.

But this time a lot of survivors, mostly women, had had enough of Dam Doi and its never-ending bloodshed. Their bedding and pots over their shoulders, they had clustered around a flight of American helicopters that had landed behind the hamlet, pleading to be taken out, anywhere. I think a few of them finally did leave, but most of them are still there.

"I shall leave my bones in Dam Doi," an old woman told me. "Where else have I to go? The fate of this place is black, but so is my own. My husband was killed during the French war, and both my sons died here in this one. Death means nothing to me any more."

The same day, I visited another district capital hamlet about twenty miles away, called Cai Nuoc. The same thing had happened at Cai Nuoc during the night, and here, too, the district chief was dead. More than forty defenders had been killed.

The pattern was always the same—the officials, soldiers and their families were brutally slaughtered, but the rest of the townspeople generally were not touched, except by stray bullets.

In this same province of An Xuyen there used to be two tiny hamlets, called Thoi Binh and Cha La, up in the northwest part of the province along a canal. Both places were at the edge of the big forest I mentioned earlier in the chapter, occupied by the Viet Cong's fierce U Minh Battalion.

Another hamlet called Thoi Binh still exists, but the Thoi Binh farthest up the canal is gone.

There used to be a little garrison there, with about a score of militiamen to defend the place. As usual in such cases, the men had their wives and children with them. There were sniping and probing by the Viet Cong nearly every night, but the post held. It held, that is, until Thoi Binh's last night, when the Viet Cong swept in, in a mass attack.

The following morning, a post farther down the canal had a ghastly visit. A large sampan came down the river. In it were the bodies of all the Thoi Binh defenders, mutilated by bayonets and acid poured over the faces. Also in the sampan were the surviving widows and children, who had been forced by the Viet Cong to ride the sampan downstream. Slogans were painted on the sampan, saying, "Don't get in the way of the National Liberation Front or the same will happen to you."

The hamlet of Cha La on the same canal was wiped out and leveled the same night. The only thing left standing was a sign bearing the name of the hamlet. Later that day, U.S. Air Force fighters ran an air strike on the sign to blow it out. It seemed like bad propaganda to leave only the sign standing.

At another hamlet farther north in the Mekong Delta, a hamlet chief (newly arrived and inexperienced) had been trying to collect government taxes and get young men registered for the national draft.

One night the Viet Cong came in, tied him to a stake in the center of the market place, and forced all the other villagers to come and watch. Among them were the chief's pregnant wife and child. They all watched as the man was slowly disemboweled. The child was then decapitated. Finally, the widow was tied to the same stake and also disemboweled.

I could fill up many more pages of similar incidents I have seen, but it would be merely repetitive, and besides, I don't like remembering them. The noteworthy thing about all of them is that they show a clear pattern of terror directed against those who oppose the National Liberation Front in one way or another. But beyond this, the terror is directed on general principle against officials—especially energetic or competent officials. Perhaps each dead district chief means relatively little in himself. But the mortality rate of district chiefs in some places, such as Dam Doi, is not conducive to recruiting civil servants. A district chief is paid about $40.00 a month, and the only other financial incentive is graft. The corrupt civil servant is swiftly singled out by the Viet Cong for assassination, if only to please the people. In any case, assignment to places like Dam Doi in the past has generally been the result of incurring the displeasure of officials in Saigon, and has happened in many cases as punishment or even personal revenge.

It is a cruel assignment, which in some cases is tantamount to the death sentence.

Politics often are merely an excuse for terrorism.

I know a young woman named L. whose family was trapped in the cross fire between the French and Ho Chi Minh's Viet Minh, with tragic results. The case is typical of what still goes on.

L., who was ten years old in 1946, was the daughter of a Vietnamese civil servant under the French colonial province chief in Ben Tre, a Mekong River Delta town about fifty miles south of Saigon. Her mother was a schoolteacher. The family was fairly well off, and had a fine house near the center of Ben Tre. Things were happy for the family, even during the Japanese occupation of World War II. L. remembers making tourist trips up the Mekong into Cambodia during the occupation, and sharing the lunches of friendly Japanese troops. Japanese occupation reached the southern part of Viet Nam only late in the war, and was never very oppressive. The hatred for the Japanese felt in North Viet Nam never had time to develop in the south.

L.'s father, a man named Tet, worked for the French, but his sympathies were on the side of the nationalists. He began to cooperate with the Viet Minh.

Tet had a neighbor in Ben Tre who was jealous of his nice

house and prosperity. There had been bitter feelings for years between Tet and this neighbor.

After the end of World War II, a seesaw battle began between the returning French and Ho's Viet Minh, which was now operating in the open (with Japanese blessings) as the legal government of Viet Nam.

The battle swept repeatedly over the Mekong River Delta, and never was really resolved there. But in one of the French advances, Tet and his family moved back with the Viet Minh, out of Ben Tre. They went to live in a small, peaceful hamlet, where the Viet Minh held complete sway.

L. remembers many happy days living, for the first time in her life, as a peasant girl. She, her sister and five brothers enjoyed living under a thatched roof. They liked playing with livestock, and the whole family relaxed in the lazy, apolitical peasant atmosphere.

The Viet Minh used to hold daily song rallies in back of the hamlet, marching around and saluting the big red flag with the yellow star every morning. Tet was one of them, and was even armed with a fine, big hunting knife he had bought on one of the family vacations in Cambodia.

There was always the rumble of distant artillery, but the war got no closer. The situation began to stabilize into definite areas of control. But what the family didn't know at the time was that their old enemy from Ben Tre was now a fairly high ranking Viet Minh officer. One day he denounced Tet to the local commissar as a French spy. Tet was arrested by the Viet Minh and taken to a jungle jail.

He was not particularly badly treated, and Tet's frantic wife was permitted to take food to his cell. After a few weeks, he was released, with no more explanation than he had been given when he was arrested.

Time passed, and there was no more trouble, but the family was uneasy. They knew they were being watched.

One day, an old friend of Tet came to him and asked him to accompany him to Ben Tre on a business matter. Ben Tre by now was in French hands. There was some worried discussion, but in the end, Tet went. The business was finished in several days, and Tet came back safely to his family in the hamlet.

But again, the old enemy denounced him, saying Tet had gone to Ben Tre to carry information to the enemy.

L. was asleep, her head resting against her father's shoulder when they came. It was about 2 A.M., and they dragged Tet roughly from his bed. He was not permitted to take any clothes. Mrs. Tet pleaded with the men in black, and the children screamed. But Tet was gone. A muffled shot sounded somewhere off in the dark jungle.

As a postscript, Mrs. Tet managed to raise the family with her earnings as a teacher. Some of the children went to Europe to take degrees. At this writing, two of the sons are in the Vietnamese Army, fighting the new enemy—the Viet Cong.

But usually there is no happy ending. Strangely enough, Viet Cong terror is often blamed on the Americans. The reasoning is that the Americans have the power to stop the terror but refuse to do it.

Recently I stopped at a hamlet called Go Den on the main delta highway, only fifteen miles south of Saigon. The night before, a police check point on the road had been destroyed by Viet Cong rocket launchers and machine-gun fire. The guerrillas had then poured into a militia training camp on the other side of the road and killed about forty of the trainees in their beds.

The militia post was typical of outposts all over the nation.

Built in the old French style, the post was triangular with mud walls on all sides and a small mud tower with gun slots at each corner. The whole thing was surrounded with tangles of barbed wire, and could be entered only through a barbed wire gate in one wall, leading over a little moat by footbridge. Inside were half-a-dozen long wooden barracks buildings and a locked, concrete arms room.

The Viet Cong had not come through the gate. They smashed each of the corner towers with rocket launchers, and set up machine guns at two of the corners. Between the two guns, the whole post was covered.

About ten of the militiamen, some of them wounded, dashed from their barracks when the shooting began, and ran for the gate. But a Viet Cong had set up an automatic rifle trained on the gate, and each man who came through tumbled into the moat, a burst of slugs through his body. The leftover defenders were all either shot or bayoneted by the Viet Cong clean-up crew. The guerrillas shot the lock off the arms bunker, and carried off about one hundred good American weapons, including several machine guns and mortars.

In all the shooting, the town of Go Den was not touched, and there were no accidental casualties.

While I was sorting through the remains, a Vietnamese policeman came running up to me, tears streaming from his eyes.

"My God, why didn't they come to help us?" he said in French. "They were so close. When the attack began, I called them by radio, and they answered, but they never came until this morning. Why couldn't you Americans with your helicopters have come to help us, at least, if our own soldiers wouldn't come? If you can't help us, why don't you get out of Viet Nam completely and leave us to die quickly?"

After a while, I learned that the "they" the policeman was complaining about were two full battalions of crack Vietnamese paratroopers, a battalion of regular army troops, some other smaller units and a good supply of armored cars and tanks— all no more than ten minutes' drive away down the road. These units were all bivouacked in the area as part of the government's ambitious "pacification plan."

There is no question that these units were available at the time of the Go Den massacre, and I have never been given an explanation by any of the responsible officers as to why they didn't come. But that is the way this war goes.

Oddly enough, while peasants often blame America for Viet Cong slaughters, it works the other way around, too.

Not long ago a U.S. Army helicopter was flying over the same province in which Go Den is located, and drew heavy enemy ground fire from a hut in a small hamlet. The helicopter wheeled around, dived at the hamlet, and emptied its rocket pods into it. The whole community became an inferno of explosions and flame. Five civilians, definitely not members of the National Liberation Front, were killed.

Later, American civilian field workers moved into the hamlet to make some reparations.

"I'm sorry this happened," an American told the hamlet chief.

"Oh, we understand," the old man said. "Your helicopter was right to fire. It was the Viet Cong's fault for starting it.

"The Viet Cong will be back tonight, but this afternoon we shall hold a protest rally against the Viet Cong to express our anger."

Viet Cong terror is not confined to government officials and soldiers and their families. Many a schoolteacher has been dropped from his bicycle by Viet Cong bursts. Teachers, unless they are neutral or pro-Liberation Front, are regarded as dangerous elements by the Viet Cong. In Viet Cong "liberated areas," the Front has its own schools and teachers. These schools are always clean and orderly, and bedecked with paper Viet Cong flags cut out by the children.

Rural Catholic priests are sometimes shot down, although they generally are first given several warnings to leave their parishes. Even Buddhist monks have been assassinated.

There is a word used in Viet Nam a great deal by the experts on guerrilla warfare (or, rather, on "counterinsurgency"). That word is "infrastructure."

Broadly speaking, "infrastructure" means all organized authority. Presidents and politburo chairmen, province chiefs and province commissars, armed forces and their command structure, petty officials all the way down the line, secret agents, terrorists and propagandists, doctors and aid men, public works employees and communications technicians, even teachers and religious leaders—all of these are considered part of the over-all "infrastructure."

As a general definition, infrastructure is the people and machinery essential to hanging a government and a nation together.

The Saigon government has its infrastructure (or at least tries to) and the Viet Cong has its own separate infrastructure.

From the beginning of its operations in the late 1950s, the Viet Cong has made its primary objective the cutting apart and dissolving of the government system of authority, and substitution of its own. It is a slow process that has been compared with dripping acid on the steel frame that holds a large structure together. It is highly selective, since, according to the rules of Viet Cong warfare, the acid must not spill any more than necessary on the bulk of the structure, only on the supporting frame.

Officials and "cadres" must be killed, but the mass of people must not be hurt. Fortifications, canals, roads and offices must be blown up, but installations that will be useful after an anticipated Viet Cong victory must be left alone. To date, the Viet Cong has never tried to sabotage the big, new Japanese-built hydroelectric plant at Da Nhim, even though the plant is extremely exposed and sabotage would be easy. French plantation officials are kidnapped for ransom nearly every week, but the rubber trees themselves are left alone. The French plantation men are practically never killed and are almost always released after payment of ransoms. The reason is that each Frenchman employs several thousand Vietnamese plantation workers. The closing of a big plantation would be a staggering economic loss for thousands of workers, who would blame the Viet Cong instead of helping it.

One of these plantation managers, Claud Salvaire, manager of "Catecka," the largest tea plantation in Viet Nam, told me of his own experience with the guerrillas.

"During the height of the picking season, we hire about five thousand workers who get paid by the bushel. They make good wages. A few hundred more work in our processing plant [at a hamlet near the central Vietnamese town of Pleiku].

"A lot of these men and women are Viet Cong, of course. I know who some of them are. One day, one of my workers complained to me that he and all the others were not getting any sleep, because the Viet Cong kept them up late listening to propaganda lectures.

"I went to see a man I knew to be a high-ranking Viet Cong organizer, and complained to him. He smiled and said he would see what he could do. A few days after that, the nightly lectures ended. But daytime lectures began, right in the fields. Production sagged. There's nothing much I can do.

"The government and the Americans would like to help. The Americans at their camp over in Pleiku often come here to my house for dinner. But I have to be careful.

"We needed power for our processing machinery, and it happens that there is a good river on this plantation. So we built a little hydroelectric dam that works beautifully and gives more power than we need. The government province chief sent me several companies of his Civil Guards to protect the dam and the powerhouse.

"Of course, I never had any faith in the Civil Guards. Their noncommissioned officers are all lowland Vietnamese, but the privates are all montagnards [primitive mountain tribesmen of different ethnic origins from the Vietnamese].

"The montagnards and Vietnamese have always hated each other. These NCOs treat their men like dirt, sitting around playing cards with each other all day long. Naturally, the men hate them and refuse to take this job seriously.

"At any rate, when American advisors first started moving to Pleiku, they had almost no equipment for their camp, no generators or anything. They were nice people, and I wanted to be friendly. So I offered to run a line out to their camp from my hydroelectric generator, at least until they got settled in. They were pleased, and it was done.

"But two days later, my hydroelectric plant was blown to bits by a huge bomb, practically under the noses of the Civil Guard. And a note was left on my door saying: 'Power for the plantation, yes, power for the U.S. aggressors, no.'

"Eventually, I had the generator rebuilt, but without a line to the American camp. It hasn't been disturbed again.

"You see how I live. I am in the hands of God—or, rather, of the Viet Cong."

That was a long time ago in 1962, in the wind-swept, open prairies of Pleiku Province. Salvaire survived all that, only to meet a killer in Saigon. A plantation worker Salvaire had fired caught up with him in Saigon one weekend, and planted a knife in his stomach. Salvaire lived, but went back to France to recuperate.

Viet Cong terror extends to the big towns and cities as well as the countryside. The key tools are bombs and grenades.

The object of a city bombing generally is both symbolic and practical. Americans are the most frequent targets of such bombings.

A major object of Viet Cong terror bombing is to isolate American advisors and officials from the Vietnamese by making Vietnamese afraid to associate with Americans. The bombings are therefore as much for propaganda purposes as they are to destroy people and things. The technique is fairly effective.

On February 18, 1964, Tran Nam Trung, chairman of the Viet Cong's military committee (and commander-in-chief of Viet Cong forces), issued the following communique, which was broadcast by "Liberation Radio":

> For more than two years, the U.S. aggressors' army has continually enlarged the crime-studded war against the patriotic movement of the South Vietnamese people. The U.S. troops have not neglected any savage act to terrorize and massacre our compatriots.
>
> The situation has now become more serious than ever. The South Vietnamese people have no course other than to resolutely devote all strength, at any price, to carry out to the end the armed, comprehensive protracted war of resistance in order to defeat the U.S. imperialist aggressors and the traitorous lackeys to attain the final goal: Peace, independence, neutrality, democracy and prosperity in the country.
>
> In order to create favorable conditions for the liberation troops and the People's Armed Forces to attack the enemy more strongly and intensively, and to destroy the enemy forces as much as possible, and with a view to sparing our compatriots and foreign [neutral] nationals living in South Viet Nam, as well as officers and enlisted men of the lackeys' armed forces who actually are on the side of the people, the National Liberation Front's Central Committee's Military Committee announces the following:
>
> 1. Effective immediately, the compatriots from all walks of life living in areas under the enemy's temporary control are requested

to stay away from places where there are U.S. aggressor troops, such as billets, restaurants, dance halls, clubs, theaters and so forth. Let the compatriots positively join the liberation troops and People's Armed Forces in destroying and annihilating the enemy.

2. Foreign nationals should not collaborate in any way with the U.S. aggressor troops. In other words, they should not, under any circumstances or in any place, fraternize with or live with the U.S. aggressor troops. Foreign nationals should also not use any means of transport of a military type.

3. Officers and enlisted men in the southern [Saigon] army and the personnel of the southern administration who are patriotic but who have not had occasion to contribute to the people's struggle for the liberation of South Viet Nam should seek to stay away and refuse to take part in the criminal acts of the U.S. aggressor troops and their lackeys.

The military committee earnestly calls for patriotism from the compatriots, for understanding from the foreign nationals, and for clear-sightedness and awareness of the situation from the officers and enlisted men in the southern army and the personnel in the southern administration. Let them seriously comply with the points set forth in this communique.

Many Vietnamese are in fact nervous about being in public places with Americans. Vietnamese bus drivers generally will not take Americans as passengers, and if they do, most of the Vietnamese passengers get off. Terror works.

Even concerning Americans, the Viet Cong is reasonably selective in its targets. "Liberation Radio," the Viet Cong's clandestine propaganda transmitter, has said that American women, children and civilians will not be targets of bombings unless they frequent military establishments. Viet Cong leaflets even apologized after a number of American women and children were badly wounded in 1964 in two huge bombings—the American community theater and the American baseball park.

But dependents or not, the bombings go on. Grenades fly over the hedges around American-occupied villas, and bombs are heaved into American military buses and jeeps, barracks and billets, and, most of all, bars.

Bar bombings almost always are grisly.

The author on a helicopter mission.

HELICOPTER WAR—U. S. Army UH1B helicopters scoot across a rice field over Vietnamese troops, ready to machinegun enemy opposition. *(AP Photo by Huynh Cong La)*

A wrecked government 105-mm howitzer pokes from the rubble of a post razed by the Viet Cong. (U. S. Army Photo)

THE VIET CONG—A 13-year-old girl guerrilla of the Viet Cong is tied to a hut while undergoing interrogation by government troops. (AP Photo by Horst Faas)

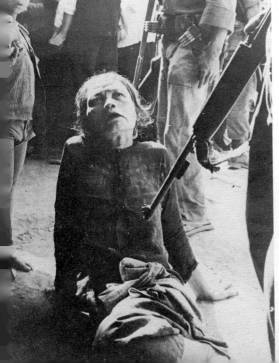

THE VIET CONG—An old woman, the mother of a Viet Cong guerrilla, pleads with government troops for the release of her son. (AP Photo by Horst Faas)

THE VIET CONG—A guerrilla surrenders from his hole. *(AP Photo by Horst Faas)*

THE VIET CONG—Guerrilla prisoners, their arms bound, are loaded aboard a helicopter. *(AP Photo)*

**AMBUSH LOOKING FOR A PLACE TO HAP-
PEN**—Vietnamese troops and an armored car
moving along a road in the Mekong River
Delta, in the kind of formation most likely to
result in a bloody ambush by the Viet Cong.
The troops are huddled together, and no
flank sentries are posted. *(AP Photo by Horst
Faas)*

WAR TROPHIES—A Vietnamese Marine and a Viet Cong prisoner
carry the heads of three Viet Cong away from an engagement 20
miles southeast of Saigon. The severed heads are suspended from
the pole with vine strung through their ears. Heads are collected
by both sides in the Vietnamese war. *(AP Photo)*

Bottom center: **PADDY-FIELD KEEL HAULING**—This Viet Cong prisoner failed to talk. He died being towed across the fields by an M113 armored personnel carrier. *(AP Photo)*

Bottom right: **COUP DE GRACE**—Vietnamese militiamen try to strangle a wounded farmer by stamping a stake across his throat. The man was hit repeatedly by machinegun fire but still was alive when troops reached him. The strangling effort failed, but the man died a short time later in his wife's arms. (Incident described in Chapter 1). *(Photo by Malcolm W. Browne)*

PASTORAL SCENE—Life returns to normal at a hamlet 40 miles from Saigon in the wake of a quick little battle. Someone will come around later to pick up the bodies. Each has been wrapped in a type of straw mat used in Viet Nam both as a mattress for the living and a shroud for the dead. (*AP Photo*)

Bottom left: **DEATH IN THE NURSERY**—A bullet-spattered bench, a cluster of bodies and a doll at a government outpost near Cai Be in the Mekong River Delta, overrun by Viet Cong. (*AP Photo by Marcellino Roxas*)
Bottom right: **TERROR BOMBING**—A Saigon bar frequented by Americans, blasted by a Viet Cong bomb. Five were killed and 26 wounded in this blast. (*AP Photo by Horst Faas*)

UNITED UNTO DEATH—A peasant and his wife, their arms still linked, as they were when caught in the crossfire of Vietnamese war. (AP Photo by Ray Jewett)

DELTA BURDEN—Carrying this kind of load has become routine in the life of Mekong River Delta. (AP Photo by Horst Faas)

FUTURE LEADER?—One of South Viet Nam's rising young officers known as the "young Turks"—Brig. Gen. Nguyen Chanh Thi. (Mentioned in Chapter 11) *(AP Photo by Michel Renard)*

NAPALM—A young casualty of an airraid on the Mekong River Delta. *(AP Photo by Horst Faas)*

I was especially moved by one, at which I arrived just a few minutes after the explosion. This particular bar had a very good five-piece combo, and was well known as a good place to dance. None of the five Americans seriously hurt by the blast died, but seven Vietnamese—most of them taxi girls—were killed.

One wall was blown out of the bar. The party decorations hanging from the ceiling lay in a smoky jumble with chunks of bodies, and the whole floor was slick with a mixture of blood and shattered glassware.

Next to the orchestra stand in the corner, a foot still wearing a fancy, high-heeled shoe was standing upright, its body somewhere in the jumble on the other side of the room.

Besides this kind of bombing, there are many bombings for personal revenge or even by accident. Deserter soldiers turned robbers often use grenades against the houses they intend to rob. Grenades sometimes drop from their pins by accident when soldiers go to movies. Fragmentation grenades in crowded movie theaters result in awful casualties.

Many people dabble in bombing in Saigon, and the Viet Cong is by no means always the culprit. Bombing in Saigon has been for many years an accepted mode of political expression.

In French colonial days, there were notorious bombing factions everywhere, including some of the French themselves. Nor has the Saigon government itself, in recent years, been above an occasional discreet bombing. U.S. intelligence men are certain that a good many of the low-power bombs that exploded in Saigon during Diem's last year in power were actually of government origin. Such bombings can always be blamed on Viet Cong, Buddhists, or anyone else against whom a government wishes to stir up American wrath.

In late 1964, a huge bomb in Saigon's plush Caravelle Hotel blew out the entire fifth floor of the building. A number of people were hurt, but no one died. The Caravelle is the usual hotel for wealthy visiting foreigners—diplomats, high-ranking military officers, rich tourists, congressmen, visiting news correspondents, and so on. It also houses the Australian and New Zealand embassies.

The bomb was apparently planted by a well-dressed Vietnamese, who had rented an entire corner suite of the Caravelle (at about $30.00 a day). He left the bomb in a closet of the suite in such a way that damage would be heavy but loss of life probably minimal. This kind of bombing is not the Viet Cong style. For one thing, it is expensive, and the Viet Cong prefers bombing on a shoestring. But it happened at a time the government was in chaos and there was rioting in the streets. Any one of a dozen factions, including the Nguyen Khanh government itself, might have stood to reap some psychological advantage from the Caravelle bombing.

Some of the Viet Cong bombers have been caught. Most have been students in their teens.

The Viet Cong has a youth organization called the "Volunteers for Death," of which Cell 65 and Cell 67 have been identified as the primary troublemakers in Saigon. Bomb throwing is considered an honorable and worthy occupation by these people, who show no remorse whatever if they are caught.

Up to this point, I have concentrated on Viet Cong terror. But terror in Viet Nam is a two-way street. It probably would be unfair to describe the Vietnamese as an unusually brutal people. But at the same time, I have personally witnessed more brutality in Viet Nam than in any other country of Asia.

Torture has been an adjunct to interrogation for many years in South Viet Nam, and there are no prospects that this pattern will change in the foreseeable future.

To the average American, all forms of torture are revolting. But given the situation in Viet Nam, distinctions must be made between degrees of torture.

The Vietnamese police probably use the mildest forms, in interrogating political (or Viet Cong) prisoners.

There is a small, American field generator used extensively in Viet Nam for powering pack radios. The device is mounted on a tripod and is operated by hand cranks on both sides, turned by one man. The generator produces a high enough voltage to produce a severe but not fatal shock.

The "ding-a-ling" method of interrogation involves connection of electrodes from this generator to the temples of the subject, or other parts of the body. In the case of women prisoners, the electrodes often are attached to the nipples. The results are terrifying and painful, but subjects are not permanently damaged. This technique is often applied at provincial interrogation centers by police, and in the field by soldiers.

Another method involves the near drowning of the subject. In late 1963, a young Vietnamese woman working as a secretary at the British Embassy in Saigon was arrested on grounds that she had provided shelter for a Buddhist monk wanted by Diem's police. She described her experience this way:

"I waited in a room with some other prisoners, who were led off one at a time for interrogation. Finally my turn came. I was taken to a bare office where there were two desks and a bench. The man interrogating me was seated at one of the desks.

"He asked me if I knew anything about the monk. Actually, I did, but of course I denied it. Then two other large men came into the room. They ripped off my dress and forced me to lie down on the bench, tying me tightly to it with pieces of rope. Next to the bench was a bucket of filthy water. Some of this was poured over my face and I choked and vomited. Then a big cloth was placed over my face—tightly—and the water was poured on it. I couldn't breathe. Just as I was about to lose consciousness, the cloth was taken off. Then one of the men beat me on the soles of the feet with a heavy club. I screamed terribly from the pain. The other began beating my stomach with his fist. The cloth was put over my face again, and this time I passed out. When I came to, I was ordered to dress and clean up the room. They told me I would be questioned again tomorrow."

It happened that this woman was not questioned again, because the following day, Diem was overthrown in a bloody coup.

But the wet-cloth interrogation technique is still used. It has at least the merit that it is not fatal and leaves no physically harmful effects.

Presumably, the "mild" forms of torture sometimes leave psychological effects, however. At this writing, nearly a dozen former political Buddhist prisoners are patients at the Cong Hoa

Hospital, Viet Nam's main military hospital. All are highly disturbed mental patients. They were released from Diem's prisons nearly one year ago.

Major General Nguyen Khanh, one of the military premiers who followed the Diem regime, went to visit these patients at the hospital recently. They screamed and went berserk. Khanh was told by embarrassed hospital attendants that the patients always reacted that way at the sight of a military uniform. Khanh left, promising to return later in civilian clothes.

But some of the forms of torture employed are more sinister, in that they maim or disfigure. Most of these are used in the field by Vietnamese troops on Viet Cong prisoners or suspects, and the object is to extract tactical intelligence.

They can involve beating and cutting, or worse. Many a news correspondent or U.S. Army military advisor has seen the hands whacked off prisoners with machetes. Prisoners are sometimes castrated or blinded.

In more than one case a Viet Cong suspect has been towed after interrogation behind an armored personnel carrier across the rice fields. This always results in death in one of its most painful forms.

Vietnamese troops also take their share of enemy heads.

Americans have learned to be suspicious of Vietnamese claims of victory over the Viet Cong, and are usually satisfied with the validity of these claims only when they see visual evidence, such as bodies.

One day, an American battalion advisor was seated in his headquarters shack in the Mekong Delta when a grinning Vietnamese officer walked in and said, "Big victory. We killed seventeen Viet Cong today." The American smiled doubtfully, and said, "Where are they?"

"Oh, out there near the road, about five kilometers from here."

"But, Nhut, you know we have to have evidence before we can report that on the American side."

Nhut scratched his head and walked out. The American thought the matter was ended. But an hour later, Nhut returned and asked the American to step outside. Outside, a truck had parked, surrounded by grinning Vietnamese rangers. In the truck were seventeen bloody heads, stacked like melons.

But by and large, things like this in the field appear to be more acts of revenge and hatred than merely adjuncts of intelligence interrogation. Many soldiers enjoy beating up Viet Cong prisoners. The subjects of interrogation so often die under questioning that intelligence seems to be a secondary matter.

In 1963, the American advisory command began experimenting with small, field lie detectors for use by Vietnamese troops on Viet Cong suspects.

The innovation drew wide international publicity, most of it unfavorable. Leading American publications attacked the little lie detectors as nothing more than toys, which in the hands of unskilled operators could result in nothing but injustice. The criticism was probably valid.

But seasoned field men here regarded the criticism as wholly irrelevant.

"Stuff like that gives me a pretty good idea of how little Americans know about the war we're fighting here," a U.S. Army Special Forces officer told me.

"Sure, those lie detectors would be no good in a U.S. court of law, but this ain't a U.S. court of law, it's Viet Nam. I figure it this way. These little lie detectors must give the defendant a clean bill at least some of the time. As it is, when the Rangers or Airborne get their hooks into some guy, he doesn't stand even a chance. The lie detector would give him some chance. And it might cut down the unpleasant preliminaries to the executions."

American advisors in Viet Nam generally don't like the torture they see applied almost daily. They are required to report what they see on special forms through the American command chain. Occasionally, they actively interfere with procedings, sometimes offering a cigarette or a candy bar to the captive. But they cannot interfere too often without provoking the hostility of the officers and men they are supposed to be advising. And, like it or not, they must learn to make distinctions between various degrees of torture.

Some Vietnamese regard Americans as hypocritically soft-hearted.

"You don't like the methods we apply to prisoners and the way we do business in the field," a Vietnamese commander told me once. "But you have nothing against the use of artillery barrages, and air strikes using heavy bombs and napalm. Have you ever visited a hamlet hit by napalm after your planes have finished?"

I have visited such hamlets, and there is no question that the results are revolting. Unfortunately, the Viet Cong builds bunkers so skillfully it is rarely touched by aerial bombs or napalm, except in cases of direct hits. But huts are flattened, and civilian loss of life is generally high. In some, the charred bodies of children and babies have made pathetic piles in the middle of the remains of market places.

Artillery also causes heavy accidental casualties.

Most Vietnamese officers have been trained in French or American patterns. A young infantry officer leading his company across an open field that is suddenly taken under fire from a tree line tends to react instinctively. His men are in the greatest danger, and pinned down helplessly, so he calls for artillery support or an air strike on the tree line. The barrage or strike comes. Almost invariably, behind the tree line is a hamlet, which is destroyed, with heavy civilian casualties. The Viet Cong plans things this way, and reaps a substantial propaganda harvest every time it happens.

The nonselective terror of artillery and air strikes led one American infantry officer to say: "This is a rifleman's war, and I'd be happy if they took every plane and every cannon out of the country. They do more harm than good. To pick a needle out of a haystack you need tweezers, not a bulldozer. And the best tool for picking out Viet Cong is the rifle."

This attitude was expressed even more forcefully by Father Hoa, the seventy-five-year-old fighting priest mentioned earlier in this chapter, whose men were butchered by the Viet Cong at Dam Doi and elsewhere. Father Hoa, who received the Ramon

Magsaysay Award for outstanding service in Asia for 1964, said at his acceptance speech in Manila:

> When fought as an international war, we have no chance to win. How can we explain to a mother when her child is burned by napalm? And how can we expect a young man to fight for us when his aged father was killed by artillery fire?
>
> Indeed, how can we claim to be with the people when we burn their homes simply because those homes happen to be in the Viet Cong controlled territory?
>
> Many have asked me why are we not winning in Viet Nam? My answer is simple. The misplacement of the order of importance. The Magsaysay way is: Winning the people first, winning the war second. I am afraid in Viet Nam today, the order is reversed.
>
> I can talk plainly like this because I am a soldier as well as a priest. Fighting is necessary in order to protect the people from being physically harmed by the armed communists. But arms are useful only for defensive purposes. Our offense is to rely solely on winning the people because as soon as the people understand what communism means, and as soon as they have faith in our ability to protect them, and as soon as they have confidence in our integrity, the battle is won.

In the long run, Father Hoa and others like him who oppose terror in general are probably right. But a strong case can be made for the application of specific terror to specific people. Even Americans have been forced to concede that terror can be an extremely useful weapon in this strange war. And in 1964 American officials for the first time endorsed and backed a campaign of selective terror in the Viet Cong style, for use against the Viet Cong.

Hand-picked Vietnamese troops were organized into a few guerrilla squads. Working closely with rural secret agents, they began penetrating Viet Cong liberated areas by stealth at night. Viet Cong commissars, key members of the clandestine enemy "infrastructure," began to die mysteriously and violently, often in their own beds. On each of the bodies was left a piece of paper, about four inches square, printed in black leaving the white outline of a grotesque, human eye.

In some areas, the appearance of "the eye" began to mean terror and sudden death—for the Viet Cong, for a change. The paper eyes, 50,000 copies of which were printed by the U.S. Information Service in Saigon, turned up not only on corpses but as warnings on the doors of houses suspected of occasionally harboring Viet Cong agents. The eyes came to mean not only assassination but that "Big Brother Is Watching You."

At this writing, it is difficult to assess the effect of "Operation Black Eye," but it will be interesting to see whether this and similar experiments in controlled terror succeed in turning the psychological tables on the Viet Cong.

This much is known: Government death squads are frequently finding empty beds in houses where they have planned raids. So few people have known in advance what the exact raid targets were that, in these cases, the empty beds could be accounted for only as the result of fear, not prior enemy intelligence. It seems that Viet Cong officials have had to adopt the policy of sleeping in a different place each night—a tactic that for years has been forced on almost all government district officials. Even Vietnamese Premier Nguyen Khanh adopted the procedure in Saigon, to foil possible assassination attempts against him.

No one likes moving from place to place all the time, and it is difficult to sleep well knowing someone is out to get you. If for this reason alone, Vietnamese and American officials are pleased with the chance to play tit for tat on the Viet Cong.

All modern wars have been terrible in a general way. In World War II, the devastation wrought on Coventry, Hamburg, Berlin, Stalingrad, Hiroshima and Nagasaki, among many other cities and towns, resulted in unthinkable loss of life, maiming and tragedy. But compared to Viet Nam, I think, wars like this have been ghastly in a relatively impersonal way. Viet Nam is a highly personal war, in which specific terror against specific people or groups of people is a principal weapon.

Part of the new face of war here, as I see it, is the use of terror for terror's sake.

Chapter 8

Red, White and Black Propaganda

It was dusk when ten strangers arrived in town. The sleepy little hamlet of Ap —— rarely had visitors, and this was something worth investigating. For many years, the war had been faraway and life had not changed much at this hamlet in the past thousand years. The day's plowing was over, and the water buffalo were back, tethered in their open sheds next to the huts. Rice was steaming in big aluminum pots over charcoal fires, and the smell of *nuoc mam*, the ubiquitous Vietnamese fermented fish sauce, was heavy in the air.

The strangers all carried guns, but they were smiling as they walked into the cluster of huts. As they came into town, their leader passed an old, bearded resident and deferentially saluted, one fist in the other closed hand. *"Chau bac. Manh gioi?"* ("Hello, Uncle, are you well?") the stranger politely inquired.

The old man responded with equal politeness, but looked the strange group over closely. The leader, who called himself Thuan, was wearing a wide-brimmed bush hat, a black shirt tucked into khaki military trousers, and sandals made from sections of automobile tire and leather thongs. A rifle was slung carelessly over his shoulder. Thuan was a bright-eyed, intelligent-looking man of about thirty, whose face was deeply tanned.

One of the others wore a white shirt and gray trousers. He also had a rifle, but incongruously squinted through spectacles. He looked more like an impoverished student than a peasant. Several others wore the black, baggy trousers and blouses of farmers, and conical, palm-frond hats.

The only one in the party without a gun was a young woman of about twenty-five, also dressed in black farm clothes and rubber-tire sandals, but with a guitar over her shoulder. Her face was serious, but her wide eyes were warm and friendly.

"My people have not had anything to eat in two days, and we are very hungry. I wonder, Uncle, if we could impose on your hamlet for a little rice? We would be happy to work for you in exchange," Thuan said.

A dozen or so villagers had gathered around the group.

"Certainly," the old man said. "You shall eat your fill."

A stranger with an empty stomach is never turned away by a Vietnamese farmer, whose hospitality to poor people is almost limitless.

There was some talk, as the old man made arrangements as to which stranger should be entertained by which family. The strangers were obviously tired and ready to relax, as they unslung their guns and leaned them against palm trees.

"It is very kind of all of you," Thuan remarked. "Earlier today we passed through a hamlet where we hoped we could get something to eat, but while there was plenty of food, it was impossible."

"Why not?" someone asked.

"Oh, the same old story," Thuan went on conversationally. "The Americans had dropped poison all over everything. No one can eat the rice there without a terrible death."

The strangers made agreeable guests. Each family was warmly complimented on its excellent cuisine. Besides, the strangers, who obviously traveled most of the time, had all kinds of interesting stories about faraway places, even the great city of Saigon.

After dinner, Thuan suggested that the visitors repay their hosts with some entertainment. The strangers gathered in one of the larger huts, and the young woman sang and played her guitar. She had a soft, sweet voice, and her songs were the sad, old-fashioned songs of lonely fishermen poling sampans. Eyes of some of the older villagers were moist with nostalgia, and quite a crowd gathered around the hut to listen. Someone produced a few bottles of strong "33 Export" beer, and it was a nice party.

At length, one of the villagers asked the pleasant strangers if they would care to stay overnight.

"No, many thanks all the same," Thuan said. "We must keep going. But perhaps we shall return again before long."

The ten strange travelers slung their rifles and disappeared into the night. But a few days later, they did return—this time, during the midday siesta. They were greeted with smiles and were offered rice.

"No, thank you," Thuan said, "we have eaten. But we came to repay our debt to you. We noticed some of your houses need repairs, and we would like to work on them. Also, we noticed the last time we were here that some of your children look sick. Miss Nga, the girl who played her guitar for you, is a nurse, and this time she has brought some medicine."

This time, the young woman carried a kit bag over her shoulder instead of a guitar, and was wearing a Red Cross armband.

"All of us must be able to do many things in order to help the people effectively. We have had to learn these things in the National Liberation Front," Thuan said.

The woman turned toward a group of children and singled out one whose face and scalp were covered with sores and scabs. She gave the boy a light kiss on the head and then applied some ointment to the bad spots.

As Nga busied herself with other children, five of the men wandered over to a clearing where an old man was cutting bamboo and building a frame for a new roof panel.

"Let us lend a hand," one of the friendly men with guns said. Quickly and expertly, the free labor force hacked lengths of bamboo to size, and lashed them together.

Thuan wandered from house to house, exchanging greetings with each occupant. The man who looked like a student also wandered around the hamlet, stopping to chat with all the young men.

At two thirty, the squad gathered as if by signal in the middle of the hamlet.

"We must be on our way again," Thuan told a bystander. "Before we go, we should like to sing a song together, our song of freedom. Some of you may know the words and may join us, if you like."

In a circle, standing at rigid attention, the ten visitors began, "Viet Nam Men Yen . . ." (Beloved Viet Nam). As the old Viet Minh song rambled along, the glint of recognition shone from the eyes of most of the villagers. It was a song they used to sing but had not heard since 1954.

The agitprop ("agitation and propaganda") squad moved away in single file across the paddies. But they came back again and again and again. With successive visits, the squad began holding "group meetings" for discussion of important problems. At first the meetings were all in the middle of the hamlet, but later they began to separate into groups. The young woman, Nga, gathered around her most of the women in town. Thuan talked to the men. The student talked to the young people.

The talks were always short and informal on simple themes.

One day Thuan would tell the people, "We had to shed our blood to destroy the French devils and throw them out. The fighting spirit of the Vietnamese people proved too much for the colonialists. But sadly for us, the fight was not over in 1954 when the People's Army stormed into Dien Bien Phu. A new aggressor came, with bombs and germs and poison. But the Liberation Front will destroy the new aggressor, too! *Da Dao My!* (Down with America!)"

And the student said: "The Americans are trying to spread hatred between the religions of Viet Nam so that Catholics and Buddhists will kill each other, so that Hoa Hao and Cao Dai will kill each other, so that Vietnamese will destroy Vietnamese, and the Americans can drink our blood. How do you like that? *Da Dao My!*"

And Nga said: "My sister, who was only sixteen, died because of these Americans. They raped her eighty-two times, and then cut off her breasts and hung them from a tree. The Liberation Front is the only hope for Vietnamese women. *Da Dao My!*"

And one of the men in conical hats said: "After the war of

liberation, I was given five hectares of land by the Viet Minh, and I lived happily with my family. But the Americans and their lackeys came and threw me out. Now a rich man who lives in My Tho owns my land and I have nothing. The only hope of the farmer is the Liberation Front. *Da Dao My!*"

And another man said: "The Liberation Front grows every day, and all civilized countries recognize it as the only legitimate government of Viet Nam. Only the Americans and their lackeys oppose us. The world is on our side. *Da Dao My!*"

And so it went, day after day. The villagers listened and said little.

But one day, Thuan and his group arrived at about dusk, laughing among themselves and talking excitedly.

"I have something very good to tell you today," Thuan told the villagers who quickly gathered. "Today the Americans and their puppet troops tried to destroy a hamlet twenty kilometers from here that had been liberated by the People's Self-Defense Forces. But the puppet troops got a nasty surprise. Our people killed three hundred of them, including fifty Americans. It was a glorious fight."

Thuan's face suddenly clouded. "But of course," he added, "I'm afraid they will be back. And I'm afraid they may even strike here. Our people need so many things that are so hard to get . . ." he trailed off. "Of course, if you could help us a little—it wouldn't involve fighting, or anything—just some help from all of you, as we have tried to help you."

"What is it you need?" someone asked Thuan.

"We need things to defend ourselves. Most of all, we need foot traps to snare and wound the enemy, halting his advance. They are easy to make. You take ordinary nails, hammer barbs into the ends, and sharpen them. Then you plant four or five nails upright in a board or a block of concrete. Even a child could make one. Would some of you children help us defend our homeland?"

Several children stepped forward, and the demonstration began. The visitors sang as they worked and made a kind of game of it. A few of the women joined in.

At the end of a week, most of the hamlet was involved in

making nail boards. A makeshift forge had been set up, and two children delighted in pumping the bellows as the charcoal fire glowed cherry red. The agitprop team had brought several large bags of American cement to the hamlet, with which they made concrete blocks for the nail boards. The children loved it. The cement bags were still marked with little American "hands-across-the-sea" stickers.

For several days, Thuan's team failed to return. When it finally came back, two of the men were carrying a body on an improvised litter.

"This poor woman was murdered by the puppet troops in her hamlet a few kilometers from here," Thuan announced. "She must have a decent burial, but it is not safe there. We shall bury her near here."

The villagers watched the burial, and some of them were plainly angry. "Damned Americans," one of them muttered. "Everything was peaceful around here until they showed up."

After the ceremony, Thuan called the villagers together. He spoke persuasively and was such a familiar figure that he was by now regarded as something of a village leader. His gallantry and good looks had softened several feminine hearts.

"I have something important to tell all of you," he said. "The aggressors probably will come here. They have heard that we are making nail boards and that we are angry at the atrocities they have committed. We must be ready to save ourselves. We can do it easily, but we must prepare. If we do not prepare there will be terrible bloodshed and suffering. For your safety, we must show you what to do.

"First they may try to come to collect taxes. You must not let them, because they will use the rice you give them against us. Tell them that rats have destroyed your stores. Hide most of your rice, and give some of it to us for safekeeping.

"Second, they will try to round up all of your young men for conscription into their puppet army. Many of our people have cut off their own fingers and toes to avoid this, but this is not necessary. The main thing is that all the young men should be ready to hide somewhere away from the hamlet when they come. You young men should have a leader to help you avoid the pirates. You, Xuan, would you like to accept that responsibility?"

Flattered, the peasant youth nodded his head in agreement.

And so it began. Each day, Thuan held drills for the young men, who would scatter into the fields and jungle. Some hid in rice paddies, and Thuan showed them how they could breathe under water through a straw without being seen. Others hid in secret tunnels that were beginning to honeycomb the hamlet.

The agitprop team worked as hard as anyone else on the tunnels and some other fortifications they decided might be useful. Mud embankments with gun ports began to go up, so skillfully camouflaged they looked like normal paddy dykes. Sharpened bamboo stakes bristled from these embankments, and nail boards were planted in the water fields around them.

And the visitors were out in the fields, too, helping with the plowing and the business of keeping the farms going.

"We have a saying in the Liberation Front that '*tam dong*' will save us all," he told the villagers once. *Tam dong* means likeness of thought and action.

"We work together, eat together and live together. Sometimes, we must fight together," Thuan added.

The songs and rallies continued, and the slogans were repeated and repeated.

One day, Thuan pointed out to the villagers that they would be better off if they could defend themselves while the Liberation Front team was away.

"Xuan, you and your men are tough and brave. Isn't it too bad that all you can do if the enemy comes now is run away in the face of the running dogs?"

Xuan agreed that it was.

"Wouldn't you prefer to have some self-protection, like these guns of ours?"

Xuan, who was only seventeen, strongly agreed. He had been interested in those shiny guns ever since he had first seen them. It would be nice to have a pistol stuck in one's belt.

"Well, unfortunately, the People's Self-Defense Forces don't have any to spare. We have to make everything we use, or else seize it from the running dogs. We shall show you how to make some swords and daggers, which are certainly better than nothing. We can also make some good grenades."

More weeks passed as Thuan's group taught the young people the rudiments of weaponry. And now, the youths held a little parade every morning with their homemade swords. They stood in ranks, proud as peacocks, and sang the patriotic songs in front of a brand-new flagpole. On the pole was a huge red and blue flag with a yellow star in the center—the colors of the National Liberation Front.

Early one morning Thuan and his team came into town with a prisoner whose hands were tied behind his back and who staggered along with a rope around his neck. It was the local government district chief. He was bloody and bruised, and his khaki uniform was slashed and torn in a dozen places.

Three of Thuan's men dragged him to the flagpole and lashed him to it.

"Comrades, come here. I want to show you an enemy of the people," Thuan shouted. People gathered curiously.

"This man," Thuan said, "is Lieutenant Nguyen Dinh Thao, the U.S. lackeys' district chief. We caught him last night while he and his men were raiding a hamlet not far from here. They were arresting all the young men to put in the puppet army, and were stealing rice from the people. You all know him, I'm sure. His pocket is bulging with the money he has extorted from you and the rest of the people."

Several villagers grunted as they recognized the hated tax collector.

"This man has had many chances. We have warned him many times," Thuan said. "But the Liberation Front can extend mercy and charity only to those who are on the side of the people. This is one of the running dogs—and he must pay his penalty."

Thuan nodded in the direction of two men in black standing near the bound district chief. One unsheathed a dagger, stepped in front of the struggling officer, and spat in his face. Then, with a series of swift strokes, he plunged the knife into the district chief's belly five times.

THE AMERICAN PLANNERS FOR VIET NAM—Former U. S. Ambassador Henry Cabot Lodge, Ambassador Maxwell D. Taylor (at the time this picture was taken, chairman of the Joint Chiefs of Staff) and Secretary of Defense Robert S. McNamara. *(AP Photo by Horst Faas)*

AMERICAN DEAD—An American paratroop advisor, killed in combat with the Viet Cong, is carried from the field by his comrades. *(AP Photo by Horst Faas)*

UNDER THE GUN—American school children in Saigon board their school buses under the watchful eye of an American guard. Viet Cong terrorism at the school is an ever-present threat. *(AP Photo by Horst Faas)*

Bottom left: **THE VIET CONG**—A guerrilla prisoner gets a cigarette from an American with whom he was trading shots a few hours earlier. *(AP Photo by Malcolm W. Browne)*

Bottom right: **FOREIGN CORRESPONDENTS**—Foreign correspondents were regular targets of secret police attacks in Saigon in 1963. Among them were David Halberstam, center, of The New York Times, and Peter Arnett, extreme right, of the AP. Plain-clothes secret police agents at left have just beaten and kicked Arnett, who was covering a demonstration. An instant after the author took this picture, other agents smashed his camera, but the film was not damaged. *(Photo by Malcolm W. Browne)*

PROTEST BY FIRE—The following photographs by the author record in sequence the suicide by fire of Thich Quang Duc on June 11, 1963 in Saigon. This event triggered the Buddhist uprising that led to the overthrow of Ngo Dinh Diem. *(AP Photos by Malcolm W. Browne)*

9:30 AM

9:33 AM

9:35 AM

10:00 AM

STUDENT MOB—The chaos of Saigon has been punctuated from time to time by bloody riots, in which students have attacked each other with rocks, machetes, and hatchets. *(AP Photo by Horst Faas)*

COUP IN SAIGON—Coups in Viet Nam can be bloody or quiet. The city always continues its existence more or less normally, even during coups. Here, a boy scout troop pedals away from the Saigon zoo under the guns of rebel armored cars. *(AP Photo by Horst Faas)*

The officer screamed and pitched forward, hanging from his bindings. The second man in black, carrying a heavy sugar-cane axe, stepped up to the dying man. Three strokes of the axe, and the district chief's severed head lay in the mud at his feet. A sharp groan came from the watching villagers.

Thuan turned to two village youths who had been watching with their mouths open. "Take him down and bury him in the fields somewhere. We shall take care of the head. It will go back to his district headquarters as a warning to others." There was something new in Thuan's tone. He was commanding, not requesting. The two youths hesitantly walked up to the bleeding body and began their assignment.

The days passed at Ap—— and life underwent changes. One night the roar of artillery interrupted the peaceful croaking of the geckos, and ten shells landed in and around the hamlet. A man, three women and two children were killed. Thuan's team was not there at the time, but arrived at sunrise.

"It is horrible," Thuan said sympathetically. "But we must let others know what the aggressors have done here. I want all the women in this hamlet to join with other women in a demonstration planned for Saturday to denounce the imperialist atrocities. Ten thousand women will march in the province capital with banners showing the people's indignation against these cruel shellings. Miss Nga will tell you about the arrangements, and we will provide sampans for you to get into town. You need not worry about the running dogs making trouble for you in the province capital. They are afraid of the people seeing them brutalize defenseless women. Those of you with babies and young children should take them along. They also can carry banners."

At the demonstration, things worked out exactly as Thuan had predicted. There were not quite ten thousand marchers. In fact, there were only about three hundred. But they made an impressive sight as they straggled through town, their hand-painted cloth banners burning with indignation and their eyes streaming tears. Finally, police chased them out of town, but not until everybody had seen the women and their banners.

Thuan and his team were not there, but had remained at Ap—— to discuss a new project with the men of the village.

"It is not enough to run from the aggressors every time," Thuan was yelling from his usual place in front of the flagpole. "When we can, we must hurt him. It is our duty to defend our fatherland by force when we can. But we need weapons and we need men. I know that there are many young heroes here who are eager to undertake this work. You, Xuan, for example."

Xuan grinned and saluted. He felt he already had been accepted by this glamorous group of leaders, and was proud of his status.

"I want you to gather the self-defense squad you command for an important secret meeting tonight, at which we shall discuss the most important mission you ever have had. It is time for us to prove our steel."

Xuan was tense. He had suspected for some time that the daily drilling with homemade swords and clubs was leading to something, and now the time of decision had come. Above all, he must not show cowardice.

At eight o'clock that night, Xuan and nine other badly frightened hamlet militia boys arrived at the hut Thuan had designated. None had wanted to come. But none had wanted to show fear or cowardice. All were curious and excited.

Inside, a single candle flickered. Pieces of cloth had been hung around the thatched walls to prevent light from leaking through. Thuan and two other men dressed like him, both strangers, sat at a large table on which several bottles stood. In the middle of the hut was another table on which an enormous tray filled with mud had been arranged. Miniature buildings, walls and watchtowers had been built out of mud in the tray, rows of bamboo toothpicks marked fences and barricades, and threads were stretched to represent barbed wire. The whole thing was obviously an exact model of a government outpost, complete with miniature flag.

"Ah, my friends, it is good to see you are punctual. We have serious business to discuss tonight, and two of our comrades from the People's Army have joined me to help explain things. But why do you look so serious? This is a joyful occasion. Let us celebrate your initiation into manhood with a drink."

The bottles contained a powerful rice liquor distilled in the Mekong Delta, the taste of which is suggestive of diesel fuel, and which burns all the way down. Each of the youths choked down a swallow or two and felt better about the whole thing.

"The job we are about to give you is really not difficult, because our comrades of the National Liberation Front have planned everything to the last detail. If you act like the revolutionary soldiers you now are, your mission will be completely successful. And you will have good weapons as your reward.

"There is one thing you must remember, though. From this point on, everything you do must be in secret. You cannot turn back now. If you betray your comrades through cowardice or malice or by accident, the Liberation Front will deal with you as traitors. The government district chief we brought to your hamlet was a traitor to the people. Do not forget what you saw."

The recruits fidgeted but said nothing. Then Thuan turned the meeting over to one of the two strangers—a man who spoke with a hard, nasal voice, and who seemed interested only in the model on the table.

"There are ten aggressor troops in this post," he began. "In each of the watchtowers at the three corners of the triangle is a sentry with a rifle. Each sentry has a bamboo log, on which he knocks once in a while. When this happens, each of the other two sentries knocks on his bamboo in reply, to signal that everything is all right. Actually, all of these men have been living in the post for nearly ten months. In all that time, nothing has happened to them, and Liberation forces have kept away. Therefore the sentries are usually asleep.

"As you see, the watchtowers are connected by mud walls on each side of the triangle. The outside of these walls is covered with bamboo spikes. In front of the walls is a moat filled with water and mud. Outside the moat are three concentric barbed wire fences.

"Inside the post, six other soldiers sleep in this building, and their officer sleeps alone in this one. Their ammunition and extra weapons are kept in this small building, which has a padlock on the door.

"The only entrance to the post is through a gate facing this canal. The gate is blocked by a movable barbed wire barricade, and boards crossing the moat are pulled in every night.

"Our plan is simple but depends on strict discipline, silence and camouflage. We shall take two sampans, approaching the hamlet from opposite directions. The sampans will stop two hundred meters from the post, and we shall crawl the rest of the way. Three of you will have wire cutters, with which you will make corridors through the barbed wire at three different points, each one close to a corner tower but to the rear of the sentry inside. Each sentry has a chair and this chair always faces forward, so you need not worry about being seen.

"Three others will carry explosive charges through the fence and place them against the walls of the towers. They will not be spotted, because you will be working so close to the sentries you will be under their fields of vision. At exactly 2 A.M., the fuses of each charge will be started. These fuses burn for only eight seconds, so you must get out of the way quickly. When the charges go off, everyone will throw all the grenades we shall give you into the post. Then you will wait while three of us from the People's Army clean out the running dogs with machine guns. When we give the signal, you will all go over the wall into the post and finish off anyone left with your daggers. One of us will shoot the lock off the arms hut, and then we shall all leave carrying everything that seems valuable to us. Besides their weapons, they have a radio we want. We also want their documents, money, food and everything else."

The lecturer paused and looked around.

"From this moment on, you are under the discipline of the People's Armed Forces," he said. "You know what that means."

All of them did. Each night for weeks on end, various members of Thuan's squad had lectured them until they almost were falling asleep on the fifteen points of secrecy, the twelve points of discipline, and the ten-point soldier's oath. Each knew the whole catechism by heart.

The whole group left the hut and marched along a dark trail to a clearing where a full-scale dummy post had been marked out on the ground. There were no walls or buildings, but stakes and lengths of string marked the outline of the towers, moats and walls. A canal ran nearby.

All night long, Thuan, the two strangers and the ten recruits practiced assaults on the dummy post. After each rehearsal, one of the strangers would criticize the exercise, lacing his remarks with sinister irony.

"Well done, Duc," he told one recruit. "You moved in bravely. Of course you are now dead, since you approached the tower from the wrong side and your guts were shot out by the sentry. But I'm sure your mother will be proud of you."

Finally, the instructors were satisfied, and the recruits marched home to bed. They were under orders to sleep all day, since the following night would be the real attack.

Two mornings later, as a glaring red sun was just slanting up over the flat horizon, the ten recruits straggled back into town in twos and threes. Their black clothing was torn to rags, and they were covered with ugly cuts.

But each one was grinning broadly, and each one was carrying a brand-new weapon. Xuan, the recruit leader, had a Tommy gun slung over his shoulder, a pistol stuck through his belt and four American grenades hanging from the belt. The operation had been a complete success, and the enemy post had been wiped out without a single Liberation Front casualty. Mothers and sisters rushed to embrace their returning soldier boys with relief. Nothing had been said about the operation, but everyone in the hamlet had known more or less what was going on. Thuan and the two strangers had not returned with the recruits, but had said they would return to the hamlet in a few days.

Each recruit had a war story to tell, and each was strutting like a peacock with his new weapon. Each was ready for a new operation of some kind.

Thuan and his team did return again and again. There were more and more lectures and meetings, and schedules were worked out for every resident of the hamlet. Two new buildings were placed in the central market area—an information booth and a new primary school. Miss Nga was assigned to take care of both of them as a combination teacher and information officer. The two buildings were decked out with paper Liberation Front flags made by hamlet children on inauguration day, and there were speeches and songs along with a hamlet feast. Thuan's group even presented a musical play, in which Thuan acted out the part of an American helicopter, flapping his arms around his head like rotor blades. Thuan fell crashing to the ground when Xuan and Miss Nga pointed dummy rifles at him, and the whole crowd laughed at his antics.

Xuan, the hamlet recruit leader, was obviously fond of Miss Nga, and was always bringing her choice pieces of fruit. In return, she would often sit with him under a tree reading to him aloud from one of her Liberation Front books. It was rumored that she was allowing Xuan to call her *em.* (Little Sister, or Beloved.)

Work went on constantly. Big clay pots were buried up to their lids in most of the huts for use as air raid shelters. Secret hiding places also were dug under most of the hamlet, often under the charcoal stoves of the mud floors. One large hiding place could be entered only by diving into the canal and swimming through an underwater tunnel in the bank. The roomy hiding place had air vents skillfully concealed by bushes. Each man and woman was drilled daily on the procedure to be followed in case of an enemy attack.

For a while, Thuan personally supervised some recruits in the building of a rather large underground chamber with a bell-shaped roof pierced by three ports aboveground, each facing in a different direction. Thuan was very fussy about the exact shaping of the interior of this chamber, and explained that a sentry must occupy it all day long, listening closely. The shape of the walls would amplify sounds coming through the ports in such a way that an approaching helicopter could be heard from a distance of up to fifteen miles, he explained. Furthermore, the sentry would be able to tell exactly the direction from which the helicopter was coming.

So little by little, Ap—— became a Viet Cong "Combat Hamlet." Of course, there were residents who didn't like the idea. Older people, especially, were afraid that all these preparations would expose the hamlet to war.

But it was too late to object. Thuan's crowd controlled everything, and the young recruits ruled the roost. Every man, woman and child was somehow committed to the new way of things, and to back out would mean banishment from the hamlet, or worse.

Besides that, everyone had been organized into cells, mostly of five persons each. There were self-defense cells for the men, first aid cells for the women, flagmaking cells for the children, work cells, building cells, agricultural cells, and, above all, political study cells. Nearly every cell included one member from Thuan's group, who kept a close eye on things.

Thuan and the steady stream of strangers now passing through town had insisted that the membership of each cell be kept secret. At first, it had seemed like a game, and many refused to take the thing seriously. But those who failed to turn up for cell meetings were punished. Usually, the hamlet central committee would confiscate rice stocks from the uncooperative cell member.

Each cell chairman was a member of the hamlet committee, but somehow the committee always seemed to go along with what Thuan proposed. And Xuan, who now was chairman of the self-defense cell, had a lot of say in things too, despite his youth.

In all this time, a period of a year or so, the National Liberation Front was unhindered in its work at Ap——. No government official ever came around, and the war never touched the hamlet itself, except for the shelling incident.

The self-defense cell, initially only ten recruits, grew to more than fifty men under arms, all of whom had participated in occasional forays on government posts. Casualties were light, and most of these operations were successful.

Xuan and a few others eventually left the hamlet. They had been spotted by Liberation Front talent scouts, as tough, reli-

able soldiers, and had been asked to join a higher echelon of
fighters—the regional liberation guerrillas. These guerrillas
ranged throughout the whole province, and were assigned
missions much more important than merely knocking out isolated
enemy posts. They specialized in big ambushes, often taking
on even enemy armored columns.

If Xuan did well in the regional forces and showed continuing
political development, he probably would graduate into one of
the regular main force battalions, such as the famous 514th—the
scourge of the upper Mekong Delta.

Good news and encouragement were continuously pouring
into the hamlet. Several transistor radios were kept at the information hut, all tuned to "Liberation Radio." The news reports
each day gave glowing accounts of victories by the Front against
Saigon forces and the Americans. There were lots of statistics—
how many enemy helicopters shot down, how many Americans
killed or captured, and so on. One report said that 90 per cent
of Central Nam Bo (Viet Cong terminology for the central
Mekong Delta area) had been liberated, and residents of Ap——
were prepared to believe it.

But reports each day also told of ghastly new atrocities being
committed by the Americans—disemboweling women, violating
children, eating the livers of peasants, dropping napalm over
whole communities, and—most of all—spreading poison over
crops.

Even neighboring Cambodia was complaining at the United
Nations about American planes from Viet Nam dropping deadly
yellow powder over border villages. (Just for the record, American planes do drop chemicals to kill vegetation in Viet Nam, to
deprive guerrillas of cover along roads and canals. The harmless
substance they drop is a purple spray, not a yellow powder, and
it is dropped only on scrub growth, not crops. The Vietnamese
Air Force does drop the same spray on rice crops in Viet Cong
areas to deprive guerrillas of food. But the chemicals apparently
are harmless to animal life.)

The graphic accounts of American atrocities inevitably
brought blood to a boil. Many of the hamlet residents had seen

the French Foreign Legion in action, and were prepared to believe anything of the big-nosed alien troops.

Besides the radio, news bulletins were circulated in the hamlet each day—at first, on mimeographed sheets, but later in the form of a six-page printed newspaper. The newspaper apparently was published in the delta capital of My Tho, right under the enemy's nose in some city print shop.

The radio and newspapers also told each day of the support the outer world was giving the National Liberation Front. Professor Nguyen Van Hieu, the Front's ambassador at large, was given a standing ovation in Jakarta or Prague or Havana. The English aristocrat, Lord Bertrand Russell, had come out against the imperialists in Viet Nam. Even American college students were demonstrating in favor of the Vietnamese National Liberation Front in Times Square in New York City. Most of all, the fraternal socialist bloc—North Viet Nam and People's China—was standing by to help.

So, all in all, it looked from Ap —— as if things were pretty well sewed up for the National Liberation Front. In any case, Ap —— was now prepared to fight the imperialists and their lackeys to the death, and Thuan's mission had succeeded to the last detail.

I have not mentioned the name of the hamlet where all this happened, for the reason that I have drawn the details from several hamlets as a kind of composite. But I want to assure the reader that none of it is fiction. I have a real hamlet in mind for most of this story, and the protagonist of the story, Thuan, was real.

I saw Thuan's shattered body among others that fell at Ap —— one afternoon when a government task force happened to take them by surprise. The hamlet had fought well, and its defenders managed to shoot down three American helicopters. All the huts in town were burned down, but the artillery and bombs never touched the underground hiding places, and casualties were comparatively light. When Saigon troops came in, they found, as usual, only women and children and a handful of old men.

But Thuan had made one of his rare slips and had got caught out in the open. Next to his body I found a bloodstained pocket notebook with his name inside and a photograph of himself with a pretty girl. The book was meticulously written in longhand, and obviously had been dictated by some instructor from a handbook on insurrection.

In common with all such field manuals, Thuan's notebook had several homespun remedies for curing the diseases of oxen and men.

I have no idea whether any of these remedies work, but they are all standard elements of Viet Cong medical lore, and their application presumably makes propaganda agents more popular with the people.

Thuan's book was a kind of how-to-do-it summary of Viet Cong insurgency. The most important section had to do with propaganda.

The reader may be familiar with the writings of Mao Tse-tung, General Vo Nguyen Giap, and the other standard writers on Asian "people's warfare." But there are writers at lower levels who must translate the theory into more practical instructions. These writings cover every practical subject to which a guerrilla is exposed, and generally are given in question and answer form, like a kind of catechism.

Since the cutting edge of the Viet Cong is political propaganda, let me introduce here a translation of most of the section of Thuan's field manual headed "Propaganda Mission." Thuan himself was a highly successful agitprop team leader, and there must be something to the instructions.

PROPAGANDA MISSION

Question: What is the importance of a propaganda mission? What should you do in carrying out this mission with people in general and youths in particular?

Answer: A propaganda mission is designed to attract people's interest and stimulate their thoughts, and also to expand our party's policy and ideology.

Question: What are the four ways by which this mission is carried out?

Answer: 1. Increase feelings of discontent on the part of the people before trying to mobilize their patriotic sentiments; 2. Explain to the people the efforts being made by the enemy to divide us from the population; 3. Educate the people about our struggle in South Viet Nam; and 4. Stress the importance of our Front for the Liberation of South Viet Nam (which already has legal status in Viet Nam and throughout the world). Also, educate the people about our party's basic policies, about North Viet Nam, about socialism, and other world news.

Question: What are the consequences of widespread application of propaganda at meetings and so forth, which, however, lacks work in depth?

Answer: No valuable result can be obtained if a propaganda mission is carried on in width only, that is, superficially, but not in depth. The public can never understand the subject well, because at most meetings you cannot explain everything in detail. Only by carrying out your propaganda mission secretly and at the grassroots level can you succeed. You should divide your work according to three separate zones: The liberated zone, where you can push hard in width as well as depth, the contested zone, where most of your operations must be in depth and in secret, and in the enemy zone, where all must be secret and in depth.

In towns, do as much as you can, but do it in depth using maximum caution. Avoid wasting the time of our people. In places where the enemy has strong fortifications, work only in depth.

Question: How should youths be approached on the question of joining our forces?

Answer: Revolutionary spirit among our people is now high. Now is a favorable time for talking our young men into our army and into reporting enemy activity to us, for educating youths about our policy, for teaching them about the struggle of the classes, about present and future victories, and about the sacrifices of a revolutionary combatant.

Before the departure of a recruit, a ceremony should be arranged and a meeting of a Liberation Front cadre with the recruit's family should take place. Front committee members will arrive later to work out personal problems for the recruit. At the recruit's request, his family will have support from our group and from the people.

Question: How should propaganda be carried out opposing enemy military conscription?

Answer: Explain to the people the deep significance of the current drafting of youths by the U.S.-imperialist clique. Opposition to the draft should be carried out in three ways: Refuse to comply with the draft notice, desert after being drafted, or get the people themselves to prevent the drafting of a youth. If a youth is drafted, a dramatic and tragic departure ceremony should be arranged by the Liberation Front.

Question: How should religious subjects be handled?

Answer: Denounce religious leaders who ally themselves with the imperialists. Our policy is to separate them. We must tell the people that no soldier should be a member of any religious organization. Among religious persons, organize a system whereby traitors working under the cover of religious robes are denounced. We must, however, be very careful in our judgments.

Question: How should you react to enemy propaganda in your area?

Answer: Enemy propaganda techniques sometimes have a bad influence on the people. We should react promptly to this, leading the people's thinking in the opposite direction, and instilling in the people a spirit of mutual assistance and mutual struggle. Revolutionary counterpropaganda and counterattack should be carried out simultaneously.

For example, if religion is mentioned in enemy propaganda, we must plead for freedom of religion. We must point out to the people that it is the policy of the U.S. and its lackeys to exterminate religion, and we must give some concrete evidence of it. Thus we not only are rejecting the enemy's propaganda but we are attacking him directly.

Question: What is our policy concerning cultural matters?

Answer: The performance of popular shows for the public is one of several ways for carrying out propaganda after attracting popular interest. The Front should promote this type of work and organize programs. But be careful in choosing the actors for such shows.

Question: How should the agitprop team approach the problem of educating children?

Answer: The mission undertaken by the team to educate children is most important. The main goal is to bring immediate educational benefits to the children, to help build the future of the nation. Schools should be built in conformity with our new type of life—well ventilated, neat and clean, but cheap. Teachers must be well educated because they are the engineers of future generations.

Programs of education should include political, social and domestic topics. The program of mass education should be pushed.

Question: What is the proper behavior of the propagandist?

Answer: A propagandist should be modest, he should learn from the people, and he should teach what he has experienced to the people. This helps to consolidate his position. He should be patient and his behavior should be exemplary.

Question: What is the current role of the party and popular organizations compared with the time of the resistance war against the French?

Answer: Throughout the history of our revolution, events usually have been initiated by the people. Only a popular organization can defeat the enemy. Our giant party organization originally was formed from large popular gatherings. We must always work closely with the people, for the people, and in the interest of the people.

During the days of the Resistance [the Indochina War, which ended in victory for the Viet Minh in 1954], popular organizations constituted the rear lines of our forces. *But in the current fight, which centers so strongly on the political field, any mass organization should be regarded as a combatant unit.* (Italics are author's.)

Thuan's manual continued for many more pages, but I think this suffices to indicate the tone. It is similar to many other manuals captured in battle, although there often are regional differences in propaganda themes.

Because of extremely primitive communications in many parts of South Viet Nam, Viet Cong propaganda can contradict itself from one area to another without danger of exposure. An interesting and dangerous instance of this developed in September,

1964, when 2,000 mountain tribesmen, trained and armed by American Special Forces as irregular guerrilla troops, rebelled against the Saigon government.

In itself, the incident was acutely embarrassing to the United States. For three years, Americans had been training the tribesmen into crack soldiers, capable of fighting in well-disciplined units.

The mountain tribesmen of Viet Nam are racially very distinct from the lowland Vietnamese, and all of their thirty-odd tribal languages are linguistically different from Vietnamese. Communication between the tribesmen and the lowland Vietnamese is normally in French, the only language universally understood.

The tribesmen and the lowlanders have been mutually hostile for centuries. Most Vietnamese regard their highlanders as savages and treat them accordingly. The highlanders don't like it, and feel that total foreigners—French or Americans—are likely to treat them with more dignity and respect.

It happens that the highlanders are the dominant racial group in many of Central Vietnam's sparsely populated provinces. Hamlets often are separated by many miles of trackless, jungle-covered mountains, where only the tribesmen know their way around. These provinces happen to be prime infiltration routes for Viet Cong from Laos and Cambodia, and the guerrillas generally have been careful to keep their fences mended with the tribesmen.

Years ago the Viet Cong understood the necessity of having friendly or at least neutral tribesmen in these areas, and began cultivating friendships. Viet Cong organizers frequently settled down in tribal hamlets, marrying the daughters of hamlet chiefs.

Recognizing the potentialities of the hostility between the tribesmen and the lowlanders, the Viet Cong managed to put the feud to practical use. Rather than preach unity of highlanders and lowlanders, the Viet Cong propagandists talked of creating an autonomous tribal kingdom, completely independent of lowland Viet Nam, in the event of a Liberation Front victory.

The first serious threat to Viet Cong dominance in the high-land jungles came directly from America in the early 1960s. The American Special Forces troops had a knack of working with the highlanders, and turned many of them against the Viet Cong. Of course, the highlanders remained anti-Vietnamese in general. The irregulars were delighted to kill Viet Cong for the Americans, but they probably would have been just as happy killing any Vietnamese.

American efforts to transfer their training and leading role with the highlanders to the Vietnamese largely failed. And in September, 1964, five tribal camps revolted from Saigon authority. At three of them, the tribesmen butchered Vietnamese officers and officials, but made it plain they wanted the Americans to stay on to lead them. This was a direct slap in the face to Saigon, and had a chilling effect on relations with Washington.

Premier Nguyen Khanh was all for blasting the rebel camps to destruction, but the Americans objected. For one thing, American officers were being held more or less as hostages at one of the camps. For another, the Americans felt that many of the tribal demands were justified. But at the same time, America was committed to supporting Saigon against rebellion, and therefore faced an ugly dilemma.

Finally, Saigon laid down an ultimatum to both the rebels and the Americans: If in twenty-four hours the main rebel camp had not surrendered, it would be attacked and destroyed, with or without Americans inside.

In the end, American officers inside the camp persuaded the rebels to surrender after extracting a promise from Saigon that no reprisals would be taken. Then the Americans pulled out and Vietnamese troops poured in.

The net effect of this was that both the tribesmen and the Vietnamese were angry at America. And the Viet Cong agitprop men were quick to capitalize on the situation.

The tribesmen were told that this was clear evidence the Americans could not be trusted and really were just as bad as the Vietnamese. If the Liberation Front wins, the agitprop men said, both the Americans and the Vietnamese will be thrown out of the area, and the tribesmen will be free to build their own nation.

But in propaganda beamed at Vietnamese, other agitprop teams took precisely the opposite line. The Americans for years had been arming and training the savages as part of a plot to exterminate Vietnamese, they said. Even after twenty-nine Vietnamese were slaughtered, the puppet Saigon government was powerless to take strong measures against the insurgent savages because of Uncle Sam's meddling in Vietnamese affairs, the line went.

During the summer of 1964, Saigon saw a simple and striking demonstration of Viet Cong agitprop technique applied to religious dissension.

For several days, there had been rioting between gangs of predominantly Buddhist and predominantly Catholic youths. The government had adopted a hands-off policy, and security police and troops were under orders not to interfere in the street fighting. The apparent idea was to let the gangs fight themselves to exhaustion, at which point resumption of government controls would be welcomed. But the fighting grew worse, and a dozen or so youths were slain with machetes, hammers and hatchets.

One afternoon, an army jeep equipped with loudspeakers was stolen from one of Saigon's compounds. A few hours later, two men in military uniform were seen driving the jeep slowly past the main Buddhist headquarters compound. The loudspeaker was blaring a warning that Catholic youths from a suburban community called Ho Nai were coming to burn down the compound that night. The jeep next turned up about three miles away in front of the North Vietnamese refugee settlement at Ho Nai, which is predominantly Roman Catholic in faith. Here, the loudspeaker warned that Buddhist gangs were coming that night to attack the settlement and burn its church.

According to the best police and intelligence information available, neither the Buddhists nor the Catholics had any intention of fighting each other that night, until the mysterious jeep passed their respective strongholds. But after that, both sides were off and running, armed with clubs, spears, torches, axes and pushcarts filled with bricks.

Police managed to halt both mobs peacefully and turn them back, but bloody chaos was averted by only 500 yards. There is every evidence that the jeep (found later parked in a back alley) had been hijacked by two well known Viet Cong agents.

Viet Cong propaganda has been known to appeal to a Vietnamese instinct for savage humor.

For many years, Saigon legends have linked Mme. Ngo Dinh Nhu, the once powerful sister-in-law of the late President Ngo Dinh Diem, with various amorous adventures. One perennial story has to do with Mme. Nhu and a U.S. Army colonel. Another links her in a tragic adventure with one of South Viet Nam's leading young generals, whose wife is supposed to have shot Mme. Nhu through the arm.

I have never seen a shred of documentation for any of these yarns, but Saigon's cocktail circuit intelligentsia accepts differing versions of the Mme. Nhu stories as established fact.

In any case, the Viet Cong evidently saw grist for its mill in the stories. One morning, traffic on a key road out of Saigon was halted by a bigger-than-life display in the middle of the pavement. The display consisted of enormous dummies made in the likenesses of the American ambassador and Mme. Nhu, lying compromised on a layer of gigantic dollar bills. The themes of capitalism, miscegenation, current rumors and the idea of Viet Nam being sold out to the American imperialist all were wrapped up neatly. To safeguard the handiwork, a small sign had been placed in front of the figures reading: "This monument is mined."

Buses, cars and boats are regularly stopped by agitprop teams and passengers get lectures. Recently, two large ferryboats headed in opposite directions across a main branch of the Mekong were stopped, and all their passengers were taken ashore. The crews of the boats served at gunpoint as chefs and hosts to a picnic, while agitprop actors put on a political skit for the passengers. The passengers were twelve hours late getting home.

These interludes do not always have pleasant endings. On

the highway north of Saigon to Dalat, two missionaries once were driving with their wives and children when they were halted at an agitprop roadblock. The Viet Cong agents had just begun questioning the carloads of people they had halted when an approaching American helicopter was heard. The Viet Cong fled, but not before machine-gunning the missionaries to death.

Viet Cong propaganda works both secretly and openly, and has many outlets. Some of its techniques seem subtle and clever, others seem childish and stupid. But it works.

It is practically impossible to measure the effect of any single piece of propaganda. But one thing that can be more or less measured is recruiting. The success of a recruiting campaign is directly related to the effectiveness of the propaganda of the side doing the recruiting.

Since 1960, the fighting strength of the Viet Cong has grown dramatically, despite casualty losses that probably number as high as 50,000. Only a small part of Viet Cong increase in strength has resulted from infiltration of North Vietnamese communist troops into South Viet Nam.

At this writing, American intelligence men believe that up to 30 per cent of the men in each newly organized Viet Cong unit are infiltrators and the rest are local recruits. As units reach fighting and political maturity, the infiltrated organizers move on to new units. The infiltrated organizers work only with the Viet Cong's "main force" units—the equivalent of the regular army. Regional guerrillas and local hamlet defense groups, numbering between 60,000 and 80,000 men, are all locally recruited. From this it can be seen that on a national basis the percentage of Hanoi-trained infiltrators in the Viet Cong army is probably quite small, say, about 15 per cent, at most.

The rate of infiltration of agents into South Viet Nam is believed to have been more or less constant over the years.

But at the beginning of 1964, for example, Viet Cong "main force" strength was rated at around 27,000 men, with up to 80,000 other guerrillas and local forces under arms.

In the following six months, according to the most reliable intelligence estimates, the Viet Cong suffered an estimated

10,000 battle casualties. But its main force strength reached about 34,000, with the other groups under arms still rated at about 80,000. This represented a net gain for the Viet Cong of 7,000 fighters in a six-month period, or a gross gain (allowing for the casualties) of around 17,000.

The Viet Cong has never hesitated to use force or coercion in drafting young people into its armed forces. But experience in Viet Nam has shown that it is not enough to draft a man to make him fight. The kind of military successes achieved by the Viet Cong during the first six months of 1964 are not suggestive of bands of unwilling, frightened draftees, but rather of hardened soldiers.

From the beginning, the Viet Cong has laid much heavier stress on rice-roots propaganda work than have either the Saigon government or American propaganda agencies in Viet Nam.

In late 1964 the Viet Cong felt that it controlled 77 out of South Viet Nam's 237 administrative districts so completely that agitprop activity no longer was required. But the other 160 districts were considered "contested," that is, up for grabs by both sides. In each of these contested districts, at least two Viet Cong agitprop teams of about ten men and women each were at work.

Saigon's Information Ministry also fields information teams of about ten members each, equipped with three-wheeled scooter trucks, loudspeakers, movie projection equipment and various "visual aids." Saigon has about twenty of these teams in operation throughout the country.

In itself, this gives the Viet Cong a sixteen-to-one numerical edge in personnel assigned to propaganda work. This would be dangerous in itself, but what makes the matter decisively worse is the respective quality of the opposing teams.

Saigon information teams are supposed to spend their time in the countryside, especially in contested areas. This is dangerous work. The Viet Cong regards its own agitprop teams as the basic cutting tools of the National Liberation Front, and looks on enemy propagandists as prime targets, even ahead of regular troops.

It probably would not be just to say that Saigon's field propaganda workers are dragged in off the streets, given a few thousand piastres and told to go to work. But this is not far from the truth.

The work of these teams is not really very difficult. On a typical mission, the team is sent to some hamlet with its scooter truck, sets up its movie screen and projector, shows the movie, passes out brochures and leaflets and leaves, as quickly as possible. Most of the leaflets and brochures are printed by the U.S. Information Service in Saigon or Manila.

Rarely if ever do government propagandists stay around for more than a few hours, and the whole approach is based on mass communications rather than the "living together" and audience-participation techniques of the Viet Cong. Viet Cong propagandists generally are peasants, but the government men are not.

To American ears, propaganda is a bad word, and Americans often feel a little queasy about using either the word or the technique. This reticence is reflected at every level in Saigon's programs.

In the U.S. Army there is an organization devoted to "psychological warfare," and an exact counterpart of this has been designed and built in the Vietnamese Army. It is primarily a force of technicians, who know such arts as printing aerial leaflets, recording tapes for loudspeakers, and so on. As such, it has about as much prestige as a fighting organization as, say, the chaplain's corps, or the special services section for troop recreation. The emphasis is on electronics and machinery rather than with direct contact with the "target people."

On the civilian side, the U.S. Information Service has what it terms "information programs." These, again, are essentially duplicated by information programs of the Saigon Information Ministry.

These programs are different from propaganda campaigns, their administrators say, because they are predicated on truthful reporting rather than distortions and lies. The theory behind this approach is that eventually the truth will out, and it is better to keep things clean rather than face exposure and possible humiliation later.

Unfortunately, in Viet Nam, where communications are so poor and people get so little chance to travel very far and check things for themselves, the truth rarely does out. The average propaganda lie is very apt to go unchallenged indefinitely.

It is simpler and safer for the poorly trained and paid government propaganda worker to make his rounds and hand out his presents, than to get really involved in hamlets. Presents include school notebooks in which a few pages of government "message" have been inserted, pencils stamped with Vietnamese flags, and children's tee shirts printed with big Vietnamese flags. (The Viet Cong regularly tears the offensive pages out of the notebooks, cuts the flags out of the pencils and dyes the tee shirts black.) The most acceptable USIS item is a monthly magazine called *Huong Que* (*Rural Spirit*) which consists mostly of helpful hints to Vietnamese farmers on agricultural problems. It contains no propaganda (except for the fact that it is available only at government information centers) and the articles, written exclusively by Vietnamese, apparently are really useful.

Atrocity propaganda, for better or worse, has an important impact on Viet Nam. In a war, there never is a shortage of dismembered bodies and other horrors to photograph for such use.

The Viet Cong has always made constant use of atrocity themes, and recently the Saigon government and USIS began concentrating on atrocities themselves.

A bus ran over a Viet Cong mine about twenty miles south of Saigon not long ago, and more than twenty civilians, mostly women and children, were killed. Before the blood had clotted, Saigon cameramen were flown to the scene, and the result of their work was printed by USIS on tens of thousands of leaflets. Within hours, planes were sprinkling these leaflets over the province, with appropriate captions.

There was an immediate reaction. At the province capital of Tan An, several hundred peasants staged what appeared to be an authentically angry demonstration to denounce Viet Cong atrocities. Several days later, two ranking officers of a local Viet Cong battalion defected to the government with their weapons. They said they were disgusted that the Front had wantonly blown up the civilian bus. (In fact, the mining probably was an accident, but the Viet Cong was nevertheless successfully saddled with the responsibility.)

This kind of thing was repeated many times, especially in the Mekong Delta. If nothing else, government atrocity propaganda seems to have made the Viet Cong more cautious about accidental attacks on civilian vehicles in the area.

An American propaganda expert summed up the essential difference between red and white propaganda in Viet Nam this way:

"There is a basic rule, applicable to all Vietnamese propaganda from whichever side, called 'tam dong.' Freely translated, 'tam dong' means 'likeness in thinking and ideology.'

"The Viet Cong propagandist breaks it down into the slogan 'live together, eat together, work together.'

"This means that the Viet Cong propagandist is expected to spend all his time with his psychological targets, blending in completely with their whole existence. Too many of the people on our side are just not willing to do this. They like to wear white shirts and sleep in soft beds. We send out our Vietnamese field workers on dangerous missions, and more often than not they go on sick call instead, or find some other excuse not to go. When they do go, they spend as little time in the target area as they can get away with. These workers are not peasants themselves, and they don't like or understand peasants.

"Too many American officials, especially those at USIS, have assumed for too many years they can cover the field using mass communications methods. You can count on your fingers the number of Americans devoted to propaganda activity who actually get out in the field on any regular basis.

"Within these limitations, our propaganda program has to be divided according to three basic groups—the Vietnamese who have had virtually no contact with Saigon authority in thirty-five years or more, the Vietnamese who have had little or no contact with Saigon since Vietnamese independence in 1954, and the others.

"For the first group, most of whom live in Viet Cong base areas, the only kind of propaganda with which we can reach them is threatening. We drop leaflets saying, in effect, surrender or die. We mention that this year, 20 per cent of the men in this or that village were killed by government troops, and say that next year another 20 per cent will die unless resistance ends.

"For the second group, we concentrate on the meaning of Vietnamese independence and nationalism. We point out that Viet Nam is no longer under the foreign domination of France, and we concentrate on the responsibilities of free citizens in building a new country. This group makes up about half of the Vietnamese population, incidentally. That's some indication of how much control the Saigon government has over its population.

"For the last group, centered mostly in the larger towns, our main approach is bringing people up to date on what has happened since the end of the Ngo Dinh Diem regime. For one thing, people are no longer forced to give their labor and time, building the hated strategic hamlets. We point out all the benefits being offered by the new revolutionary regime, and describe its aspirations for peace, prosperity and democracy.

"But obviously all this is done by mass communications.

"The most important thing is the thing our side is not doing nearly enough of—getting out and talking and living with the people. What's really needed is the personal touch, and that's where the Viet Cong is beating us so badly."

Some years ago, the Saigon government opened an agency called the Ministry of Civic Action. In successive coups, the ministry was closed down, but its functions remained on the books. In brief, civic action is the sending of propaganda agents skilled in social service work into contested or enemy areas following military operations. Civic action workers are supposed to build schools, dig wells, help harvest crops and so forth, while putting the message across.

On the American side, U.S. Aid mission civilian officials and military S-5 officers are supposed to work with the civic action people. At this writing, the former minister of civic action, Ngo Trong Hieu, is in jail on charges of gross corruption. At best, the average civic action agent looks down on the peasants he is expected to convert as inferior beings.

But beyond reluctance to face dangerous situations, unwillingness to take initiative and flagrant corruption, civic action officials often have shown lamentable lack of planning and coordination with related agencies.

I once visited a hamlet near the southern tip of Viet Nam where a civic action team was at work. The day before there had been a bloody firefight, and the hamlet was still reeling from the effects of war.

It was clear that the brunt of the civic action job had been shouldered by a young American Negro army captain. This captain with one interpreter was wandering throughout the hamlet outskirts, talking to peasants and trying to form an idea of what was needed in the area. His polite manners and obvious sincerity apparently were softening up a lot of the peasants, especially the older ones.

One peasant told him rats were eating most of the rice reserves in the hamlet. He promised to get them rat poison within a few days. Another said water supplies were desperately short, partly because government soldiers had smashed most of the clay reservoirs in which rain water is kept. (Most of the surface water in the area is brackish because the canals are tidal and near the sea.) The captain promised to investigate the possibility of bringing down deep well drilling equipment.

One woman complained that her son, a government militiaman, had been arrested by district authorities recently, after his post had been wiped out by the Viet Cong. He had managed to run into the jungle while all his comrades in the post were slaughtered. The American said he would try to get the youth out of jail.

He talked to an old and obviously influential villager about building a new market place for the hamlet. Wherever he went, he seemed to be making friends.

But in late afternoon, someone must have reported seeing a small group of Viet Cong moving through the opposite end of the hamlet from where the American was working. Without warning, two A1H fighter planes swept in with rockets and cannon, and blasted half of the hamlet to splinters and embers, with charred pieces of bodies strewn in all directions. From then on, the American found it impossible to talk to anyone in the remains of the hamlet.

In other cases, civic action teams have been sent to innumerable hamlets on the heels of regular military units to find the hamlets robbed blind. Vietnamese soldiers are not issued food on operations but are expected to pay for the food they confiscate. They rarely do pay, especially when they are in areas considered Viet Cong territory, but help themselves to all the chickens, ducks, eggs and rice they can carry away. This makes things tough for the propagandists.

Vietnamese peasants like to be shown respect by the soldiers even in government-dominated areas, and they don't like doing anything free for the army as a matter of principle. Complicating matters, most soldiers are Central Vietnamese, while the war is hottest in the south. Central and Southern Vietnamese don't like each other.

A large group of peasants interviewed by an American team in a Mekong River Delta province disclosed that they would not willingly carry even battle casualties for the Saigon troops.

"They force us to do this work, and they have no right to," one peasant said. "If they would pay us even a little for it, we wouldn't mind. That way we would be equals."

The Viet Cong also confiscates food and labor, of course, and this is a strong point for government propagandists. But the Viet Cong very often makes a show of issuing receipts or worthless pay certificates for the things it takes, which sometimes mollifies the peasants.

The jargon of the propaganda specialists includes the term "black propaganda," which should be mentioned at least in passing at this point, because it is so close to the Vietnamese way of life. In substance, black propaganda is the art of putting words in the other guy's mouth and then blaming him for them.

The "signed confessions" obtained by the Viet Cong from American and Vietnamese prisoners are a crude sample of the technique. Such confessions invariably attest to atrocities, the use of poison gas and germ warfare, and so on.

At a slightly more subtle level, government agents dressed to look like Viet Cong (complete with battle flags) have sometimes come roaring into coastal towns, firing in the air, and throwing around leaflets denouncing God, motherhood and the local province chief. The idea is to make the Viet Cong look bad and local authorities look good.

Local residents are rarely fooled by these shows, but American military advisors (who never are given the word in advance) have sometimes had some nasty shocks. On a few occasions, Americans actually opened fire on the "Viet Cong" before officials hastily told them what was going on.

Many American experts believe black propaganda is dangerous because it can easily misfire if handled with clumsiness.

This writer had an irksome exposure to black propaganda once during a period when the Ngo Dinh Diem government was particularly angry at foreign newsmen.

A document purporting to have come from the Saigon Central Committee of the National Liberation Front was quietly circulated to most embassies in the city. The document consisted of instructions to Viet Cong agents as to how to get in touch with "sympathetic" foreign correspondents in the city, and there followed a list of ten names and addresses. My name headed the list.

Copies of the document had come from the government Information Ministry. Because of certain internal details, it was immediately clear to American authorities that the document was phony and even traceable to a specific functionary in the ministry. But clumsy or not, it was enough to start rumors going, which was one of the main objects of the exercise. Incidentally, for the record, I never have knowingly met or been approached by any Viet Cong agent in Viet Nam, although it is probable that I have met some of their undercover people. I have also met Viet Cong officials outside Viet Nam, in Laos and Cambodia.

There is strong evidence that terrorist grenades sometimes are used as black propaganda. Many American intelligence officials believe Saigon agents have from time to time exploded grenades and then blamed the Viet Cong to generate a public reaction.

Saigon residents are used to this kind of thing. When something happens in town, residents often suspect black propaganda at work, or even double black propaganda. ("The Viet Cong threw that grenade, knowing that we would suspect the government of throwing it with the idea of blaming it on the Viet Cong.") South Viet Nam is a nation in which twisted, devious thinking is the rule, and nothing is accepted at face value. Another sample:

"The government deliberately lost that battle in order to alarm the Americans into giving us more aid." And conversely,

"The Viet Cong deliberately lost that battle to give the Americans a false sense of security."

Americans are widely regarded as gullible people ready to swallow all black propaganda. Perhaps we have, on too many occasions.

In any case, if Americans are gullible, it is my judgment that Vietnamese are probably the least gullible people in the world. They tend automatically to reject all official statements as lies, regardless of the source. Furthermore, they assume that every organization and every person acts wholly out of selfish motives. It is utterly inconceivable to the average Vietnamese that America might be trying to help Viet Nam in any genuinely altruistic way. The more altruistic American aid looks, the more suspect it is. If a Vietnamese is told that some American has volunteered to serve another tour in Viet Nam, he is apt to reply, "Yes, our girls are pretty, aren't they?"

On July 29, 1964, Vietnamese Foreign Minister Phan Huy Quat formally charged the Viet Cong with making black terrorist propaganda to stir up trouble between Viet Nam and neighboring Cambodia. His charge appears to have a lot of supporting evidence.

Certainly, the Viet Cong is interested in keeping relations between Cambodia and South Viet Nam bad. Two of the efforts to be realized from this are that Cambodia is more likely to remain a fairly safe haven for anti-Saigon guerrillas, and that Cambodia and South Viet Nam are not likely to undertake joint action to patrol the frontier. Besides this, the madder Cambodia gets at Saigon, the more likely it is Cambodia will move away from an ostensibly neutral international position to one more closely aligned with North Viet Nam.

In any case, somebody attacked a string of Cambodian border villages in July, 1964, with fairly heavy loss of life for the villagers. The Saigon government occasionally raids Cambodian border hamlets, but almost always apologizes afterward. In any case, from the evidence I have seen, it is very unlikely that any Saigon units were near the area in question when the attack happened. There is no question, on the other hand, that there was an attack. Cambodian villagers in the wrecked hamlets said they were certain the attacking troops wore Saigon uniforms. This mystery probably never will be solved to the satisfaction of everyone, but I think it is quite likely that Quat was right in deciding that the Viet Cong, disguised as government troops, pulled off the raids.

This kind of thing leads Vietnamese to mistrust everything, even if they see it with their own eyes.

I think it is indicative of the lack of trust Vietnamese have in each other that the bodyguards of the president (or prime minister, or whoever happens to be in power) invariably are Cambodians, not Vietnamese. Also, Vietnamese hire Chinese as cooks, maids and domestics. They do not hire Vietnamese, unless they are too poor to afford anything else. Most Vietnamese families believe that Vietnamese servants cannot be trusted.

It is my opinion that this deeply ingrained suspicion, skepticism and cynicism make the average Vietnamese almost wholly immune to any propaganda that depends on mass communication techniques.

Airplanes with loudspeakers, for instance, are an amusing novelty in Viet Nam, but have little effect. A ghostly voice coming from high in the clouds is always an attention getter, but I have yet to see a Vietnamese taking the words themselves very seriously. The attitude seems to be that the Americans have come up with another impressive gadget, but that one shouldn't read too much into it. After all, the plane is miles away from my hamlet, my jungle, and my whole frame of reference.

South Viet Nam is a professional propagandist's nightmare. Everywhere he turns, he faces apathy, mistrust and hostility. His biggest chance of success seems to lie in making friends with individuals on a personal basis, establishing his credentials, and then, cautiously, putting his point across. It is slow and often frustrating work, but no short cut is apparent.

The Viet Cong lacks technology, but it more than makes up for the shortcoming with its propaganda skills. Furthermore, the Viet Cong and its prototypes have had a quarter-century head start in their propaganda operations over the United States.

The Viet Cong has repeatedly said at its organization meetings that it does not hope to win a victory by military means alone. Most of all, the Viet Cong expects a political victory. And in this, propaganda is by far the most important weapon.

It appears so far that the Viet Cong has outgunned Saigon and its American ally in this field.

Chapter 9

War on the Family Plan

It had been raining hard every day for several months, and the Plain of Reeds forty miles west of Saigon was an almost unbroken sheet of water. From the air, there is a peculiar beauty in this kind of landscape, especially at certain times of day or night. There had been a particularly heavy series of helicopter raids on the area at that time, and one image in particular sticks in my mind: a vast expanse of flooded fields just before dawn, a great full moon mirrored in the glassy surface of the fields, and the dark silhouette of a flight of helicopters speeding across the face of the moon in the fields.

Of course, from the ground, the whole thing seems much less attractive. The Chinese-scroll quality of the setting becomes a mass of neck-deep mud, and the helicopters no longer look like wild geese but merely the instruments of destruction they are.

There is a town called Go Dau Ha in this area that stands only a mile or two from the Cambodian border. It is a very busy, prosperous town, largely because of the tremendous smuggling trade between South Viet Nam and Cambodia that goes on nearby. The buildings are the substantial yellow stucco kind that characterize Viet Nam's affluent society, the streets are paved and fairly clean, and the downtown section has many open air coffee shops, a number of billiard parlors and a few movie houses. Just outside town, the smugglers' market flourishes. On the Vietnamese side, one can buy Cambodian silver, and various Chinese medicines and foods not available in Viet Nam. On the

Cambodian side, popular items are good Vietnamese cattle and cigarettes.

The Plain of Reeds also is one of the strongholds of the National Liberation Front, and I had come to Go Dau Ha to watch an operation against the Front.

The operation commander had set up his headquarters in a large, two-story wooden house in a compound at the edge of town. The small compound was bulging with troops, and a pair of 105-millimeter howitzers had been dug in emplacements next to the back porch. A column of thirty M113 amphibious armored personnel carriers stood pulled up in the road outside the compound gate waiting for opening of the operation in the morning. They were under especially heavy guard, because two nights earlier a child had wandered up to the gate with a big metal box that looked something like a pie tin. No one paid much attention to the boy and his box, although someone had noticed him putting it down next to an armored car parked outside the gate. Ten minutes later, a heavy explosion ripped open the armored car, killing its dozing, four-man crew.

The operation commander liked the plans for the new operation and was confident of a victory in the morning. Reports had it that a battalion of Viet Cong was operating out in the open about fifteen miles away from Go Dau Ha, and since M113s had never been used in this sector before, he was counting on giving the enemy a nasty surprise. At dinner in town that night, he was a model host to his officers and the American advisors, and he broke open four bottles of a delicious Vietnamese strawberry wine he had been saving.

After dinner, under the light of a gasoline lantern on the porch of the headquarters house, the commander spread out his maps once again for a final conference with his officers and advisors.

Final intelligence reports were plotted on plastic overlays, and lines of march laid out in red crayon. Every once in a while, a large wriggling gecko would lose his footing on the wooden porch ceiling and come slapping down on the map, to the extreme annoyance of the strategists.

The officers and American advisors were sleeping inside the house. They had glued newspaper over the walls and ceilings of the rooms to keep plaster dust from falling over them every time the howitzer battery fired.

The howitzers kept firing all night long at intervals of about twenty minutes. Each time, the guns fired only six or eight shells. But to a man sleeping only a few yards from a howitzer muzzle, each shot is like an electric explosion in his brain, and there is a feeling of panic and unspecified horror every time.

The task force was tired as the men slapped cold water in their faces at three thirty the following morning. A thin drizzle was falling, and breakfast was cold rice and glasses of hot, weak tea.

By 4 A.M., the column of clanking M113s, each loaded with about fifteen soldiers, was moving down the road with lights out. Five miles out of town, the column stopped. Someone off in a dark field to the left of the road had been signaling with a flashlight. A squad of troops dismounted and went out into the field to investigate. Twenty minutes later they were back, having found nothing. By 6 A.M., the column reached a point on the muddy road where the operation was to jump off across country. Drivers have to see the dykes and holes they must drive across, and cross-country travel is impossible at night. So the column halted until the sky became light a little before 7 A.M.

Then began the long, spine-jarring trip to the objective. Unlike conventional tanks, M113s do not ride smoothly but take every bump in the terrain and seem to magnify it. The squat, slab-sided machines moved in a wave a mile long across the flooded fields, like a menacing herd of rhinoceroses. Atop each machine, a soldier manning a big .50-caliber machine gun gazed forward, looking for targets. I was sitting behind the gunner of the M113 on the extreme left flank of the formation.

Abruptly, firing began somewhere off to the right. Someone had seen movement in a tree line about two miles away and started shooting. Our vehicle surged ahead at full speed toward a hamlet, the outlines of which were barely visible in the tree line.

Plunging up and down dykes, we narrowed the distance from the hamlet to about 800 yards, and then our gunner spotted two tiny figures in black running in front of one of the huts. The big gun began hammering out tracers. The mixture of powder smoke and exhaust gas from the M113 engine was nearly suffocating as we charged on. Geysers of mud and water were spurting in the fields ahead as the slugs hit. Now we were only 200 yards out, and could see the two figures running fast to the left, apparently aiming for some protective scrub growth. We altered course slightly to head them off. The gun continued to pour out tracers, but because of the lurching motion of the M113 none of it was very accurate.

At 100 yards out, the geysers of water finally were spitting up all around the two running figures, and we evidently had the range. Any second now they would go down in a mangled pulp of flesh and shattered bone.

The two figures suddenly stopped and threw up their arms in surrender. The lieutenant commanding our vehicle ordered the gunner to cease fire as we closed on our captives. The troops leapt out to grab them.

Our two guerrilla prisoners turned out to be brothers, eight and nine years old. One had fallen or been hit by something, and his hand was broken, a spear of bone protruding through the muddy skin. Both boys looked at us incuriously, and neither face registered any trace of emotion. One boy had a coil of electric mine-detonating wire over his shoulder, and the other had two grenades slung from a rope around his waist. The boys were roughly stripped of their gear.

The hamlet ahead of us was deserted, except for one old man. The boys were given a rope and ordered to tie the man's hands behind his back. They did it.

The lieutenant in charge of our platoon walked up to the boys and asked them where the Viet Cong had gone. No answer.

"Well, then, where have they hidden their weapons and supplies?"

No answer. One of the boys spat into the mud in front of him.

"You'll answer my questions, or you'll be sorry," the lieutenant said. No answer. The officer pulled out his .45 automatic and pointed it in the face of the older boy.

"Where did they go?" The boy did not answer, but gazed straight into the officer's eyes.

Furious, the officer fired three quick shots into the ground in front of the boy's feet. The boy did not flinch or answer.

The lieutenant snorted and walked off, shouting to a subordinate: "Have them help search the ponds for weapons." The boys were led off, and began sullenly wading through the hamlet ponds as ordered. I don't think they were very helpful in the search. After twenty minutes of combing fruitlessly through the hamlet, the troops climbed up on their vehicles, and the boys and the old man were shoved through the back hatch of one of the M113s.

None of the new passengers had ever ridden in one of these machines, and none knew that you must hold on to nylon straps hanging from the ceiling or there is danger of being badly hurt. Pieces of machinery and loose oilcans fly around the interior of the vehicle every time it hits a bump. So our three captives were pretty badly scraped and banged up as we moved on to the next hamlet, and soldiers laughed when the bedraggled trio was hauled out again. The boy's broken hand had been hurt some more, and was now bleeding profusely, but his face was still emotionless.

This hamlet, too, was deserted. But from one of the huts, a soldier let out a whoop. He had found a huge, silk Viet Cong flag. Another soldier, poking a stick in muddy holes he passed, also hit it lucky. One of the holes contained a young man with a rifle, who popped up like a jack-in-the-box when the stick gouged his shoulder. Here was an authentic prisoner, and four or five soldiers took turns beating him up until he was bloody and unconscious. They shot him later, but not until the American advisors were safely out of the way.

By this time, the M113 crews felt a certain satisfaction with their operation, and the Viet Cong flag had been attached to the radio mast of one of the vehicles. The huge red, blue and yellow banner looked rather strange flapping over the vehicle.

It was time to leave, and there seemed no point in taking along the three prisoners. The two boys were ordered to untie the old man, which they hastily did.

"All right, go home, and let this be a lesson to you," the lieutenant told the boys. The old man sat down on a log and watched as the M113s prepared to leave. The two boys trudged off across a field without a backward glance.

Those two boys were tough little guerrillas. If they survive, they will grow up to be tough big guerrillas.

War is a family matter in Viet Nam, and a Viet Cong family has Viet Cong children.

There is nothing extraordinary about women and children getting involved in wars. Most wars claim civilian lives. In some wars, women and children are active participants. History has seen many phenomena like the Children's Crusade of the Middle Ages. Women and children seem to have a particular tendency to get involved in guerrilla operations, and played major roles in the undergrounds of Europe during the Nazi occupation.

But there seems to me a peculiarly personal quality to family war in Viet Nam. Fighters on both sides very often take their families with them, right up into the front lines.

I saw another incident in the Plain of Reeds that struck me as poignant in a characteristically Vietnamese way.

Viet Cong guerrilla tactics are not always letter perfect. The enemy sometimes makes bad mistakes, too, which cost him dearly. It happened once that a battalion of Viet Cong was moving rapidly from one province to another across the Plain of Reeds, and made the fatal mistake of moving in large groups without adequate camouflage.

The battalion was under the command of a Viet Cong brigadier general, who had the reputation of being an excellent guerrilla officer, but who had spent most of his combat career in Central Viet Nam, and who was new to the Mekong Delta. It often happens when Viet Cong move from one area to another that they take their families along. This general had brought his young wife and infant son.

The general had not counted on being spotted as quickly as he was. The Vietnamese army swooped down in helicopters and M113s, and cut his battalion to pieces. The fight was such a disaster that for months the National Liberation Front continued to issue critique papers on the mistakes made and how they should have been avoided. Some of these secret critiques happened to fall into American hands, which is why I know of them.

In any case, one government unit even managed to catch the Viet Cong command post in a hut, flat footed. A machine gunner spotted four men running through a thicket behind the house, and cut all four of them down with one burst. They were the general and his three top aides. It was a brilliant coup for the Saigon forces.

A half hour later, the shooting was over and the troops were collecting their war booty—an impressive pile of enemy bodies and weapons. While this was going on, an American captain heard a whimpering sound in the direction of the spot where the Viet Cong officers had been killed, and saw a flutter of movement in the thicket. He walked over, his Tommy gun at the ready.

Huddled on the other side of a dyke was a young woman stripped to the waist, her blouse wrapped around an infant that she was trying to nurse. The blouse was covered with blood, and it turned out that the baby had been shot through the belly.

The pathetic pair was the family of the dead Viet Cong general.

The American hastily stripped off his field shirt and put it over the shoulders of the young mother. Within minutes, a helicopter on the ground had been ordered to take the mother and baby to a Saigon hospital as priority casualties. Some of the Vietnamese officers were angry in a polite way about this display of American softheartedness, but did nothing to interfere.

Tears were running down the woman's face, but she nodded when told to get aboard the helicopter with her baby. That was the last I saw of those two, but I learned later that the baby survived, and the softhearted Americans were taking care of mother and child financially.

I think it is quite likely that the mother remains a hard-core believer in the National Liberation Front, and the baby probably will grow up to be a guerrilla. But that is one of the tragedies of this kind of war.

It works both ways. Thousands of little government posts manned by militiamen dot South Viet Nam, and most of them have brassieres and diapers hanging out to dry on the barbed wire. Each post actually is a little community of military families, leading an existence quite isolated from the rest of the country-side. I know of one such post in eastern Kien Hoa Province that went without supplies or contact with the outer world for six solid months in 1964. The post was literally forgotten, and not a cartridge or a piastre reached it during the whole period the mighty leaders in Saigon were fighting among themselves for control of the capital. Somehow, this little post of ten men, seven women and a liberal sprinkling of children went right on with its war routine, even doing a little fighting.

In the center of a sea of Viet Cong domination, this post could easily have been annihilated by the guerrillas at no cost to themselves. It is difficult to understand why this didn't happen, unless by some unlikely chance even the Viet Cong felt some pangs of compassion.

More often than not, the Viet Cong feels no such qualms. The guerrillas do not make a point of killing women and children, but in overrunning a post, it is difficult to avoid.

Accidental civilian casualties are much more often caused by the government side than the Viet Cong, because of artillery and air strikes. The usual justification given for this is that if civilians persist in living in Viet Cong zones they have to be prepared to take the consequences. But the consequences can be ghastly.

In the last week of September, 1964, an intelligence report reached a province headquarters in the Mekong Delta that thirty sampans loaded with Viet Cong troops were moving down a nearby canal. Within minutes, the sector commander was on the radio telephone to Saigon, talking to a mustachioed young Air Force officer in the operations room at the Tactical Operations Center. With commendable speed and efficiency, the young officer issued a scramble alert, and within three minutes, a flight of A1H single-seaters was roaring down the runway.

The fighters found the thirty sampans with no difficulty, and the whole run was duck soup. Within fifteen minutes, every sampan had been blown to matchwood.

It wasn't for several days that the sector chief found out who had been in the sampans.

A trigger-happy field intelligence agent had seen and correctly counted the sampans, but his guess as to what was in them was not correct. They were all civilians, most of them women and children. Twenty-seven were killed and thirty seriously injured. The Air Force announced blandly that it would take steps to avoid a recurrence of such accidents.

But similar announcements have been made after many of the hundreds or thousands of such incidents in the past, and basically nothing changes. The Air Force sometimes saturates areas with bombs weighing up to 500 pounds. Some of them go off immediately, but the others are timed to explode many hours later, presumably after the Viet Cong has come back. Or peasants, who simply think it is safe to return to work. This kind of thing, regardless of whatever tactical advantage it may have, is to my mind little short of slaughter. It is not difficult to conceive of a farmer or his wife joining the National Liberation Front merely as an act of revenge after one of these accidental massacres.

On the other hand, there is a tendency among Westerners to regard women as the frail sex. The Vietnamese do not so regard their own graceful and beautiful women, nor should they. Women make dangerous guerrillas.

There is one woman in particular who has become a legend in the upper Mekong Delta, especially Long An Province where she most often operates. Her name is Kim Loan, she is a small woman in her mid-thirties, and she commands a large Viet Cong combat team in one of the most bitterly contested areas of the nation.

Kim Loan used to be a family woman. She was the wife of a Viet Cong district commissar and the mother of two small children.

In 1963, Kim Loan's husband was killed in a clash with government troops. She is said to have identified his mangled body without betraying a sign of emotion. A few days later, she took her children to the home of her dead husband's sister in Tan An, twenty miles south of Saigon, and disappeared.

From then on, Kim Loan went on a one-woman killing spree, even sometimes tackling groups of soldiers singlehanded. On various assassination jobs, she captured first one pistol and then another. Since then, she has always worn two pistols.

At first, the Liberation Front assigned her mostly to tax-collection chores, which she carried out with brutal enthusiasm. She once visited a government official at his home in the dead of night, and demanded money. The official refused. She whipped out a pistol and slammed it down on a table in front of her.

"Talk to my pistol," she said. The man trotted off to his bedroom and brought back a wad of bills. Kim Loan spat contemptuously and slammed her other pistol on the table.

"Talk to my other pistol," she said. "I want everything you've got." The man went off for a second trip and brought back a more satisfactory sum.

Kim Loan quickly gained a reputation for extraordinary daring, shrewdness in military tactics, and dedication to exterminating Saigon authorities. She rose rapidly through the ranks, and in little over a year after her husband's death, she was placed in command of all Viet Cong intelligence and subversion throughout a large sector of populous Long An Province. As a sector military commander, she has headed a Viet Cong politico-military machine that has made continuous progress during a period when Saigon and Washington were bringing maximum pressure to bear on precisely the same province. An entire government division was assigned to the area, and all kinds of special civilian aid and propaganda teams went to work in the province, but Kim Loan and her legions gained increased mastery of the countryside.

As a Viet Cong bigshot, Kim Loan was assigned two permanent bodyguards, each armed with a submachine gun. She also generally traveled at the head of a twenty-man assault platoon. One month, she returned to her home village in a remote part of the province, and recruited thirty-three men into the Viet Cong army.

Kim Loan's brutal but colorful style began to become a kind of latter-day Joan of Arc legend on both sides. She was regarded with a mixture of awe and delight, and anecdotes about the female gunslinger have become favorite conversation pieces in the cafes of Tan An.

There is even a touch of the miraculous about it all in some eyes. Kim Loan has had so many hair-raising narrow escapes, that there are those who say she turns into a monkey if cornered in a tree, or turns into a fish if boxed in near a canal.

But legendary or not, Kim Loan was kept under sharp surveillance by Liberation Front political commissars. Basically she was a vengeful fanatic rather than a coolheaded leader, and besides this, her methods were often a little too brutal. These qualities do not rate high in Viet Cong field manuals.

And one day in 1964, Kim Loan went too far. A minor Viet Cong official had failed in a mission assigned by Kim Loan. She told him quietly that he was a coward, and then shot him down in cold blood.

Top-ranking Viet Cong commissars relieved Kim Loan of her command, and packed her off to a base area on the Cambodian border for several months of political indoctrination. For one thing, Kim Loan was not a communist, and the leadership felt she could not be trusted without initiation into the party.

Evidently Kim passed her course, because after a few months she turned up again in Long An Province. But this time she was stripped of her pistols and troops, and apparently was assigned as a full-time intelligence operative. She reportedly dresses as an old woman now, and is using a fourteen-year-old boy as her lookout.

The boy's mother was deeply worried about her son's association with the terrible Kim Loan, and one day actually approached an American civilian operative in Tan An on the matter.

"I don't want my son killed," she said, "and he will be, if he stays with Kim Loan. If there's anything you could do, if you ever see him, you will have a mother's thanks."

It will probably come to pass that Kim Loan is caught in some trap or betrayed into government hands. But her legend is likely to persist long after she is gone. She is perhaps more responsible than any other single individual for the frustration of Saigon and Washington efforts to "pacify" one of the most critical provinces in the nation on Saigon's back doorstep.

The women of Viet Nam are as tiny and fragile looking as any in the world. They stand about five feet high, their waists are likely to be eighteen inches or less around, their legs are slim and in proportion, and their features sweet and gentle. But the impression all this creates is a living lie.

These same gentle little women rule their families and husbands with an iron hand, and in the cities women control an enormous share of all commercial enterprises as well. The traditions of Viet Nam are entirely different from those in Japan and North Asia, where the women have a decorative but somewhat subservient role.

The fiery Mme. Ngo Dinh Nhu gained enormous international notice during the last two years of her late brother-in-law's reign over South Viet Nam. But she is not a particularly extraordinary Vietnamese. Mme. Nhu could crush a political opponent with the flick of an eyelash, and often did. Even while smiling demurely, her eyes often shone with a deadly hardness that could mean prison or death for someone. And when addressing crowds, her cold fury sometimes reminded me of the Hollywood versions of ancient pagan goddesses demanding a blood sacrifice. I have seen the same stigmata in many another Vietnamese woman.

I always had the feeling that Mme. Nhu despised and hated men, including those closest to her.

One afternoon, I was ushered past a pair of stuffed tigers into her sumptuously furnished reception parlor at Saigon's Independence Palace. The First Lady entered, wearing, as usual, a gorgeous *ao-dai*, cut low at the neck in the style she always affected. The *ao-dai* in itself, a close-fitting silk dress that hangs to the ankles and is slit to the waist, is worn over loose white or black silk trousers. It is one of the most beautiful and graceful feminine garments ever devised.

We talked over tea for three hours that afternoon, mostly about politics. I was struck by the frequency with which she attacked or criticized this or that man, always suggesting some approach to a problem she felt was better.

At one point, we were discussing the corruption of some ranking government officials, and she said:

"The President [Diem] is much too softhearted. He will always protect his friends, even if they betray him by doing wrong things in the government. The President is like a child, and sometimes I get so angry with him I could slap him."

I could hardly believe my ears. I had met Mme. Nhu only two or three times before at receptions, and was, for all practical purposes, a stranger to herself and her family. Furthermore, this conversation was not a casual social call. I was there as a foreign correspondent, working a story for The Associated Press. She read my story (in which I quoted her exactly) and she sent me a note saying she had liked it. I don't know whether or not Diem read the story, but if he did, it is safe to guess that he did not like it.

Another time, Mme. Nhu was playing hostess to an American television crew, and felt the parlor was not an appropriate place for the interview. She wanted the presidential reception room itself. It happened that Diem was using the reception room to entertain some state visitors, but Mme. Nhu strode in rather coldly and ejected the whole party, President and all.

There was a spark of fanaticism about Mme. Nhu. With a stroke of the pen, she outlawed divorce, dancing, beauty contests, gambling, fortunetelling, cockfighting, prostitution, and a hundred other things dear to the hearts of Vietnamese men. Neither her husband nor his brother, the President, ever dared interfere with these amazing legislative decrees.

She spoke wistfully sometimes of her blighted childhood in Hanoi, her teen-age marriage to Ngo Dinh Nhu, and the life of danger and struggle that followed.

She even declared war on her family. In 1962, she drove her sister to attempted suicide by forbidding the sister to see the Frenchman she loved. In 1963, Mme. Nhu disowned her parents,

Tran Van Chuong, the Vietnamese ambassador to Washington, and Mme. Chuong, the Vietnamese observer at the United Nations. Both of them had bolted from the Diem regime after Saigon troops raided insurgent Buddhist pagodas, and both of them resigned from their posts. A bitter public feud between Mme. Nhu and her parents immediately followed, which, as far as I know, has never been healed.

Mme. Nhu organized her own party, the Vietnamese Women's Solidarity Movement, and her own army, the Vietnamese Women's Paramilitary Corps. Her daughter, a sixteen-year-old slip of a girl at the time, was one of the first to join. Little Le Thuy swiftly learned the manly arts of judo, marching and shooting, and I have seen her shoot balloons out of a man's hand thirty yards away with her .45 automatic.

Mme. Nhu tried during her last year in Saigon to destroy the integrity of the free foreign press, and in the process she made life extremely dangerous and difficult for my colleagues and myself. I think if she had had complete free reign, she would certainly have arranged for at least some of us to die. I know from personal experience that Mme. Nhu could be the most dangerous enemy a man could have.

But for all that, Mme. Nhu had (and has) a breed of daring and courage that must always command respect, even when it is aimed against principles that Americans hold sacred.

I have written at some length of Mme. Nhu, because I think there are elements of her in many Vietnamese women, albeit on a less spectacular scale. And a lot of these women are Viet Cong. Men and women revolutionary guerrillas have been meeting and marrying in the jungles of Viet Nam for the last thirty years or more, fighting government forces side by side, and raising children to do just the same thing. For such families, revolution is not merely a campaign, or even a war. It is a way of life.

A good many attractive and talented Vietnamese girls have been siphoned off by the Viet Cong recruiting machine not as guerrillas but as spies. There are tales about some of these girls that make the Mata Hari legend seem pallid.

One is worth recording, in that it involved an American

tragedy, and somehow typifies the tangled, wretched relations that can develop between Vietnamese and Americans. I happened to know some of the people involved in this one.

A certain American officer named B. was sent to Viet Nam as part of a group of experts in strategic military intelligence. For a long time, he was stationed in a horribly desolate jungle post in the mountains, where it is usually cold, almost always drenched with rain, and where supplies must be dropped by air when the weather is good enough for flying. It is one of the least agreeable places in Viet Nam. There are no diversions, and the work is lonely and usually frustrating.

B. was pleased to be reassigned to a mountain detachment in more civilized surroundings, but on his arrival there he found a letter from his wife back in the States. She wanted a divorce.

B. had always been a hard-working and conscientious officer, and he had a keen mind. But he was really miserable about the news from America.

The weeks passed, and B. struck up a friendship with a very attractive Vietnamese girl in town. The girl not only was beautiful, but extremely intelligent and able to talk with the officer almost as an equal. The friendship warmed into romance. The girl and her family were hard up, and B. began helping them out financially. B. seemed to be a happy man again, and more weeks passed.

Somehow, B. got involved in directing a counterintelligence operation at his new duty station that began paying off. The object of this investigation was to crack a dangerous Viet Cong espionage ring. The evidence looped in many directions, but B.'s inquest finally led him directly to the girl he loved. There was no question that this girl and her family were important Viet Cong secret agents.

I have no idea how long this terrible conclusion had formed itself in B.'s mind before he did what he did. But it is a fact that one night, in the privacy of his quarters at the American detachment, B. blew out his brains.

Vietnamese families themselves often are tragically split by politics and war. There are thousands of officials, officers and soldiers in South Viet Nam with brothers or sisters or fathers or sons fighting for the Viet Cong or serving in important posts in Hanoi. Sometimes, during *Tet*, the lunar New Year festival in January or February, divided families get together for secret reunions. *Tet* is a time when both sides stop fighting completely, and there have even been instances of Viet Cong squads joining government troops for dinner.

The Vietnamese war is fratricide, in the most literal sense. I know very few families in Saigon or the provinces who do not have at least some distant relatives on the other side. And there is no apparent geographical patterns to the divisions. Some of North Viet Nam's top officials are South Vietnamese, and vice versa. One of Premier Nguyen Khanh's top aides was considered once for the post of ambassador to West Germany but did not get the post because his brother already was the North Vietnamese ambassador to East Germany.

Situations like this are regarded by Americans as tragic ironies. There is a general impression that Vietnamese are fed up with incessant war and political strife, and would be happy just for a little peace and security. This is unquestionably true in many cases.

But Saigon and Washington planning is largely predicated on the conclusion that the Vietnamese peasant wants security more than anything else. To this end, various "pacification plans" have been put into operation, and Vietnamese are told they can have security only if they will co-operate.

I think there are two flaws in this reasoning. One is that the Viet Cong also offers security, and the guerrillas view the Saigon government and the Americans as the force disrupting security.

The other and more important flaw is that security is apparently not the primary motivation of a Viet Cong guerrilla and his wife and children, who go out to do battle together against the Saigon forces. If security were the prime goal, a life in the Viet Cong could hardly be less attractive. But as Viet Cong casualties increase, so does its recruiting, at an even greater rate.

This is the nature of what the great Asian communist theorists call "people's warfare." It means nothing less than mobilization of every man, woman and child. The man who engineered the Viet Minh defeat of France at Dien Bien Phu in 1954, General Vo Nguyen Giap, described the total involvement of "people's warfare" this way:

> The application of this strategy of long-term resistance requires a whole system of education, a whole ideological struggle among the people and party members, a gigantic effort of organization in both military and economic fields, extraordinary sacrifices from the army as well as from the people, at the front as well as in the rear. . . .
> Each inhabitant is a soldier, each village a fortress, each party cell and each administrative committee a staff.[1]

More than any other aspect of the new face of war, the involvement of entire families is critical. The practitioners of "people's warfare" do not distinguish nearly so sharply as the West between terms like soldier and civilian, politician and officer, front lines and rear lines, or any of the pigeonholes into which conventionally trained tacticians slice up their campaigns.

The new enemy may just as easily be an eight-year-old boy with a mine as a helmeted soldier in jack boots. And while you may beat him on the field of battle, he may win the day in the privacy of a rural cell meeting. He may also beat you in a religious temple, and the following chapter seeks to show how.

---

[1] *People's War, People's Army,* by Vo Nguyen Giap, Foreign Languages Publishing House, 1960.

Chapter 10

Buddhists, Communists and Poor People

The long, brown joss sticks that burn at Buddhist holy places and homes throughout South Viet Nam generate a pleasing fragrance said to find favor with ghosts. But the smell of joss sticks is one that I shall never be able to dissociate from the ghastly smell of burning human flesh.

The two odors mingled June 11, 1963, at the intersection of two busy Saigon streets, to create a political explosion, the effects of which are still felt in Washington and elsewhere. I was there, and it happened like this:

On Monday, June 10, I got a telephone call at my office from a young Buddhist monk named Thich Duc Nghiep whom I had known some time. Duc Nghiep became well known to Western newsmen later as official press spokesman for the Buddhist rebels, by virtue of his fairly fluent English. At this writing, he is in the United States studying for a master's degree in comparative religion.

"We shall hold a meeting tomorrow morning at eight A.M.," Duc Nghiep said. "I would advise you to come. Something very important may happen."

For nearly a month, top Buddhist monks had been holding marching street demonstrations and hunger strikes in Saigon, all aimed at wringing concessions from the authoritarian Ngo Dinh Diem regime. Demands included one for government permission to fly the five-colored Buddhist flag in public. The Buddhists also wanted an end of alleged government favoritism to Catholics, an end to arbitrary police arrests, and "social justice for the nation."

The whole thing had been touched off on Tuesday, May 8, 1963, when Buddhists observing the birthday of Buddha were forbidden to fly their flag in the streets. A pagoda protest meeting organized by the powerful young monk Thich Tri Quang had been tape recorded, and the Buddhists demanded permission to broadcast their recording on the local government radio station. Permission was denied, and several thousand Buddhist marchers led by monks headed from Hue's Tu Dam Pagoda for the radio station in the center of town.

As the marchers approached the radio station and surged around its entrance, the local military commander, a major named Dang Sy, had a bad case of jitters. He ordered troops and armored cars to move in.

Several grenades, apparently thrown by trigger-happy soldiers, exploded in the midst of the crowd. A few of the marchers (including children) were crushed under the tracks of the armored vehicles. Eight persons were killed on the spot, and, of the scores wounded, several died later.

The people who died in the Hue incident became the first of the Buddhist martyrs in what was to become a fierce struggle to destroy Ngo Dinh Diem and his family.

The Diem government, rather than back down, applied increasingly harsh measures against the Hue Buddhists, and the pleasant little city on the banks of the Perfume River became an armed camp. In another incident later in the summer, marchers with arms folded were blocked at a street barricade, and staged a sit-in on the pavement. Troops dispersed them by hurling glass containers of acid, which splashed over demonstrators and sent more than seventy of them to the hospital.

The masses of the nation were stirring, and the showdown was nearing.

In Saigon, demonstrations by monks during the first month after the Hue incident were orderly and staged with military precision. Monks would converge at key parks around the city in taxicabs and bicycle taxis with such perfect timing that formations of three or four hundred saffron-robed Buddhists appeared to materialize from thin air, under the noses of security police.

Street marches, especially on Tuesdays, became so frequent they appeared to be losing their impact. Tuesday was the day of choice, because the ascension of the spirits of the dead from the Hue incident was said to be marked by seven-day intervals, and the victims had died on a Tuesday.

Some time in late May, one of the English-speaking monks at the cluster of concrete buildings known as An Quang Pagoda had given a visitor a piece of blood-chilling intelligence. He said that two monks were planning to commit suicide publicly in support of Buddhist demands—one by disembowelment and the other by burning. The Buddhist high command (consisting of about ten top monks, including Tri Quang) had not yet authorized the suicides but was considering them, the informant said. Nothing further was said about this plan, and many people wrote it off as an idle threat, on grounds that the nonviolent Buddhist faith would never condone suicide.

But something special was in the air the morning of June 11.

I arrived about a quarter to eight at the small pagoda off Phan Dinh Phung Street where I had been advised to go. The concrete pagoda building was set in about thirty yards from the street with a muddy alleyway as an entrance. In the rear was a small courtyard, jammed with yellow-robed monks and gray-robed nuns. Loudspeakers nailed to trees and corners of the pagoda building were blaring in rapid Vietnamese.

More monks and nuns, all of them standing, were jammed in the main pagoda room, where another loudspeaker was howling.

I was shown to an alcove in which a large, gilded Buddha statue stood, and asked to sit down at a low table. Six or eight women wearing the white dress of mourning were busy preparing tea. One of them brought me a steaming glass cup of tea, and tried to smile politely, although tears were coursing down her face.

My monk informant, Thich Duc Nghiep, spotted me and came over. He whispered in my ear, "I advise you to stay until the very end of this, because I think something very important will happen."

At exactly eight o'clock, the jabber of Vietnamese from the

loudspeakers stopped and the chanting of prayer began. One monk led the chanting with a microphone and another one next to him kept time, beating rhythmically on a gourd.

"Na Mo A Di Da Phat," the ancient prayer begins, each word equally accented on the same monotonous note.

It is the most hypnotic kind of chant I have ever heard, and on that hot June morning, clouds of incense in the air, I found even myself affected. All the monks and nuns joined that chant, quietly at first, then with rising, hammering volume, as the verses were repeated over and over, the tempo speeding up slightly.

Eyes all around me were fixed straight ahead, almost glazed in the absorption of fervor. But at exactly 9 A.M. it stopped.

Monks and nuns, who apparently had drilled their procedure many times, lined up in the alleyway, moving out into the street in two ranks. Some unfurled banners in Vietnamese and English calling on the government to answer the Buddhist demands. In a minute or two, the procession of 350 or so monks and nuns was formed and moving. At its head was an innovation in the street marches—a gray sedan with four or five monks riding inside. It seemed strange to me at the time that monks were now riding instead of walking.

Police ahead of the procession cleared the streets as usual, keeping clear of the marchers, and not interfering, except to shunt traffic and crowds away from the line of march. Preceding the Buddhist car by about a half-block, a white police jeep kept pace. At that time, the main crackdown on Buddhists by government officials was in Central Viet Nam, not the Saigon area.

People leaned from shopwindows along Phan Dinh Phung, and children stared at the passing procession.

The marchers reached the intersection of Le Van Duyet Street, one of the most important boulevards in Saigon, always jammed with heavy traffic. On one corner of the intersection stood the massive, gray Cambodian consulate building, with its stone lion statue. On two other corners were apartment buildings, and on the fourth corner, an Esso service station. At precisely the center of the intersection, the Buddhist car stopped, apparently stalled. The police jeep was already halfway down the next block.

The marchers began to move past the car, and then abruptly turned left into Le Van Duyet, quickly forming a circle about thirty feet in diameter, of which the car formed a link. It was now nearly 9:20 A.M.

The monks in the car had gotten out, and one of them had opened its hood. From inside, he pulled a five-gallon gasoline can made of translucent plastic, filled to the brim with pink gasoline. Three other monks were walking from the car side by side to the center of the circle. One of them placed a small brown cushion on the pavement, and the monk in the center sat down on it, crossing his legs in the traditional position of Buddhist meditation known as the "lotus posture." This monk was the Venerable Thich Quang Duc, destined to be known throughout the world as the primary saint of modern Vietnamese Buddhism.

The three monks exchanged a few quiet words. The two who had flanked Quang Duc brought the gasoline container quickly to the center of the circle, and poured most of it over the bowed head and shoulders of the seated monk.

The monks stepped back, leaving the gasoline can next to the seated man. From about twenty feet away, I could see Quang Duc move his hands slightly in his lap striking a match. In a flash, he was sitting in the center of a column of flame, which engulfed his entire body. A wail of horror rose from the monks and nuns, many of whom prostrated themselves in the direction of the flames.

From time to time, a light breeze pulled the flames away from Quang Duc's face. His eyes were closed, but his features were twisted in apparent pain. He remained upright, his hands folded in his lap, for nearly ten minutes as the flesh burned from his head and body. The reek of gasoline smoke and burning flesh hung over the intersection like a pall.

Finally, Quang Duc fell backward, his blackened legs kicking convulsively for a minute or so. Then he was still, and the flames gradually subsided.

While the monk burned, other monks stood in positions at all four entrances to the intersection, holding banners reading: A Buddhist Priest Burns for Buddhist Demands.

City police at first watched in stunned horror, and then began running around aimlessly outside the circle of Buddhists. One of them radioed headquarters, and three or four fire trucks arrived with a platoon of helmeted riot police carrying fixed bayonets. The riot police charged down the street in a wave, but stopped short in confusion a few yards from the circle. As the fire trucks moved down the street, several monks leaped in front of their wheels, and other monks chocked themselves behind the rear wheels, making movement impossible without crushing someone.

All the while, leading monks with portable electric loud-speakers harangued onlookers, both in Vietnamese and English, with a highly emotional explanation as to why the suicide had taken place.

A black delivery truck with large Buddhist flags painted on its sides arrived, and monks unloaded a wooden coffin. The flames by now were completely out, and monks tried to transfer the charred body to the coffin. But its splayed arms and legs were rigid, and could not be forced into the box.

Seven monks shed their saffron robes (wearing brown robes underneath) and made a kind of sling to carry the body. The circle broke and formed into a procession once again, the body at its head. Marching a few blocks more, the group arrived at Xa Loi Pagoda, the main Buddhist pagoda in South Viet Nam, where a bell was tolling mournfully from the concrete tower. It was 10 A.M. sharp, and the demonstration was finished.

Quang Duc was the first of the Buddhist monks to die by fiery suicide the summer of 1963. He also was the only one to die with such elaborate public trappings. The other suicides all were sprung by surprise without processions. In Saigon, one young monk arrived in a taxi at Saigon's central market place, walked to the center of the traffic circle, and set himself afire. Three American newsmen attempting to photograph the incident were badly beaten by police. Another young monk, his clothing apparently impregnated with gasoline in advance, died on a street corner facing Saigon Cathedral one bright Sunday morning, as Catholic worshipers were arriving for mass. A policeman tried to beat out the flames, but without success.

Two monks in Hue burned themselves to death inside their barricaded pagoda, with no outsiders as witnesses. Another monk burned to death in front of a soldier's memorial, completely alone, in the coastal town of Phan Thiet. And a thirty-three-year-old nun died in flames near her pagoda outside another coastal town, the seaside resort of Nha Trang. In all, seven died, all with the blessings of the Buddhist high command.

Thich Quang Duc's body was taken for cremation at the Buddhist cemetery just outside Saigon, and monks in charge of burning the body claimed that Quang Duc's heart would not burn. A singed piece of meat purporting to be the heart was preserved in a glass chalice, becoming an object of worship.

Quang Duc's ashes were distributed to pagodas throughout the country. The yellow robes in which his body had been carried were cut into tiny swatches and distributed to Buddhist followers everywhere. Pinned to shirts and dresses, these bits of cloth were thought to have miraculous healing properties, and also were symbols of the Buddhist uprising against the government. At one point, police tried to crack down on wearers of the yellow cloth, but there were too many of them.

Tidings of miracles spread throughout the land. In the evening sky over Saigon, thousands said they could see the weeping face of the Buddha in the clouds. Traffic was jammed everywhere as crowds of people stood gazing into the sky.

Tens of thousands of followers poured through Xa Loi Pagoda each day to worship before the heart in the glass chalice.

The series of pictures I took of the death of Thich Quang Duc came to have an existence of their own as they circulated around the world. They meant many things to many people.

An acquaintance in Lisbon wrote me that my photographs of Quang Duc's death were being sold in back alleys by hawkers of "feelthy pictures." A group of prominent American clergymen used one of the pictures as the basis for full-page advertisements in the New York *Times* and Washington *Post,* over the heading: "We, too, protest." Their protest was aimed against American support of the Diem regime.

Communist China reportedly printed millions of copies of one of the pictures for distribution throughout Asia and Africa. These pictures were captioned: "A Buddhist monk gives his life in the struggle against U.S.-Diem imperialism." Someone in Dar-es-Salaam, Tanganyika, wrote me a long letter praising my "revolutionary spirit" in taking the pictures. It was not long after that the communist movement in Tanganyika began to attract international interest.

In a conference with U.S. Ambassador Frederick E. Nolting, Jr., President Diem asked if it were true that I had bribed the monks to set up the suicide so as to get an eye-catching picture. The question, absurd though it was, may have been sincere. It was an indication of the suspicion and hostility Diem entertained for the foreign press in general. Actually, I suspect this particular idea was planted in Diem's mind by his brilliant and ever-scheming younger brother, Ngo Dinh Nhu. Nhu certainly knew better, but he hoped to discredit both the Buddhists and the foreign press.

It was characteristic of Diem in those days that he had such slight contact with the realities of his exploding nation and the war that he tended to accept as fact anything told him by his ruthless brother, the "political counsellor."

The Quang Duc pictures also had an impact in Washington. I have been told that when Henry Cabot Lodge went to see the late President Kennedy about being assigned as ambassador to Viet Nam, Kennedy had a copy of the Quang Duc photograph on his desk. Quang Duc's death probably was one of the factors that finally turned the State Department and White House against Diem, altering the course of Vietnamese history, to some extent.

Things have changed in Viet Nam since then.

At this writing, the retiring, Central Vietnamese monk named Thich Tri Quang who masterminded the 1963 campaign is a powerful national leader. What Tri Quang and his coleader,

Thich Tam Chau, say, must be taken seriously by any leader of the government.

The handful of monks who command the movement ride to the premier's palace in limousines, and are certain to be heard for as long as they like. A ripple of anger on the part of the monks is enough to cause a cabinet reshuffle or even an army command reorganization. The Buddhist youth movement, sometimes uniformed, has become a kind of paramilitary force for the faith. In some cities, Buddhist youth groups have carried out arrests on their own, beaten up rival groups, maimed and killed. So have Catholic youth groups.

In any case, the Buddhist leaders have created a political force in South Viet Nam second in strength only to the Viet Cong.

In neighboring Cambodia and farther west in Thailand, Buddhist monks have long cast their shadow on the political scene. When Prince Norodom Sihanouk, fiery young ruler of Cambodia, holds any important public ceremony, a stall is always reserved for the monks, to whom Sihanouk pays his respects before beginning. This is such an institution that it is taken for granted. Buddhism is a much more embracing faith in Cambodia than in Viet Nam. It has been estimated that something like 90 per cent of all Cambodian males shave their heads and enter monasteries for a period of time at least once during their lives. The stay in the pagoda may be only a few weeks during a summer vacation, or it may be many years.

It is not difficult to become a monk in either the Hinayana or Mahayana branches of Buddhism that dominate Viet Nam, Cambodia, Thailand, Laos, Burma and Ceylon. No special credentials are required, and novitiates are fairly short. Even a few Westerners have become Buddhist monks in these countries.

Some of these Westerners are among the most bizarre and colorful types I have ever run across outside a Greenwich Village coffee shop, by the way.

One of them, a German who had taken the Buddhist name of the Venerable Anaruda, arrived in Saigon in late 1963 from India for a look at the crisis. He stayed for several weeks at Xa Loi Pagoda, where he was treated much like the army *oberleutnant* he once had been. Despite his yellow robes, he looked more like a Prussian officer than a monk, as he ordered the little Vietnamese novices around and had them shave his head.

Anaruda disliked newspapermen in general, but one afternoon while he was having his head shaved, I got him talking. Before World War II he had joined the French Foreign Legion in North Africa, from which he eventually deserted. Making his way through a series of desert adventures reminiscent of those of Lawrence of Arabia, Anaruda was conscripted into the German Navy, in which he fought until the middle of the war. Later he went into the regular army. I'm not sure what happened then, although I suspect he was assigned to the Eastern Front and eventually deserted. In any case, he wound up in India after the war and became a Buddhist monk. He never explained what he was doing in Viet Nam, but spoke vaguely of carrying important messages to and from India. He finally left as a steerage-class passenger aboard a French ship, returning to the flow of strange, homeless men and women who drift endlessly around the Far East.

Among this legion of permanently displaced persons who roam Asia—Europeans in particular—there are many professional agents of various governments. Laos, Cambodia and Viet Nam—the three former associated states of the French Indochina colony—are havens of a particularly large share of these adventurers. Some, often hangovers from the departed but not forgotten Foreign Legion, have found employment in the more unsavory occupations open to foreigners. This particularly applies to the opium industry.

There is, for example, a Corsican named Frondizi who lives in Laos and has a fleet of two-engine Beechcraft planes known throughout the area as "Air Opium." Pilots of this "airline" say they have no difficulty penetrating the radar picket around South Viet Nam at low altitude, flying at night to within visual distance of Saigon, where they make their drops. A large proportion of their "packages" are lost, they say, but for every one reaching its addressee the profits are large enough to exceed handsomely all the losses.

Laos is one of the world's primary sources of raw opium. Opium from the poppy fields of the Laotian highlands is technically illegal in Laos. But in Vientiane, particularly in the neighborhood surrounding the French Military Advisory Assistance Command compound, the opium dens thrive quite openly. Many are cheerful, family-style establishments, brightly lighted and offering Coke machines and jukeboxes as well as the standard opium benches and pipes. For less than one dollar, a patron can smoke ten or twelve pipes at such an establishment, reeling into the street at the end of the evening as high as a kite.

But Laotian opium finds its main outlet abroad. Opium smuggled into Thailand is shipped to every nation in the world. Opium, transported by small planes, is flown in large quantities to neighboring Cambodia and South Viet Nam. It is believed that a good deal of opium finds its way into the hands of the Viet Cong, which uses it as currency or credit. With gold, opium is one of the two most stable commodities in Southeast Asia, and is therefore extremely useful for guerrillas traveling constantly across national frontiers.

In South Viet Nam, the Viet Cong sometimes prints its own paper currency or chits. This currency is in piastres (or dong) which the Viet Cong claims are freely and equally convertible with Saigon piastres. In fact, however, the Viet Cong found it necessary to give this money some kind of backing of its own. Gold smuggled into Viet Nam became the primary backing of the money. It is believed that opium is similarly used as backing for paper currency in some cases.

It is possible that the Viet Cong has produced the first paper currency in history based on "the opium standard."

None of the foregoing is intended to suggest that Buddhism, the Viet Cong and opium smuggling are directly related. I am merely trying to show the confused background against which the shadow organizations of South Viet Nam operate, each one playing a part in the war in which America is so deeply involved.

Nor is opium traffic limited to society's backwash in the masses of poor people. More than one diplomatic passport has proved a boon to the smugglers. Several years ago, some Canadian officials of the International Control Commission were convicted of carrying the black, tarry liquid from one country to another.

The Indochina area is an essentially lawless corner of the earth, never more than a step or two away from complete anarchy. Successive governments in Saigon (including those of the French colonial regime) never have controlled the Vietnamese people in a very effective way. Even at this writing, various American experts estimate that nearly one tenth of the nation's population has probably never experienced any control from Saigon.

There are no anticommunist political parties in South Viet Nam with any national backing, and indeed there is very little sense of national identity anywhere. Against this background, the newly organized Buddhist machine and the Viet Cong pretty much share the field between them, although neither one could probably be considered very important in a more politically advanced nation.

At this point, I would like to discuss the nature of relationships between Vietnamese Buddhism and the Viet Cong a little.

A Buddhist pagoda in Viet Nam is a good place to get your pocket picked. This is not to say the faith condones larceny, but the swarming, jostling crowds of poor people who pack the pagodas during festival days and in times of political crisis make an ideal setting for pickpockets, beggars, social flotsam in general, secret agents—and the Viet Cong.

In South Viet Nam, Buddhism is the faith of poor people, and the Viet Cong professes to be the party of the poor.

For those who have seen the richly ornate and graceful pagodas of Thailand, Burma and Cambodia, the pagodas of Viet Nam are a disagreeable contrast. Most of the pagodas in Saigon and elsewhere in the nation are starkly modern buildings made of concrete and faced with yellow stucco. They have almost no architectural adornments, and look a little like badly Orientalized versions of Spanish mission buildings. At present, national Buddhist headquarters is a rambling compound comprising a few acres of muddy ground, an open-sided, steel barn used for

holding services, and a long row of contiguous wooden shacks.
All these shacks are fairly well furnished as offices for the top
monks, and all are equipped with telephones, filing cabinets,
typewriters, and—most important—duplicating machines.

The mobs of students, uniformed Buddhist boy scouts and
other young people who congregate at this headquarters suggest
more the atmosphere of a campfire rally than a religious shrine.

It is a far cry from the lone monk in brown robes, sitting cross-
legged before the idol of the Lord Buddha, chanting the sacred
verses to himself and keeping hypnotic time to the cadences with
the knocking of a stick on a hollow gourd.

The old Buddhist customs are still rigorously practiced.
Heads remain shaved, and the average monk, who becomes a
novice at the age of fifteen, maintains a strictly vegetarian diet
all his life. This diet excludes even milk and eggs, but does not
exclude soybean curd. Some monks are such clever cooks they
can create remarkably close imitations of pork chops and other
meats out of bean curd and various spices. The monks remain
celibate.

The monks usually live in rathole cells that bespeak more real
poverty than religious chastity. A high proportion of them has
tuberculosis. Among those with advanced cases of tuberculosis
are some of the top leaders of the Buddhist insurrection of 1963,
which led to the ouster and death of President Ngo Dinh Diem.

A very few of the Vietnamese monks are extremely well educated by any standard. Some have studied in Japan, India and
even the United States. The Venerable Thich Quang Lien, one of
the younger monks, holds a degree from Yale University. He once
greeted another Yale alumnus, an American reporter, by saying
"boola, boola!"

A few other monks currently are studying at American uni-
versities. One monk, who lives in the Vietnamese countryside, is
entirely self educated, but speaks nearly flawless English, French
and German. He is fond of discussing the works of the existential-
ist writers with an American field official who stops by from time
to time.

But in general, the educational level of Vietnamese monks

is extremely limited. All have more or less read the basic Buddhist writings in Vietnamese, but scholarship at pagodas is undisciplined, casual and lacking in program.

In short, apart from a handful of fiery, intelligent and highly ambitious young leaders, the Buddhist monks of Viet Nam are not a distinguished-seeming lot.

Nevertheless, they have become a powerful bloc in their nation, without whose active support the government itself is in extremely dangerous circumstances. The mere threat of a hunger strike is now enough to bring on a cabinet reshuffle. More serious threats by the Buddhist hierarchy can actually topple governments.

Newspaper columnists and political writers have argued for several years as to just what proportion of the South Vietnamese people is Buddhist. The Ngo Dinh Diem family (Roman Catholics) contended that less than a tenth of the nation was Buddhist. The U.S. Information Service, which tried to survey the situation, estimated that around three quarters of the population was at least nominally Buddhist, with large doses of ancestor worship, animism, Confucianism and other things thrown in. No real census of Vietnamese religious allegiances ever has been made.

The militant Hoa Hao sect, numbering perhaps as many as a million followers, counts itself as a branch of Buddhism, although its priests often carry submachine guns. The Cao Dai sect, which also claims about one million followers, considers Buddhism a kindred faith. It has been said that most Vietnamese need the services of a Buddhist monk at least three times—at birth, marriage and death.

But if many Vietnamese take Buddhism as a faith or a way of life fairly casually, they still regard the Buddhist monk as an extremely prestigious individual, no matter what his intellectual shortcomings. When John Richardson arrived in Saigon in 1961 to take charge of the CIA mission in Viet Nam, he got a strong taste of this.

Richardson elected to live in an extremely comfortable and attractive villa on a shady street. The villa has been occupied since Richardson's departure successively by Ambassador Henry

Cabot Lodge and Ambassador Maxwell D. Taylor. The CIA chief may not have known before he moved in that the site on which the villa stood had a dark and bloody past.

The site had once been occupied by a building of the dreaded French colonial *Deuxième Bureau*—the intelligence service. According to the stories, hundreds, or perhaps thousands, of Vietnamese political prisoners died of torture while being interrogated by French guards there.

During the Japanese occupation of World War II, the site was put to the same uses by the Imperial Army's intelligence organization.

After the war, during the brief period before the return of the French when communist leader Ho Chi Minh was president of all Viet Nam, Ho's Viet Minh intelligence service used the same building for political torture. Then the French took it over again. After Viet Nam gained independence in 1954, the torture camp was finally dismantled for good, and pleasant houses were built along the street.

But in the Vietnamese mind, many ghosts still stalk the site— the ghosts of men and women who died in agony, and who therefore are likely to cause all kinds of trouble. Richardson found when he moved in that he could not get servants to work for him.

In desperation, Richardson hired a team of Buddhist monks (presumably at CIA expense) to handle the highly specialized job of banishing ghosts. The team worked for about one week, chanting prayers, burning bits of sacred paper and incense, and hanging a set of octagonal, ghost-repellent mirrors around the house. Servants were satisfied that the procedure was effective (although the precautionary burning of incense is necessary at the house to this day), and Richardson no longer had to wash his own dishes.

The important thing about this story is that while Buddhism as a doctrine has very little to say about ghosts and concerns itself mostly with the freedom from worldly passions, Buddhism in Viet Nam is regarded as a bridge to the spirit world. And the spirit world is all important. Dreams, signs and portents, fortune-telling, astrology and the phases of the moon, necromancy, and all the other trappings of spiritualism are close to the hearts of practically all Vietnamese.

Among the primitive tribes people of the central Vietnamese mountains, it is considered an offense to a river spirit to so much as throw a stone into the waters of his domain. To placate the spirit after such a misdeed generally requires the ceremonial sacrifice of a water buffalo, which in turn is a pretext for the ceremonial drinking of rice wine and a fine party.

But even for sophisticated, Western-educated Saigonese, the spirits hold sway. I know a young woman who, after her graduation from a leading American college, was given a new car by her wealthy family. The girl was eager to buy her sportster and take it on a spin to the beach resort of Cap St. Jacques about forty miles from Saigon. But the moon phase and spirit portents were just not right for it. So even the boisterous spirit of youth and a bachelor of arts degree were suppressed, and the purchase of the car was postponed.

Most Saigon newspapers are forced to maintain their circulation figures by running at least one serialized ghost story in each edition.

I doubt that there is a single family hut in rural Viet Nam that does not have its little family altar with a glass jar of burning incense sticks. On the altar there generally are a few mystical characters in Chinese, and one or more yellowed photographs of departed relatives—paper symbols of ghosts.

All this is obviously a highly fertile background for all kinds of charlatanism.

It also accounts for the enormous influence of the Buddhist monk.

As a faith, Buddhism is not much concerned with material matters. It teaches that man is chained to a wheel of life, death and rebirth, which can be broken only by his attainment to the coveted "state of enlightenment."

It is not my purpose here to discuss the theology of Buddhism, but the one point I would like to make refers to the theoretical compatibility (or lack of it) of Buddhism with communism.

A book on the subject called *Buddhism Answers the Marxist Challenge* by Francis Story (published by Burma Buddhist World Mission, Rangoon) has been widely read by Vietnamese Buddhist monks. It contends that Buddhism and Marxism are not compatible. Story writes:

> Marxist materialism is scientific in so far as it follows the principles of causality, but it does not admit any causal process beyond that of matter and material agencies.
> It condemns religion because religion teaches that there is a process of causality based on moral principles. Every religion maintains that there is another life beyond the present one, and that this future life is in some way governed by the moral effects of what has been done, said and thought in this present life. This claim is nowhere made so strongly or logically as in Buddhism, with its rational teaching of Karma and rebirth, the two principles which are categorically denied by Marxism.

Vietnamese Buddhist monks in the past few years have often cited writings like that as evidence to refute American political writers who claimed they were communists.

The monks who advance such theoretical evidence are no doubt sincere in their conviction that communism and Buddhism are incompatible. Many of the Buddhist monks leading the South Vietnamese movement are refugees from communist North Viet Nam, and know by personal experience of the atrophied state of their faith under the Hanoi regime. A few even have tried to organize teams of monks to travel in the countryside, denouncing communism as they preach.

But unfortunately for American policy in Viet Nam, the Viet Cong does not regard itself as at all incompatible with Buddhism. The fifty-seven member central committee of the National Front for the Liberation of South Viet Nam (Viet Cong) claims actual membership of several Buddhist monks and one Roman Catholic priest.

Buddhist monks have sometimes run into trouble with the Viet Cong, but as a rule, the orange- or brown-clad monks pedal their bicycles over the rice paddy dykes of Viet Cong base areas without the slightest interference. The inference drawn from this by a number of American writers is that the monks are phonies, or at best, religious dilettantes.

But I think this view is based on a general American misunderstanding as to what the Viet Cong really is.

The words "Viet Cong" in themselves are somewhat misleading. They mean "Vietnamese communist," and they were coined by Saigon's propaganda ministry as a kind of catch phrase, used in much the same sense as Hanoi's invariable reference to the Saigon government as the "U.S. Imperialist Lackeys."

Probably only top Viet Cong officials know how many of the National Liberation Front's members are Communist Party members. But Western intelligence experts believe the proportion of communists is probably extremely small—limited probably to the handful of foreign-educated intellectuals who pull the wires. In other words, the Viet Cong is a true "front" organization, appealing for the support of every social class, and every educational, religious and occupational background. The National Liberation Front is supposedly made up of many dependent fronts, such as the Farmers' Liberation Front, the Women's Liberation Front, the Writers' and Artists' Liberation Front, and so on.

Supreme leadership of the Front is openly described by Front leaders as "a Marxist-Leninist party," but this party does not appear in organizational tables used by the Front, nor is it often even mentioned.

In any case, there is certainly no requirement to be a communist to join the National Liberation Front. The fact is that even fairly high-ranking Viet Cong prisoners often show a surprising ignorance of the world communist movement. The ideological battle between Moscow and Peking is usually a matter of complete indifference to them, for example. They consider themselves first and foremost Vietnamese nationalists and patriots, "soldiers for the invincible cause of freedom against the American imperialists and their lackeys."

It is obvious to Western observers that the National Liberation Front is the creature of the Vietnamese Communist Party, and has strong but subtle ties to the Hanoi regime and even to communist China. But these relationships are not so apparent to Vietnamese eyes. For many, the Front is exactly what it purports to be—the people's struggle for independence.

Viewed in this light, the theoretical clash between Marxist-Leninist communism and religious dogma tends to blur or even disappear.

If it is possible for Buddhist monks to sit on the ruling central committee of the Viet Cong, there is no apparent reason why a member of the National Liberation Front could not become a Buddhist monk, or at least a Buddhist layman. The man himself might not even notice any contradiction in his allegiances.

A number of leading Roman Catholic laymen in Viet Nam have told me they believe even their faith has a number of adherents who belong to the Viet Cong. In 1948, a devout Roman Catholic was chief of Viet Minh intelligence. He later commanded a guerrilla regiment.

Without question, the Viet Cong is the most powerful political organization in South Viet Nam, and has by far the largest following of any nonreligious group in the nation. A major reason is the "underdevelopment" of the nation.

To most Americans, I think, the word "underdevelopment" evokes the picture of a child with a belly bloated by starvation. By inference, a CARE package of powdered milk is taken as the primary weapon against underdevelopment.

Elsewhere in Asia, this image has some substance. But in Viet Nam, underdevelopment cannot be cured by bread alone. The fact is that South Viet Nam is one of the most agriculturally rich nations in Asia.

Even in bad years, the rich, green Mekong River Delta produces plenty of rice to feed the whole people, with a large exportable surplus to enrich the treasury. Fish are so plentiful in the sluggish canals and ditches of the delta they can actually be caught by hand. The pineapples, mangoes and other delicious fruits that proliferate in the area are among the finest in the world. Sugar cane and coconuts grow swiftly with little labor requirement, and ducks can be raised in huge flocks right in the rice fields. Feathers from the Vietnamese duck crop are prized as pillow stuffing, and are an important export item.

Very few people in South Viet Nam go hungry. This, of course, includes the Viet Cong guerrillas ranging over the delta. The abundance of food and the warmth of Vietnamese peasant hospitality to all poor people give the guerrillas an almost free nationwide logistic network that would cost a Western army hundreds of millions of dollars to duplicate.

The nation is rich in all kinds of salable commodities. A rich, red soil that covers most of the central highlands is ideal for tea, rubber and kenaf plantations, which have been exploited by the French for the past century. Rubies and even gold are sometimes found in or near this soil. A completed Japanese-built hydroelectric plant harnessing one of the highland rivers is expected soon to provide enough power for all Saigon, in addition to planned industrial plants around the country. Viet Nam's coast has many fine harbors. Cam Ranh harbor, according to the experts, could be made into one of the world's greatest ports. Even inland Saigon serves a heavy annual tonnage of ocean cargo, because of its deep river leading to the sea.

In peacetime, South Viet Nam could certainly attract an important share of the world's affluent tourists. Its cool mountain resorts, partly developed by the French colonialists, are near fine big game hunting in the great rain forests. Elephants, tigers and water buffalo are the prime quarries. The coastal beaches are snowy white, clean and fairly free of dangerous fish. The gigantic lobsters of Nha Trang and Cap St. Jacques are certainly worthy rivals of those from Maine.

The Vietnamese farmer is lucky to earn $20.00 a year in hard currency, but this does not mean he is impoverished. His clothing, cheap, baggy, black calico blouses and trousers, is adequate for the tropical climate. Excellent supplies for housebuilding are no farther away than the nearest grove of bamboo and palm trees.

He may even have some savings—generally in gold or opium. Even the French recognize that opium was more highly valued by Vietnamese than their paper currency, and retiring civil servants often were pensioned off in opium.

Underdevelopment in Viet Nam, therefore, means something other than mere material hardship. It is partly the lack of technology. But much more important, it is a national state of mind.

The lack of technology means that communications in many areas are almost nonexistent. Few persons in Saigon have telephones, and outside the capital, telephones are almost unknown.

Travel in South Viet Nam is an arduous and sometimes dangerous business. The one railroad line, which serves only the coastal towns, is ambushed or sabotaged once a day on the average by the Viet Cong, with frequently fatal results. There are only four or five first-class highways in the country, and most of the nation is served by rutted paths amounting to little more than trails. Many of these are permanently obstructed by the Viet Cong and even main roads are the target of incessant ambushes. Canals are also blocked or ambushed. The only sure way of getting from one point to another is by air, and this is too expensive for most poor people.

The result is that peasants of one district in Viet Nam may not have the remotest idea what is going on in another district only a few miles away. A large proportion of Vietnamese have never visited the capital of Saigon, and know it only as the place where the king or his equivalent reigns. Every once in a while, raiding parties of troops come from Saigon to collect taxes, round up young men for the military draft, and look around for illegal weapons. That is about the total of contact with Saigon.

This state of affairs is obviously an excellent background for a semiclandestine guerrilla army. For one thing, a peasant is generally not much inclined to resist the ubiquitous guerrillas, even if he dislikes them, when he knows that there is no way of calling for help.

But the real nature of underdevelopment in Viet Nam has to do with education and a man's view of the world around him.

Most Vietnamese have a primary school education, and the great majority are literate, at least to the extent that they can read propaganda slogans.

Of the small Vietnamese professional class left by the French colonialists, large numbers remained French citizens and went back to France after Viet Nam became independent in 1954. Most of the remainder live in Saigon where they make money and dabble in politics. Provinces of nearly a quarter-million people often are served by only one or two doctors, who generally grow rich because of their huge practices, and become major land-owners. Some provinces have no doctors at all.

Rural administrators generally are men with little more than a few weeks' training and salaries of only about $40.00 a month. It is said that when a man puts on a white collar in Viet Nam, he has the right to step all over his neighbors and take whatever he can get. Careers in the civil service too often are merely plat-forms for a lifetime of extortion.

This is a purely subjective judgment and perhaps open to challenge. But it seems to me that of the thousands of Vietnamese officials I have known, I can think of none who does not more or less hold the Vietnamese people in contempt. Many of these offi-cials are loudly patriotic most of the time, and mouth the stock phrases about "the courageous and all-enduring Vietnamese peo-ple." But when they are occasionally induced to speak frankly, they speak of their nation not with pride but with contemptuous apology. Certainly, their attitudes in most cases bespeak con-tempt.

This feeling of suspicion and hostility is fully reciprocated by the poor people of the nation in their relations with their rulers. I think it is safe to say that the average Vietnamese views the only good official as a dead one.

When Viet Cong terrorists publicly behead some hamlet or province official and then disembowel the wife and children as well, Americans tend to assume that this will result in a power-ful reaction by the people against the Viet Cong. Nothing could be farther from the truth in most cases. The Viet Cong often liquidates a government official precisely because it knows such an act will please the local people.

In passing, it is well to note that peasants often seem pleased when unpopular local Viet Cong commissars are rubbed out by government terrorists, too.

But if the Vietnamese people by and large are apolitical anarchists in tendency, most need some kind of higher authority toward which they can turn with a degree of trust. The humble, uneducated Buddhist monk meets this requirement. His organization demands almost nothing of the people, except enough rice and bananas to live. In exchange for the modest gifts of food solicited by the monks, the people receive powerful protection against the mysterious dangers of the spirit world, and are guided toward an afterlife that will be happier than this one.

Some, of course, turn to Catholicism. But, and again this is a purely subjective judgment, I think the discipline and restrictions of Catholicism are more than most of the Vietnamese people like to have imposed on them.

Buddhism is many centuries old in Viet Nam, and fits the country like an old shoe. This, to my thinking, is the reason that when Buddhism entered the Vietnamese political arena in 1963, its power shot up like bamboo. The potential was always there. It took the mistakes of the Diem government to bring it to realization.

Somewhat the same considerations apply, I believe, to the growth of the Viet Cong. Viet Cong forces are highly disciplined fighting units. But members are led to believe that the discipline is only a temporary evil. Once the imperialist bureaucrats are thrown out, there will be no more military conscription, no more taxes, no more interference by officials, just a happy life of private peace. If this image is exactly the opposite of reality in communist-governed nations, the South Vietnamese farmer can hardly be expected to see the contradiction. He knows next to nothing about the outer world in general, much less its politics. So far, the Viet Cong has never raised the idea of collective farms, for example. It is difficult to imagine a Vietnamese farmer being forced to live on a collective farm without rebelling. The so-called Strategic Hamlets invented by the Diem regime, which had certain similarities to collective farms, were a notable failure and a cardinal propaganda benefit to the Viet Cong.

Generalities are dangerous, but to my mind the Vietnamese farmers who make up 85 per cent of the nation's population are people who loathe controls but who will exercise them ruthlessly on others if given the chance; they are men with little or no sense of identity with Viet Nam as a united nation, but they mistrust and dislike all outsiders; they are willing to unite and fight effectively, only in the belief that they are overthrowing the controls they despise. When they are rich or educated, they generally prefer to live outside Viet Nam rather than in it.

Viet Cong propaganda takes all these characteristics into consideration and has proved highly successful.

The student who failed his examination would be delighted at the chance to burn up all the test papers, but cannot do it on his own. On the other hand, if he is a member of the National Liberation Front or one of the Buddhist youth groups that occasionally launch mass riots, he has a team behind him. The test papers get burned, and instructors are in grave personal danger if they protest.

One of the political rampages staged in the coastal city of Qui Nhon in late 1964 had its roots in exactly this cause. The student leaders of the riots all had flunked their examinations and were demanding a second chance at easier examinations. It was suggested by some of the teachers that the students might have passed if they had spent less time demonstrating in the first place and more in studying.

In summary, underdevelopment in South Viet Nam means social and political sickness. Many diplomats, politicians and other more or less qualified observers—both Vietnamese and foreign—have expressed grave doubts that South Viet Nam should even be considered a nation at all.

This view is of course academic, because South Viet Nam is a nation, for better or worse. So are the scores of newly independent African and Asian nations that now dot the map.

Western colonialism is dead, and it has left a legacy of sickness.

The battle in South Viet Nam is this: the Western world is trying to cure the sickness, and the communist world is trying to revive the corpse in a new form.

The Western world faces staggering odds. Somehow the patient must be kept from dying for another twenty years or so, long enough for the sons and daughters of a new generation to grow up as new Vietnamese, with new ideas and new ideals.

The Communists need only go on expanding their fronts and continue the infiltration of the social bases of Viet Nam, including religion. By playing on existing hatreds and fears, the National Liberation Front can go on recruiting almost indefinitely. The best human pools from which to recruit are the few loosely organized but enormously popular mass organizations already existing in South Viet Nam, of which Buddhism is now one. Somehow the Viet Cong always manages to get its finger in pies like this, and does better than the anticommunists.

Their formula is a tough one to beat.

Chapter 11

Cream and Dregs

A longshot horse finishes first, and an angry mob storms the betting window, charging that the race was rigged. The track obligingly refunds all bets, but pays off the winners.

A downtown theater sells out tickets for a live performance by a visiting singer from Paris, and five persons are hospitalized when a mob jams them against the entrance gate, trying to get seats. Elsewhere in the city, banners go up reading "Down With France."

A dentist lays down his drill and hastily tells his patient, "Pardon, madame, but a demonstration is beginning, and as leader of my party, I must be there." The astonished patient is left to spit out the filings and clean herself up.

A petty bureaucrat who earns $70.00 a month in salary steps into his Mercedes limousine and drives home to his villa.

Another government employee stalks into the office of his boss, demands a raise, gets turned down, douses himself with gasoline, and sets fire to himself.

And the marriage of a bicycle-taxi driver with a woman he picked up for work every morning makes front page news in the local papers.

This is Saigon, a city like thousands of others in Asia, Africa and Latin America, where there are only two classes—the haves and have-nots.

From the air, Saigon looks like a sprawling village, with very few tall buildings, and main streets mostly covered by arching treetops. It is hard to believe that a million and a half people live here. If you are rich (earning more than $200 a month), Saigon is a beautiful city.

Stately villas line the broad streets in the "nice" part of town, and each of these villas is shaded with tall tamarind trees. There are dozens of fine French and Chinese restaurants, and, if you're daring and don't mind the smell of fermented fish sauce, you might try one of the better Vietnamese restaurants.

Catinat Street (renamed Tu Do, meaning "freedom") and the streets near it are filled with expensive shops where you can buy fine tortoise-shell items, bronzeware and Vietnamese ceramics.

Hotels are air conditioned and comfortable. The Caravelle is the largest and swankiest of these, although getting rooms or suites there is a little difficult since the fifth floor was blown out by a bomb.

If you live in Viet Nam as a permanent resident, you will find it agreeable to spend the hottest months of April and May in Dalat, a cool mountain resort an hour away by air, where you will find all the comforts of Saigon. Your children will be having their vacation at this time, so you can take them along.

There are many profitable businesses in which you may engage, provided you have the capital to start. You can do contract work of every imaginable kind for the many American official agencies operating in the cities. You could open a bar or night club. You could start a loan agency, where you may collect 10 or 20 per cent interest a month. You might go into real estate, although investments in the countryside are a bit risky just now. Or you could open a factory for which labor costs are remarkably low.

Best of all, since you have money, you will not have to worry about all the nasty government red tape involved in getting exit visas, in case you should feel obliged to leave the country hastily.

You may know the Interior Minister socially, and he will be able to get you fixed up. Most important, you can have a plane ticket to Paris any time you want to buy one, should the roof cave in.

If you are poor, of course, you may do none of these things.

If you work in one of the white collar offices in town, you probably earn between $20.00 and $40.00 a month, and this won't go very far. Food in Saigon is cheap, but almost everything else is expensive. Your children will have to be satisfied with a trip to the zoo (admission: two cents) or a Sunday picnic at the side of the four-lane, American-built Bien Hoa highway just outside town. You can get there by bicycle.

But if you are a Saigonese, you probably are among the masses who earn even less than $20.00 a month, and you live in one of the vast slums that the visitors never see. You have no tall trees, no sporting club, and little more than your day's share of rice and fish and the thatched cubicle in which your family lives. Your cubicle is likely to be searched at night by police looking for Viet Cong, and your identification papers will be checked several times a day by someone in authority. If a fire happens to start anywhere in your neighborhood, your own dwelling will probably burn to the ground, because there are very few fire-breaks in the slums, and the houses burn like the kindling wood they are.

Your children will go to primary school, but they won't get beyond that unless you have some money. Advanced education is expensive. Your family may never see one of the Paris-trained doctors who treat the rich and become politicians. You will have to settle for midwives and traditional medical practitioners.

If you have Parkinson's disease, you will tilt back your head while the practitioner introduces the head of a live gecko (the large, insect-eating lizard) into your mouth. The savant will then snip off the lizard's tail, which will cause it to wriggle its way down into your stomach, curing your disease.

You can generally afford a ten-cent ticket in the weekly drawing of the national lottery, which could make you fabulously rich. You probably will buy one, even though you know that a former director of the lottery under the Diem regime once decamped with a half million dollars from the fund. For diversion, you can place bets on cricket fights. You can find the fighting crickets swarming in the streets during the hot season.

You can afford to drink. Local booze is awful but cheap. If you are a man under thirty-five, the government will try fairly hard to draft you. You can probably dodge this, but if they catch up with you, you can always desert later, and you probably won't have further trouble.

If you have a flair for language, you could learn enough English to become a pimp.

If you are really hard up, you can probably join a *hui*, which is a kind of private credit union. You and as many friends as possible get together, each contributing a certain sum to the *hui* fund, and then making loans from the central fund to the needy members of the group. Those who don't borrow anything draw interest from the others. It's a kind of shared risk investment, from which borrowers pay much lower interest rates than to banks or the professional loan sharks.

Chances are you are irritated almost constantly by the rich. Just pedaling your bicycle along you are apt to be forced off to the side of the street twenty times a day by honking cars. You probably dislike the drivers of these cars as much as they dislike you for loafing along in the middle of the street.

You can always get even with them by saving up enough money to become a taxi driver. As a taxi driver, your vehicle will be a banged-up little blue and white Renault *quatre chevaux*, in which you will find the shiny big cars give you a wide berth. They know that a collision with you will cost them a lot more than it does you.

If all this gets you down and you have a revolutionary bent, you can always join the Viet Cong. A recruiting agent is never far away.

Actually, the ruling class of Saigon—and, for that matter, of South Viet Nam—is pretty small. If you live in Saigon for a few years and are privy to the social elite, you probably know just about everyone who is anyone or is likely to become anyone in the event of a coup. People change jobs, of course, and sometimes people are out of jobs altogether. Recently, a number of familiar faces went to the penal colony on the island of Poulo Condore sixty miles offshore. A year ago, these people were sending other people to Poulo Condore, but some of the people they sent are now top officials again.

There are various ways to become one of the elite, but they all involve being born with a certain amount of money. To reach the top, you must have an education—preferably a foreign education, since you must speak French or English or both—and education is expensive.

Incidentally, this situation is just as true in Hanoi, the capital of communist North Viet Nam, as it is in Saigon. The three most powerful men of the north, President Ho Chi Minh, Premier Pham Van Dong and Armed Forces Minister Vo Nguyen Giap all must be classed as foreign-educated intellectuals. None of them was born into the really poor class, and each of them is as much at home discussing European art and literature in fluent French or English as he is talking Leninist dogma.

As a generality, if as a Vietnamese you have a really solid education, you are likely to rise to the top, regardless of which side you are on. It doesn't really matter what field of learning you choose, although doctors very often make out better than others. Very few Vietnamese doctors end up practicing their professions. They can do much better going into politics, or so they believe.

One case in point is Dr. Tran Van Tho, a southerner whose family scraped up enough money to send him to France to take a medical degree. He arrived in Toulouse without a sou in his pocket, but borrowed a fairly large sum from another student— a rich Cambodian—to get started. Tho made the academic grade and eventually returned to Viet Nam after 1954. He set up a private clinic in Saigon, and joined Diem's political party.

Tho let the nails on his pinky fingers grow long in the style of old-fashioned Vietnamese aristocrats, and rose through the political ranks. Eventually, he became Diem's information minister. Tho was delighted with the empire he had built. He had a fine villa, he had two secret police bodyguards to follow him wherever he went, he headed a large and important organization, and he held a post in which he could give his anti-American feelings full vent.

He worked hard for the expulsion of various American reporters. At one point, he demanded and got the expulsion of the director of the U.S. Information Service, a man he cordially hated. That was in 1962, at a time when the U.S. Embassy was doing its best to humor the requests of Vietnamese officials, no matter how shortsighted these requests were.

Tho's family life was less than perfect. The French wife he had acquired as part of his meteoric social rise deserted him, and took the children back to France. But there were lots of girls in Tho's ministry to pick from, and he could (and did) make life extremely unpleasant for them if they resisted his advances. None of them could escape by quitting their jobs, because in those days you couldn't just quit without permission of the minister. If you really wanted out, about the only thing you could do was get transferred to one of the remote, dangerous and unpleasant provinces. Such transfers generally were (and are) used as punishment within the Vietnamese civil service, and this is one of the reasons rural civil servants have so little enthusiasm for their jobs, by and large.

Tho turned out enormous quantities of propaganda highly flattering to Diem, and, more important, to Diem's all-powerful brother, Ngo Dinh Nhu.

At one point, Diem became exasperated with the politician-doctors infesting his capital, especially those who were his political opponents. He rounded up some of them and sent them to the penal island of Poulo Condore. But he also passed a doctors' conscription bill, aimed at forcing doctors into government service to practice in the provinces, most of which had no doctors at all.

Naturally, Tran Van Tho was exempt from this draft, and took delight in helping to draw up the list of doctors to be drafted. The list included all his rivals.

But Tho made so much bad blood with so many people, that in the end he became too much even for Diem. He was fired as information czar. Of course, Tho was still left his seat in the National Assembly, which entitled him to a chauffeur-driven limousine, a nice house, and other amenities. But for financial reasons, he was forced to return to his practice at least part time, so he cranked up his clinic again. That is the story of one Vietnamese doctor.

Incidentally, after the coup of November 1, 1963, in which Diem was overthrown and slain, Tho was arrested by the revolutionary government. Nearly a year later, the government shipped him off to Poulo Condore island with a lot of other former high officials, to do penance for his sins. It must be especially galling to him to have to go to the same place he sent many others. But I have no doubt Tho will someday return to public life. It gets in your blood.

Another doctor named Pham Huy Co was one of the outs during the Diem regime. Co never visited Viet Nam during the first nine years of Vietnamese independence, but maintained a practice in Paris. His practice was lucrative enough to support his political party and a flourishing anti-Diem propaganda apparatus he kept in operation. Co designed a new national flag (a red field with a yellow cross), announced himself as a staunch anticommunist friend of the United States, and, through agents, began a grenade-throwing campaign in Saigon. In 1963 quite a few of Co's grenades went off around town, one of which nearly blew the pants off a messenger of mine, who happened to be near when it went off.

Each grenade was wrapped in paper and contained thousands of little anti-Diem, pro-Co leaflets. The low-power bombs were not supposed to be dangerous, but were merely intended to make a loud noise and scatter the leaflets. Actually, a number of people were hurt by the little bombs, which turned out to be more powerful than expected.

Co gave press conferences in Phnom Penh and Tokyo, and attracted quite a bit of official American interest for a while. He seemed to be for all the things America was for. Shortly after the death of Diem, he returned to his homeland, presuming that a place in the sun would have been reserved for him. It turned out otherwise. Even his old fellow military plotters against Diem, all of whom now had good jobs, ignored him. Successive military governments also ignored him, and he couldn't even land a seat on one of the powerless civilian advisory councils. This was a bitter disappointment, and Co began organizing political meetings and press conferences. Co probably has fewer than 300 followers, all of whom have allegiances to other organizations as well. But he has defiantly branded the Nguyen Khanh government as a military dictatorship (which, in a way, it was), demanding immediate free national elections for a new government. To back up his demands, he issues several toughly worded news releases each week, which he takes around in person to foreign news agencies.

He is one of scores of Saigon politicians doing exactly the same thing. He is not willing to join forces with any of them, because he knows he would probably be outmaneuvered politically, and would again find himself on the outs. It is better to go on giving dinners for powerful people and talking up a campaign in the coffee shops. At least this way, he can remain an independent.

In a general way, this is the pattern with all Vietnamese politicians, and I mean that term specifically to include Vietnamese military officers.

Vietnamese military officers have always held roles completely foreign to the patterns of Western armies. Among other things, they command troops and run fighting campaigns. But they also administer about 85 per cent of all the people in South Viet Nam. When Diem came to power in 1954, he felt it would be a mistake to make too many changes in the French provincial administration system immediately. As it turned out, the system never was changed, and still functions essentially in the French colonial pattern, except that Vietnamese instead of French hold the top jobs.

Under the colonial system, the nation was ruled by a colonial governor through a number of ministries, most important of which was (and is) the Interior Ministry. This ministry appointed a province chief for each of the country's major subdivisions. Each province chief had his own staff, and in turn appointed district chiefs at the next lower level. District chiefs and their staffs named canton chiefs, who named village chiefs, who named hamlet chiefs.

Under the French, most of the province chiefs were army officers. This, presumably, was because the main worry of each rural administrator was the war being waged in his own sector by the communist insurgents. It was reasoned that military men were better qualified than civilians to do this work.

Diem continued the pattern. Out of some forty provinces, only two had civilian chiefs, and the rest were regular army officers—majors, lieutenant colonels and colonels. Nearly all of these officials were natives of provinces other than the ones they commanded and a majority were North or Central Vietnamese.

This geographical situation reflected the composition of the army itself, which is recruited primarily in central Viet Nam and the coastal cities. One rarely finds Vietnamese officers native to the Mekong River Delta where half the population of South Viet Nam lives, and where the war rages hottest.

Currently, every one of South Viet Nam's forty-five provinces is commanded by a military officer, as is every one of the nearly 300 districts in the country. Communities that rank as cities all have army officers as mayors (with the exception of Saigon, where a civilian was recently named). Each of these administrative officers is, of course, subject to military discipline, and is part of the Defense Ministry. He is usually outranked by regimental, division and corps commanders who wander in and out of his sector with troops from time to time.

Nevertheless, the rural administrative officer is the supreme government authority in his region, with sweeping powers of good or evil. He is so remote from Saigon he must generally work his problems out for himself, and he has basically exactly the same job that provincial mandarins of the Vietnamese civil service held for many centuries. The average Vietnamese citizen has a great deal of contact (mostly unpleasant) with his local district chief, but generally none at all with Saigon.

An ordinary army captain does not have an enviable job in South Viet Nam. If he has a job as commander of an operational company, there will be all sorts of unpleasant field duties, not to mention the danger of getting shot in combat with the Viet Cong. But if this captain happens to land a job as district chief, he becomes a little emperor. As the chief tax collector, conscription officer, judge, county prosecutor, police chief, contract officer and everything else all rolled into one, he literally has the power of life and death over his subjects. If someone chooses to give him a hard time, that person is apt to be arrested as a Viet Cong agent, and no one is likely to be the wiser. That person may rot for months or years in some provincial jail without trial or further investigation, or he may be shot on the spot. Similar pressures can be brought to bear on entire families, even on entire hamlets.

If you were a Vietnamese army captain earning $40.00 a month, wouldn't you like to be a district chief?

In general, the requirements for the job are not too exacting. The main thing is dedicated loyalty to the officers farther up the line who make the appointments. Military competence is apparently not a prerequisite. Discretion and political *savoir-faire* are.

It has been argued that in Viet Nam, the military officer has had the best general training for administrative office. U.S. Ambassador Maxwell D. Taylor said recently, "We can't afford the luxury of discriminating against a man because of the color of his coat. You have to use administrative talent where you find it."

This is no doubt true.

But it also has been argued by various political writers that the Vietnamese rural administration service is one of the cleanest in Asia. If such is the case, Asia deserves the undying pity of the rest of the world. Vietnamese army officers serving as administrators are no worse and no better than you would expect them to be. A few are outstandingly good, and their provinces or districts always are used as showcases when visitors (especially foreigners) come around. A few are so bad that popular demonstrations erupt when the Viet Cong assassinates them.

Most manage to stay inconspicuous by keeping their extortion within limits, their love-making to the local girls reasonably discreet, and their vengeance arrests confined to a handful of enemies. It is most important to keep your nose clean with the Americans these days, but this is not too difficult, because they have so few qualified field men that they can't keep tabs on everything all the time. The main thing is to avoid alienating the official just above you.

There are lots of little things you can do to make a living. If one of your men gets killed fighting the Viet Cong, the government is now obliged to pay his family a year's salary, say, about $400. This payment comes down from Saigon and goes through you. You can charge certain "fees" without too much danger of being caught. You can charge something for providing a coffin (made free by a squad of your troops), something for "funeral expenses," something for your own expense account involved in seeing to all these matters. So you split the $400 with the family, and that's that.

You probably are on friendly terms with a lot of American advisors, all of whom are anxious to stay on good terms with you (since their rating officers will have a close look at these relations before considering any of them for promotion). These friendly people generally will buy you all kinds of supplies at cost at their PX—transistor radios, ladies' hair spray, and so on. You can sell these things at 1,000 per cent profit locally, and it all adds up.

You may have been able to collect a nice haul of taxes from some hamlet one month, but there's no automatic need to turn this tax money in to your bosses, if you're discreet. You can keep it, and claim that you couldn't get your tax-collection team into the hamlet because the Viet Cong was too strong there.

To make sure the hamlet makes no trouble about all this, you can always feed headquarters an "intelligence report" that a Viet Cong regiment has camped in the hamlet, along with the recommendation that the whole thing ought to be blown off the map immediately. Generally, this will be done, and the Skyraiders will be over in a day or two to bomb the town to rubble.

I have lived in Viet Nam continuously for three years, and I have spent a great deal of time in all its provinces, returning time and time again to many districts, villages and hamlets. I have many Vietnamese friends who live in these places. If there are still those who doubt that Vietnamese national administration has ever been anything other than as I have just described it, I would invite him to accompany me on a two-week tour of the countryside to places not included in any of the official itineraries. I know that my views are entirely shared by most of South Viet Nam's top leaders, who contend, however, that they must have time to clean up the mess left by the French administration.

I do not mean to imply that all Vietnamese military provincial officers are corrupt and self-serving. Some military officials, especially those who served in the Viet Minh in the war against the French and later switched to Diem, are excellent officials by any standards. But they are exceptions. Unfortunately, most of the really intelligent, dedicated and patriotic men and women who form the stuff of sound leadership stayed with the Viet Minh.

Efforts have been made, of course, to develop an effective civilian administrative system in South Viet Nam.

In 1955, Michigan State University signed a contract with the Diem government to set up schools for a new generation of administrators. The U.S. Aid mission was working along similar lines.

Hundreds of American experts in accounting, taxes, urban renewal, public works, land development, agriculture and all the rest came to Viet Nam. A National Institute of Administration with American teachers was set up in Saigon, and began churning out budding *fonctionnaires* by the thousand. A lot of combined talent was brought to bear on this project, and there were high hopes.

But from the beginning, Diem was much more interested in the police and security programs than most of the other things. The various Vietnamese police organizations (including the dreaded "Bureau for Political Research at the Presidency") bloomed, and all of them were equipped with the most advanced American gadgets, including phone tapping equipment and other sophistications. As the Diem regime became increasingly rough on its political adversaries, one American police advisor remarked:

"I'm afraid we have unwittingly created a Frankenstein's monster here, a made-in-America police state."

Diem also liked American ideas about land development and he had visions of turning the virgin jungles of Central Viet Nam into fields of golden grain. Unfortunately, most of the land in the populous Mekong River Delta already had long been reformed by the Viet Cong, which was prepared to fight to keep it from being re-reformed. And somehow, the jungles never have turned into wheat fields.

But if Diem liked some of the new American techniques, he distinctly disliked many others. For one thing, the Ngo family was essentially a French-Vietnamese family, and in its eyes the old administrative system was not nearly so bad as the Americans were making out. Diem and his indispensable brother, Nhu, both found it easier to speak and write in French than in Vietnamese. The night they decided on the measure that was to bring about their deaths two months later, they summoned the cabinet to the palace. The two brothers, looking haggard and tired, had decided to crush the Buddhist rebellion by smashing the pagodas, arresting the monks and nuns, and clamping martial law over the nation. They scribbled the terms of their decision in long-hand—in French—and passed the paper around the table to the assembled ministers. This, according to Vice President Nguyen Ngoc Tho, who was there.

The thing Diem least liked about the Americans was their persistence about belittling existing systems and their constant introduction of revolutionary ideas, along with their open personal friendships with some of his foes.

Some of the Americans working for Michigan State University, the U.S. Aid mission and various other American education missions were pretty outspoken in their criticism of Diem. In a learned article, one of them described South Viet Nam as "a permanent mendicant," and Diem was incensed. U.S.-Vietnamese relations went from bad to worse, and one after another, the American civilian advisors were thrown out. The Michigan State mission was closed down in 1962, leaving the National Institute for Administration in Vietnamese hands. One American, Dr. Stanley Millet, was detained and questioned by police before being permitted to leave the country.

Millet had been teaching political science at Saigon University under a grant to Viet Nam under the U.S. Smith-Mundt Education Act. Millet spoke Vietnamese pretty well, was on close social terms with most of his students, and therefore was close to most of the Saigon intelligentsia, including leading political opponents of Diem.

Millet saw one after another of his friends disappear, and began to conceive a deep dislike for the Diem government. He used to express his opinions fairly openly at cocktail parties and other places the secret police regularly wired with tape recorders, and word was not long in reaching Nhu.

It happened that one of Millet's acquaintances was a man named Nguyen Van Luc, an intellectual with decidedly anti-Diem views. Luc had two sons in the Vietnamese Air Force, both of whom had been trained to fly in the United States, and who had become star fighter pilots. On February 27, 1962, one of Luc's sons, Sub Lieutenant Nguyen Van Cu, climbed into his American-built AD6 fighter at Bien Hoa Airport fifteen miles from Saigon, took off, and bombed the presidential palace to rubble. Another rebel pilot who flew with Cu was shot down by palace antiaircraft guns, but Cu's bullet-riddled plane made it 145 miles west to Phnom Penh, the capital of neutralist Cambodia, where it crash-landed.

Mme. Ngo Dinh Nhu got bruised up by the raid and a Chinese governess was killed by a falling beam, but the whole presidential family managed to get to the palace bomb shelter in time, and survived. Cu lived happily in Cambodia until the 1963 coup, teaching English to Cambodian students, and dreaming of returning to Viet Nam. He is now back, flying an AD6 fighter once again.

Father Luc, the other Air Force brother, and a lot of other people associated with the Nguyen family were arrested right after the palace bombing. And among the friends of the family was Stanley Millet.

Millet was finally allowed to leave Viet Nam, but Diem was never entirely satisfied that the American professor had not had something to do with the raid that nearly cost him his life. Nor

was Diem alone in this feeling. Many ranking Vietnamese, including some currently in high offices, feel the American CIA
is constantly active in Vietnamese politics, and was responsible
for the 1963 coup, among many other things. For the record, and
there is no reason to doubt it, Millet said he had no advance
inkling of the raid.

Incidentally, Father Luc got out of jail right after the 1963
coup, and is now one of the "ins." He is a member of the seven-
teen-member "High National Council" appointed by General
Nguyen Khanh to draw up plans for a civilian government, and
to answer charges that the Khanh regime is a military dictatorship. By the time this book is in print, Luc may very well be one
of the "outs" again, but that does not diminish the interesting
role he played.[1]

The central fact is, that despite all the power plays and re-
shuffles, the Saigon ministries, with all their red tape, favoritism,
inefficiency and politics, have not changed in any important
respect since French colonial days, and there are no prospects for
any major change. The old forms in triplicate, the rubber stamps,
the two-and-a-half-hour daily siesta and the ridiculous multipli-
cation of bureaus and employees persists, war or no war, and the
sheer inertia of Vietnamese administration is amply powerful
to frustrate any innovator. Khanh, one of the hardest-working
and driving leaders Viet Nam has had, failed completely to re-
vamp the civil service.

The problem is less one of mechanics and organization than
it is of attitudes. The Vietnamese hated the French enough to
rise up and destroy them. But after a century of colonial rule,
patterns are etched into a society.

Colonialism is not all bad. It sometimes introduces efficiency,
education and other desirable by-products. But these things are
only by-products. The reason for having a colony in the first
place is for commercial exploitation, not altruism, and the first
job of colonial officials is to make sure that nothing seriously

---

[1] Luc, in fact, was among the High National Council members arrested
December 20, 1964, when Khanh purged the new civilian government.
Luc is indeed again one of the "outs."

interferes with this exploitation. This immediately makes the colonial official a "have" and an "exploiter" among the "have-nots," no matter how benign and enlightened his social views may be.

Inevitably, a colonial class developed in the French community in Viet Nam, which lived pretty high on the hog. The Vietnamese came to hate the colonialists, but at the same time envied them. In many cases, they imitated the French ways, just as a matter of prestige. French automobiles, night clubs, clothing, and all the rest were indelibly stamped into the texture of Viet Nam as status symbols.

The same mixture of hatred and envy was extended to the French colonial official, the little king, who could have any girl he wanted, take anything he pleased, and spit on his constituents if they objected. It is a sad observation of humanity that many Vietnamese hated this kind of thing not so much because of what it was but because it was a Frenchman doing it. Now there are Vietnamese holding the same jobs and spitting on the same people, and too often it seems that nothing has changed but the color of the faces.

There is no accurate gauge of Diem's popularity (or the lack of it) since he was never exposed to a free election. But there are grounds for feeling Diem was genuinely popular with a lot of Vietnamese for a long time. For one thing, he rode the crest of a revolutionary wave, coming to power at just the time his nation became independent (largely because of the efforts of his arch enemy, Ho Chi Minh). For another, Diem had been a good provincial mandarin in his time, and had a reputation for great personal honesty, stubbornness and courage. Many talented young Vietnamese returned to Saigon from France in the first years of Diem's rule, captured by the ideal of building an independent nation of which they could be proud. In the end, these same people were dancing and singing in the streets of Saigon the day after Diem was overthrown and quietly butchered inside an American-made M113 personnel carrier.

Many reasons are offered for the sweeping hatred of Diem that characterized his final years. One is that he was a Roman

Catholic in a non-Christian country. Another is that he was a ruthless dictator. And so on. There is some substance to all these. But personally, I feel the biggest factor in the disenchantment of the Vietnamese people with the Diem regime was his failure to do anything to change the French colonial system of administration. And this fatal flaw appears to be no less true of Diem's successors.

The old attachments to the French colonial way of doing things show themselves in interesting ways not only in South Viet Nam but in the communist North, as well.

I know a Frenchman, for example, who used to be the manager of Hanoi's swankiest hotel, the Metropole. This man has recently come on hard times, incidentally. He owned a bar for years in Phnom Penh, but was finally driven out of business by new Cambodian currency restrictions. He went to work for the U.S. Aid mission in Phnom Penh as a local employee for a few months, and then Prince Sihanouk threw the Americans out of his country, leaving my friend once again without a job. I expect he is managing somehow.

But in 1954 he was the top man at Indochina's most comfortable and prestigious hotel.

The crisply uniformed French army stood at rigid attention, tears streaming from the cheeks of some officers, as the "Marseillaise" sounded and the *tricouleur* was hauled down for the last time. The ragged, poverty-stricken Viet Minh army straggled into Hanoi, looking much more like a defeated mob of guerrillas than a force which had just won a brilliant victory over a powerful European army.

The Viet Minh looked terrible, and its leaders knew and resented the fact. Hanoi was to be kept looking as shiny as possible within the wretchedly poor capabilities of the new government of the Democratic Republic of Viet Nam. And, if only as a place to entertain foreign dignitaries, Ho Chi Minh wanted the Metropole Hotel kept at its best. It was immediately nationalized, of course, but my friend was asked to stay on under contract to the Hanoi regime to maintain the hotel.

Some things had to change. Capitalist tipping was halted.

The hotel staff was organized into political cells, but polite and efficient service was rated high as a political virtue.

So the Metropole still looked good. The trouble was, the management could no longer get the imported luxuries that make a European hotel what it is. One of the first problems was tomato juice. North Viet Nam grows some tomatoes, and the government insisted they be used somehow to replace the French canned juice demanded by hotel patrons. The Vietnamese tried hard to make juice for the Metropole, but all their efforts failed. Tomato juice is tricky to make without the right machinery. Supplies of other left-over imports dwindled, hotel linen and furniture began to wear out, and decent liquor for the bar was no longer available. The Metropole's days as a great hotel were over, and my friend finally left North Viet Nam forever. Friends who can still go to Hanoi (Canadians and Indians) tell me the Metropole is now a dingy, third-rate place frequented only by down-at-the-heel Albanian junior diplomats and their like. But it still tries to keep up an attractive face.

Face, especially the French kind, is something vital to Vietnamese, and no Vietnamese likes to have his country thought of as being in any way backward or inferior to any other nation. There is nothing Vietnamese hate more than slurring references to the state of their development.

In his memoirs, one of Viet Nam's top old Bolsheviks, Bui Lam, mentions an incident in 1921 that I think is quite revealing.

In 1921, [Lam wrote], the French government held a colonial exhibition in Marseilles with a view to inducing the capitalists to invest more in the colonies in line with the policy of systematic exploitation of the colonies put forth by Albert Sarraut.

In this exhibition, shame was brought on the colonies: Viet Nam was represented by a rickshaw. But the French organizers were unable to find any Vietnamese who was willing to hire himself out as a rickshawman. In a film on Viet Nam there were scenes of children easing their bowels on beds and grown-ups calling dogs to jump up and eat the excrement.

Meanwhile, King Khai Dinh and Pham Quynh, who were visiting the French cities, kept chanting "their gratefulness for the civilizing and protecting country."

We [the Vietnamese Communist Party] were very angry, and time and again were about to set fire to the movie house. Right at that time, we read the articles criticizing the colonial exhibition, the policy of racial discrimination and of exploitation of French colonialism. All these articles, dear to our hearts, were signed by Nguyen Ai Quoc.

(Nguyen Ai Quoc, meaning more or less "Nguyen the Patriot," was one of the aliases of Ho Chi Minh, a name which also is an alias. The venerated president of the communist North was born Nguyen Sinh Cung (or Coong), changed his name at ten years old to Nguyen Tat Thanh, lived in France, Russia, America and various other countries as Nguyen Ai Quoc, signed articles written in French as "Lin," was known in China variously as Mr. Vuong, Ly Thuy and Wang Shan-er, and returned to Viet Nam to take charge of the whole communist movement as Ho Chi Minh, or, more familiarly, as "Bac Ho"—"Uncle Ho.")

If I have painted a black picture of Vietnamese governmental progress up to this point, what of the young officers and the students who are the next generation of leaders?

Let us look at a group of fast-rising South Vietnamese officers who have come to be called "the Young Turks" because of their radical ideas for improving the social structure, their vigorous methods and their Western training and orientation. Some of these officers remained loyal to General Nguyen Khanh on September 13, 1964, thus saving Khanh's regime from destruction at the hands of a coup led by some other, more conservative officers. The man on whom destiny turned that day was Sub Brigadier General Nguyen Cao Ky, reserve officers' class of 1952, commodore of the Vietnamese Air Force.

Ky, dressed in orange flight coveralls and sporting a pistol, cut a dashing and impressive figure. He controlled Saigon airport, and his position was fairly clear-cut. If the rebel army that occupied Saigon would not leave the capital within a given period of time, he would bomb the rebel units and Saigon along with them to rubble. This simple ultimatum prevailed, and the rebel officers, who had no plan or any real idea what they were doing, gave up.

So Ky was catapulted to national prominence. He had had an enviable career from the start. The French trained him as a pilot at their school in Marrakech, North Africa, where he learned the difference between good wine and bad, and grew a mustache. After Vietnamese independence, he rose rapidly through the ranks, and was sent to the United States to polish up his pilot training. He emerged as a hotshot fighter pilot qualified to fly the latest jets, and could now speak jaunty, American English. And at the age of thirty-three, he found himself as commander of the now fairly powerful Vietnamese Air Force.

Somehow, while I like Ky personally, he seems to me to be a man cut from a mold that once tried here and failed. A young French general named De Castries once cut a wide swath in Indochina, too. De Castries was known as one of the most ardent Lotharios in the Far East, and his parties were among the most spectacular and exciting that Indochina had ever seen. De Castries also rose rapidly through the ranks. But history was to assign him the job of commanding a gigantic French garrison near the Laotian border of North Viet Nam, in a valley called Dien Bien Phu. That name is still mentioned with horror by Frenchmen. For fifty-five days, De Castries and his brigade fought a doomed battle against the ragged guerrilla forces in the hills. The French at Dien Bien Phu died and fought with the valor and gallantry of a French army of another and happier age. But in the end, they were beaten by a bunch of peasants.

As I write these lines, I am sitting in a hotel room at the charming mountain resort of Dalat, about 150 miles northeast of Saigon. A few miles down the mountain, at Dalat airport, an American-built T28 fighter with no guns or rockets is parked. This fighter, a two-seater, is the personal property of the dashing Air Commodore Ky. He flies his latest girl friend (a gorgeous stewardess on Air Vietnam, the national airline) around in that T28, and they are now at a bungalow in Dalat, where one can still enjoy vestiges of the happy, old French colonial times.

I don't mean to sound like a Puritan (pretty stewardesses appeal to me, too), but Ky is now a national leader, and at this moment, Saigon is in what may be its final crisis. I can't help thinking that time is running out, even though I must say I envy Ky. He and I are the same age, and look at the difference.

What of some of the other young officers who have been involved in various coups and countercoups?

There is Major General Ton That Dinh, an old man of thirty-five, who commanded, at least nominally, the troops of Diem that raided the Buddhist pagodas on August 20, 1963; who personally commanded the troops on November 1, 1963, that overthrew Diem; who was named after the revolution to command the vital and sensitive Third Army Corps; who was taken out of that job to become Interior Minister; who was arrested and jailed January 30, 1964, by a new regime headed by Major General Nguyen Khanh (who is thirty-seven years old), and who is now at work again for the Khanh government (because of pressure from the Buddhist bloc, ironically)—all that in the space of one year.

What is Dinh like? He is engaging and forceful, and he boasts constantly. He wants to be premier of Viet Nam. He drinks hard and lives hard, and can be a canny military tactician at times.

Another of the "Young Turks" is Sub Brigadier General Nguyen Chanh Thi, thirty-seven, who also remained loyal to Khanh during the abortive coup.

Thi is a nervous little man whose eye twitches constantly, who delivers speeches that boom like thunder, who wears a mustache just like Ky's, and sports a red paratrooper beret and a swagger stick.

I got to know Thi in Phnom Penh, where he lived in exile after trying unsuccessfully to overthrow Ngo Dinh Diem with a coup on November 11, 1960.

Thi, a colonel at the time, commanded the Vietnamese para-troop brigade in 1960, and got to thinking about what it would be like to throw Diem out and set up a more forward-looking, modern government. On November 11, he ordered four para-troop battalions and some odds and ends of armor, heavy weapons companies and so on into Saigon. Thi's coup caught even Diem's secret police completely by surprise, because it had been planned so hastily. Thi quickly seized control of the whole city and placed his forces in an iron ring around Independence Palace. The coup appeared to have been a resounding success, and a lot of people, who by this time were fed up with Diem, were dancing in the streets.

But Thi had not planned ahead very far. In the years preceding Thi's coup, a variety of the Saigon intelligentsia-politicians began holding conspiratorial meetings in coffee shops and bars around town, and began to form a kind of loose organization. They agreed on only one thing—that Diem must go—and that was what held them together. The secret police kept an eye on all of them, of course, but Diem never bothered to lock them up because he regarded them as harmless. This group began meeting most often at the plush bar on the eighth floor of the French-owned Caravelle Hotel, where it was convenient to meet and entertain visiting American officials, journalists, and other supposedly influential foreigners. Hence, the organization came to be known as "Les Caravellistes." Activist Colonel Thi had got himself tied up with this bunch.

And it was to this group that he turned for political guidance after his troops had seized Saigon and placed Diem under what amounted to house arrest. Chaos and confusion immediately followed, the politicians were unable to give Thi any effective guidance, and he decided to try a parley with Diem himself.

Another rising young officer, then Brigadier General Nguyen Khanh (at this writing, Premier Khanh), had taken an interest in the goings on, but was not yet sure which way the wind was blowing. He sneaked his way through Thi's forces and got into the palace by a back entrance ("I wasn't sure whether or not Diem was being attacked by the Viet Cong," Khanh said four years later), and offered his services to Diem, mainly as a negotiator with the rebels. Negotiations came to pass, and Diem went on the radio, promising that he would step down immediately in favor of a military junta, to which he would be attached temporarily as an advisor.

Thi, the rebel forces and the politicians were more confused than ever, but Diem's promise sounded encouraging. The tank crews stretched out for siesta and lunch to wait out developments.

Developments were not long in coming. A day later, army units loyal to Diem roared into Saigon from the Mekong Delta, and the bloodshed began. In bitter fighting throughout the city, the loyalists pushed the understrength rebels back and back, the siege of the palace was lifted, Thi and a dozen other rebel officers commandeered a transport plane and escaped to Cambodia, and the coup was over.

A lot of the Saigon intelligentsia were rounded up and shipped off to Poulo Condore after that, and some were badly tortured in Saigon's secret jails (one of which, unknown to any outsider at the time, was right in the middle of the Saigon zoo near the lion house. It was called "P42," and some pretty terrible things happened there. Confinement in P42 was a valuable credential after Diem was overthrown, and a number of old P42 inmates now hold important jobs).

While Thi was in Cambodia after his attempted coup, he was a beaten and impoverished man. I took him to dinner once in a while, and good food and beer made him more cheerful. He and some of the other exiled 1960 rebels lived better after young Lieutenant Cu bombed the Saigon palace and flew to Phnom Penh. Cu, who spoke excellent English, could at least make a comfortable living teaching. Cu's little English school prospered, and was soon earning enough money to support some of the rebels who had arrived earlier, including Thi. It was obviously galling to Thi to have to accept charity from a man in his twenties, six military grades his junior, but there was no choice.

During this period, Thi plunged himself into political reading, plotting, and doing almost anything to keep his sanity. He got interested in the propaganda being sent from France by Dr. Pham Huy Co (whom I have described earlier in this chapter), and helped set up the leaflet bomb campaign in Saigon. He also claimed to have regular contact with officers still in Saigon who were planning a new coup. But in fact, Thi had nothing to do with the 1963 coup. He came back to Viet Nam, and the man who had once served as mediator between him and Diem was now his boss. Khanh sent him as far north as possible, gave him a division to command (a safe 400 miles from Saigon), and eventually promoted him to sub brigadier general.

Thi has been loyal to Khanh so far, and during the abortive coup of September 13, 1964, Thi made a show of flying down to Saigon to join the loyalist forces. That is how things stand at this writing. But I know Thi as a man with big ideas, and there is reason to suppose he may have some old scores to settle with Khanh.

I could draw more profiles of the officers of the Vietnamese Army and their careers, but to do so would be somewhat repetitious, and my object is not to confuse the reader with all the details of the constant intrigue involved.

Suffice it to say that I do not regard the Vietnamese officer corps as the most desirable pool from which to draw a stable national government.

I have already said by implication that the Vietnamese civilian politicians do not strike me favorably either.

This depressing view is shared by a lot of official Americans in Saigon, one of whom told me semifacetiously:

"The only solution to all this is to bomb the hell out of both Hanoi and Saigon, and start the whole thing from scratch, working entirely with peasants—the only stable element in the country."

It would be nice to think that idealistic young people in Viet Nam may be preparing themselves to forge a brave new world.

A month or so ago, the Vietnamese government decided to liberalize its formerly stringent restrictions on the issuance of exit visas. Airline offices in town were mobbed. Students of all ages picked up their passports and enough money for one-way trips to Paris, paid for in many cases by their families' life savings. Air France began putting on special daily flights in addition to its regular flights to handle the huge load of youthful emigrants. The large new waiting room at Saigon Airport is packed before each of these flights, as students and their families tearfully say farewell, perhaps forever. Many families are happy to have at least one son or daughter out of the country, and there is a tragic Noah's Ark quality to the whole thing.

Of course, for each student who goes there are thousands who cannot. They must make the best of Saigon. They have chosen to do so not by studying but by joining various political action groups.

Since the summer of 1963, the leading monks of the Buddhist

hierarchy have exercised enormous control over many of Saigon's young people. The monks now can get up a student demonstration of 10,000 or more on a day or two's notice.

Each of Saigon's scores of political parties also controls a student bloc, sometimes numbering no more than a hundred, sometimes several thousand. University professors in Hue and Saigon also are neck-deep in politics, and can have students and banners in the streets any time they please.

A political bloc calling itself the "National Salvation Council" was formed recently by a group of politicians in Hue, which has called for a lot of things, depending on who happens to be printing the banners at the moment. The "Council" has made its influence felt in key cities all the way down the populous coast line from Hue, although this influence stops short before Saigon. There is evidence of a penetration in depth by the Viet Cong into the National Salvation Council. Various agitators have frequently stirred council demonstrations into violence, and there has been increasing bloody rioting in some areas. The name National Salvation Council itself is peculiarly reminiscent of a National Salvation Bloc once organized by Ho Chi Minh as part of his underground apparatus.

Serious students complain that they no longer have time for study, because they are so frequently called to demonstrate or protest or strike.

"It was exactly like this when the Viet Minh was organizing the students in the delta in the late nineteen forties," a young woman told me recently. "Whenever the organizers wanted to protest something, we girls were all ordered to wear the same color dress to school to demonstrate solidarity. One day I forgot, and wore the wrong dress. They chased me out of school and hit me, and I cried all day when I got home. I wasn't against the demonstrations or anything, because I thought they were exciting, and all of us more or less believed in what the Viet Minh was doing. So I was all the more miserable for having been rejected."

There is a temptation to believe, having seen students surging through the streets of Saigon clubbing and hacking each other to death, that Vietnamese students are not susceptible to discipline. But one night recently I attended a torchlight swearing-in ceremony of 300 students into an "assault group." The political aims of this group are extremely vague, but its organizational program is not. Student leaders barked orders as the recruits dressed their ranks and files to military perfection, the leader of each file holding a torch at parade salute. The whole street was blocked by all this, of course, but police did nothing to interfere. As the recruits watched, a thirty-member student judo team belonging to one of the trained "assault groups" put on an exhibition, in which the students felled each other by the numbers, with a precision generally not seen in Vietnamese police and military judo groups. After the exhibition, student leaders barked again, and each recruit fell to one knee, raising his (or her) right arm in the old Hitler salute. The leader intoned the oath of allegiance to the nation and the assault group, and each recruit repeated the oath.

Then they all marched off in perfect step to Student Union headquarters for some iced tea and a round of student songs, accompanied by guitars. The whole thing was pretty impressive and rather frightening. These assault teams spend their Sunday mornings, by the way, out on a rubber plantation near Saigon, where they picnic and practice street fighting with clubs. A student medical team, each member of which wears a Red Cross armband, stands by and patches up the cuts and bruises.

The students involved in all this have always had the option of joining the national army, but they are not interested in this, and will pull any wire handy to avoid getting drafted. Many say in their fiery speeches that they regard the Vietnamese Army as a contemptible organization, unworthy of a student's fighting zeal.

One suspects that these assault groups eventually will find a use in Saigon, and it is likely not to be one beneficial to the cause of the Free World.

In discussing the "cream" of South Viet Nam's current leadership potential, there is one Saigon politician I have not mentioned so far. In himself, he is no more distinguished-seeming a leader than Pham Huy Co or any of the others. A one-time Saigon lawyer now in his late forties, he had a love affair in Tuy Hoa some years ago, and got in trouble with the government when his girl friend sued him for nonsupport.

In March, 1950, French authorities in Saigon threw him in jail for organizing an anti-American street demonstration during the goodwill visit of some U.S. warships.

He was among the many plotters and intriguers against Diem, too, and the Diem government had him under arrest in Tuy Hoa for several years.

In 1958, Diem ordered his release, in the belief that the man was just another one of the intellectual plotters who posed no real danger to anyone.

That man was Nguyen Huu Tho, whose present title is Chairman of the Central Committee of the National Front for the Liberation of South Viet Nam. As such, Tho is the Number 1 man in the Viet Cong, and in the event of a Viet Cong victory, he would be president of the nation. Tho looks in some ways more like a figurehead than a real leader of the Viet Cong, but there is no question at least of his nominal authority.

There is one big difference between Tho and the other Saigon politicians. The others depend on their own pocketbooks to hold together the ineffective splinter groups each one heads.

Tho, on the other hand, chose to ally himself with the most powerful political organization in Asia. And he has not wanted for expert advice and assistance.

Chapter 12

The National Liberation Front

The backbone of the Vietnamese communist movement is not Ho Chi Minh, Pham Van Dong, Vo Nguyen Giap, Nguyen Huu Tho, or any of the other worldly Bolsheviks of another generation. It is the Vietnamese peasant, sturdy and conservative in his ways, who is a courageous and intelligent fighter, provided he trusts his leaders.

Ho and the other top communist theoreticians have been saying exactly this all along, but neither their followers nor their enemies entirely believe them. To a Vietnamese communist, Ho is only a little lower than the angels. To many an American counterinsurgent, Ho is a fiendish genius sitting up in Hanoi, pulling the strings of a dirty war. To my mind, both these views fall short of the truth.

This is not to say that the reigning communist intellectuals are not important to the movement or do not control it. Regular visitors to Hanoi who also are old Moscow and Peking hands have told me that the degree of control the top Communists of North Viet Nam have over their country makes even the regimes of Stalin and Mao look like "pseudo-liberal, counter-revolutionary deviationism."

I am more concerned in this book with giving an account of Viet Cong tactics than with the Viet Cong organization. For one thing, I know of the Viet Cong organization and history only through broadcasts from "Liberation Radio" and Radio Hanoi, various intelligence reports I have seen, and other secondhand sources. I cannot say I really know much about it.

With that qualification, I will try to give a very abbreviated summary of what is known of the evolution of the Viet Cong.

Since the turn of this century various revolutionary Vietnamese groups have been active. For that matter, Vietnamese revolutionary tradition predates the time of Christ, and many revolutionary heroes still remembered in poetry, holidays, and by street names in Saigon date back that far. Vietnamese have at various times fought Chinese, Mongols, Khmers, Chams, Japanese, French, Americans, and, most of all, other Vietnamese. The history of the Indochina Peninsula (the two Viet Nams, Cambodia, Laos, Thailand and Burma) makes even the Balkans look peaceful by comparison.

The French colonized Viet Nam in the mid-nineteenth century, and thus inadvertently gave birth to modern Vietnamese communism. France provided at the same time a target of fairly universal hatred and a capital in which the revolutionaries could get organized. Paris itself became the cradle of Vietnamese insurrection. It still plays an important role.

There were several reasons for this. For one thing, while French colonial policies have often been extremely repressive, a much looser rein was kept on people from the colonies visiting France itself. A Vietnamese revolutionary was generally much safer from the hands of secret police in Paris than he was in Hanoi or Saigon. The same has been true to a large extent of Algerians and other French colonials.

A second and more important reason is that communism itself is fundamentally a European doctrine. First codified by Marx, a German, it spread in Europe and came to full bloom in Russia. Not until relatively late in the game did it make inroads into Asia, where it underwent some big changes from its original form.

Communism in one form or another was a big political force in the industrial cities of France from the early nineteenth century onward. After World War I, communism swept through Europe, and the great factories around Paris came to be known as "the Red Belt." Ho Chi Minh, the son of a rural doctor, had spent most of his youth drifting around the world doing odd jobs, such as serving as a cook's helper on the French steamship line

Chargeurs Reunis. He arrived in Paris just after the war, joined the mushrooming French Communist Party, and earned a living as a photographic technician while learning the arts of party organizing and churning out communist propaganda.

Ho rose rapidly, and his history from then on is too well known to record here. But the point is, all his initial organizational work was in Paris, to which he generally returned after sojourns in the Soviet Union and China.

There has been a large Vietnamese colony in Paris for many years. Most of the Asians you see there are Vietnamese, and if you notice such things, several times a day you will see the Vietnamese *ao-dai* worn by women as you stroll around. There are great numbers of good Vietnamese restaurants in Paris, the only city outside Viet Nam I know of in which one can buy Vietnamese food.

Thousands of Vietnamese are permanent residents of Paris, but the biggest continuing influx is in the form of students. For this reason, the largest Vietnamese concentrations are in the cheap student quarters of the Left Bank, and around the various university faculties.

At one time, Vietnamese communist headquarters in Paris operated quite openly, with a sign on the door describing it as such.

Eventually, the *Deuxième Bureau* got around to closing this hotbed of revolution, so it had to go underground. The headquarters is now a floating operation, but most often is set up in a garage building, of which the garage itself is the front. I have not ventured inside this building (I would not be welcome), but I have many Vietnamese friends who are or have been regular visitors there. Since this garage is currently the source of a lot of America's troubles in Southeast Asia, I think it is worth further description.

A Vietnamese student arriving in Paris is apt to speak rather imperfect French. He (or she) probably lacks adequate warm clothing for the bitter, academic winter. He is almost always hard up, at a loss to find some place to live, disgusted with the fare served at third-rate French restaurants, and eager for a bowl of good Vietnamese *pho*, and extremely lonely. Paris is a cold and lonely place for any poor stranger to the city.

But the student is not likely to remain in this predicament long. Within a few days, one or two friendly Vietnamese students who know all the ropes are likely to come calling on him. If he asks them how they happened to know he was here and why they are doing him this kindness, he is apt to get a rather vague answer. But these host-students and others he will meet will be to him the most solid friends he could want. They will help him find a part-time job, they will give him small loans, they will make sure he has a decent place to live and knows all the good Vietnamese restaurants, they will invite him to their homes to meet other nice young Vietnamese, and they will eventually suggest that he come to eat at the garage.

Having learned that the garage (or whatever place is currently in use) is a clandestine meeting place, the student may have some misgivings about going there. But he is in for a very pleasant surprise. There are no grim, bearded Bolsheviks inside, and no apparent conspiracy. The rooms are bright and cheerful, and filled with young people like himself. There are reading rooms, there is a pleasant common room where there may be a pretty young girl strumming a guitar, two other students bending over a chessboard, and others chatting and laughing. Everyone treats him as an esteemed friend, and nothing could be less sinister. It is a joy to hear the singsong patter of Vietnamese instead of French for a change, and the whole thing is warming.

The big surprise comes in the community dining room, where the meal is cheap but tasty. The waiters themselves are all students, most of them advanced post graduates in medicine, law and letters—the very elite of students.

In Viet Nam, such a thing is unheard of. The student, or rather, scholar, has a special place in Vietnamese society, and it is unthinkable that he would lower himself by serving food to other people. In old-fashioned, cultured Vietnamese families it is still the pattern for the husband to spend his days over his books, learned articles and poetry, while the wife earns the living and tends the home fires. The Vietnamese husband does not generally help his wife with any household chores, except in very modern families. But here, the fledgling doctors, lawyers and poets are also waiters!

The student is at first thrown for a loss as to how to address these waiters. Obviously, you can't yell "Boy!" when you want another bowl of rice, nor does it seem quite right to yell "Please, sir." But one quickly learns from the others to call the waiters "Brother" or "Comrade." The student has learned his first political lesson from the garage: There are to be no distinctions of class in addressing other people in the new club.

He will get to know the waiters later, and they will always be friendly and helpful to him, treating him as a complete equal, despite their elevated academic caste.

Time passes, and the student may become a regular part of the community house. He will be exposed to a certain amount of communist teaching from his comrades, and he will probably participate in the lively and interesting "discussion groups" and "cultural night." But no political pressure of any kind will be brought to bear on him, and the talk will be friendly, free discussion and argument. No badgering or hard sell.

If the student likes the way things are done here, and if his studies (and political attitudes) mature, he may eventually find himself as one of the waiters or group leaders. He has been closely watched the whole time, and appointments like this are made carefully. When the student's education reaches a certain level of attainment, he begins to come under extremely close scrutiny by the permanent officers of the fraternity. Questions about patriotism and the belief in the golden future of Viet Nam (North) begin to come up, and the student is shown some very interesting pamphlets. It seems that a doctor enjoys a lot of privileges in Hanoi.

Besides the opportunity of serving a growing nation, he will be provided by the state with a comfortable villa, he will get liberal food ration allowances, his children, if they are worthy, will have excellent education facilities, and he may even be entitled to a motorcar (or, more often, a motor scooter).

For engineers, lawyers, chemists, and all the other professionals, there are other blandishments.

"You are Vietnamese, and your place is not in imperialist

France but in the Vietnamese fatherland," the student is told. "You don't want to go back to the slavery of South Viet Nam, do you? Do you want to be drafted into the army of the U.S. lackeys and have your fine education spent as cannon fodder in a dirty war against our patriotic compatriots? Of course not. Why don't you come to Hanoi and join the people? You can always leave, if you don't like it."

The student may or may not take up the offer. If he does, he is apt to find that he does have special advantages, and while North Viet Nam is pretty threadbare, he gets the best of what there is. He may also leave Hanoi to go abroad, but he is not likely to do so because he is fed up. He leaves because he has reached the degree of trust that he can be safely sent once again into the lands of the Philistines. He may go to France, as a recruiting officer or party organizer. Or he may merely pass through France on his way to South Viet Nam, for a very special kind of work.

The South Vietnamese embassy in Paris also has occasional dealings with students, mostly of an unpleasant character. The embassy there frequently poses problems involving red tape and restrictions on currency exchange that students find aggravating.

A number of students were stunned one day on receiving invitations to dinner at the South Vietnamese embassy on the occasion of the South Vietnamese national day. The Vietnamese ambassador was no friend of the students, and this gesture seemed like Scrooge sending Tiny Tim a turkey. But most of the invitees came to the dinner, dressed in their Sunday best and ready to bury the hatchet.

The ambassador arrived, got them together in the reception hall, and gave them the most blistering tongue-lashing they had heard yet. The themes included squandering their parents' money, wasting the resources of their government, and other related subjects. Afterward, they all went into the dining room, gulped down their food in silence, and hurried off—some of them for a friendly coffee at the good old garage. That dinner is still remembered with bitterness by a lot of former Vietnamese students. The next year, the ambassador sent out the same invitations, but almost no one showed up.

Ho began in the early 1920s by sharing his meager supplies

of rice and salted fish with the Vietnamese sailors and students who used to visit him in his room in Paris. There was always a spare mat in the room for anyone who had no place to sleep. Ho's successors have continued this tradition. My Vietnamese-Parisian friends tell me that 90 per cent of the Vietnamese colony in France is sympathetic to the Viet Cong and helps the movement in little or large ways. This may be an exaggeration, and I have no way of knowing. But on the basis of what I have seen, it sounds not unreasonable.

This does not mean, necessarily, that the Vietnamese communist in Paris is ready to take up a machine gun against the American imperialists.

It is a long way from the cafés of Boulevard St. Germain des Pres to the jungles of South Viet Nam. I know a young married couple, for instance, who met and married as students in Paris, got interested in the garage, and talked the toughest Viet Cong line most of their friends had ever heard. They were regarded as among the toughest young revolutionaries in Paris.

But a few years after Diem came to power in Saigon, they both returned to the homeland—not Hanoi, but Saigon. The husband joined Diem's semisecret political party, became a good, solid "Personalist" (the political philosophy Diem ascribed to his regime), and got a post in a thriving government business in exchange. The couple rapidly prospered, and the old days (and talk) in Paris were forgotten in favor of more practical considerations.

This couple has been in trouble with the military governments that followed Diem, and the husband, under suspicion of flagrant corruption, has lost his job. But they have salted away enough to live for a long time with no further income, and they can always go back to Paris if things get too bad.

But Paris remains Uncle Ho's revolutionary garden, and he expects a certain amount of chaff along with the wheat. Paris is also the best of all possible rear bases for the Vietnamese communist movement, and is likely to improve with the current rapprochement between Paris and Peking.

Vietnamese are not always able to freewheel in Paris. After the French military collapse at Dien Bien Phu, a lot of my Vietnamese friends who lived in Paris at the time started carrying switchblade knives. There had been a series of wild Vietnamese celebration parties, and discharged French veterans of the Indo-china campaign took to beating up any Vietnamese they came across in the streets.

But times like that are rare.

Let me change the scene to Phnom Penh, the capital of Cambodia, a picturesque and lively little city of 600,000, and a kind of exquisite miniature of Saigon. The absolute ruler of Cambodia is a hot-tempered and brilliant young prince of the blood named Norodom Sihanouk.

In 1953, a year before Ho's Viet Minh defeated the French in battle, Sihanouk drove his own bargain with France, and won independence for his tiny country, without ever getting deeply involved in the war.

America started pouring military and other aid into Thailand, Cambodia's western neighbor, and South Viet Nam, Cambodia's eastern neighbor. It happens that both these neighbors have been mortal enemies of Cambodia since the beginning of recorded history, and Cambodians still fear and dislike both the Thais and Vietnamese. Both have taken healthy bites out of the old Khmer (Cambodian) empire, which, during the Middle Ages, was one of the greatest and most powerful empires in Southeast Asia. The old Khmer capital of Angkor Wat was built at that time, and its ruins still are among the great architectural treasures of the world.

Sihanouk claims lineal descent from the builders of mighty Angkor, and has tried hard to preserve what little there is left of his nation. Cambodia's colonial relations with France were much more cordial than those between France and the other Indochina colonies. A primary reason was that France prevented both Thailand and South Viet Nam from taking some more bites out of Cambodia. Sihanouk has not forgotten this historic fact. A highly cultivated man of parts who writes and acts in plays, composes music and captains sports clubs, Sihanouk sees himself as a combination Henry VIII and Charles de Gaulle.

He elected to keep his nation neutral after winning independence, and steadfastly turned down American overtures to him to join the Southeast Asia Treaty Alliance (SEATO). Sihanouk wanted no part of an outfit one of whose leading members was Thailand.

Increasingly, Sihanouk has leaned ever closer to the communist bloc, particularly to China. While his main economic ties are with France (Sihanouk threw the American Aid mission out in 1963), Cambodia is now receiving a certain amount of military hardware from China. He also reminds the Western powers from time to time, "If Cambodia is invaded, we are small, but six hundred million Chinese stand behind us."

Despite Sihanouk's dislike of all Vietnamese, North or South, it is no longer possible for him to turn a cold shoulder to Hanoi. There are obvious political reasons for this, but there is also an interesting ethnological reason.

Only about one third of the inhabitants of Phnom Penh, the Cambodian capital, are Cambodians. Another third of the city is Vietnamese and the remaining third is Chinese. Only Cambodians can hold public office, and public officeholders may not marry Vietnamese or Chinese. But the Vietnamese and Chinese have the lion's share of economic wealth in the city. Just as in Paris, the Communists have been the most active in organizing the Vietnamese and Chinese. Nearly all the Chinese schools in Phnom Penh are run by Peking communists, and all the Chinese and Vietnamese newspapers are communist. (This despite the fact that the Cambodian Communist Party has been outlawed and practically wiped out by Sihanouk.) Therefore, Sihanouk has a powerful Viet Cong headquarters right in his front yard, which could make terrible trouble for him if it chose.

All this means that Phnom Penh is now the major forward base of operations for the Viet Cong. Less than a hundred miles from the center of the Vietnamese war, it is a good place to print leaflets and newspapers to be sent into Viet Nam.

There are continuing reports that significant shipments of arms and ammunition are reaching the Viet Cong through Cambodia.

The North Vietnamese legation in Phnom Penh now occupies

one of the largest buildings in town, and hums with activity. (It took the building over from the Chinese communist embassy, which needed larger quarters.)

Cambodia is geographically relatively large, but has fewer than six million inhabitants, which gives it one of the lowest population densities in Asia. In simpler terms, it is full of wide open spaces (especially along its frontier with South Viet Nam) where unusual activities can be carried on without attracting official notice. These activities include Viet Cong operations.

At this point, I shall switch to Viet Nam and the Liberation Front proper, skipping over Laos, much of which is now openly controlled by the Viet Cong (or their Pathet Lao assistants) and which can no longer be considered a foreign base for the Liberation Front. It is part of communist Viet Nam.

In 1954, South Viet Nam was a nation in anarchy. Powerful private armies roamed the nation and even controlled Saigon. A band of river pirates formed a secret society called the Binh Xuyen, organized a formidable fighting force, took over Saigon's police, established a syndicate dealing in narcotics, prostitution and many other things, and turned Saigon into the vice capital of Asia.

In the 1920s, several Vietnamese religions were invented by local prophets—ostensibly to promote spiritual belief, but actually for use as covers for underground military organizations being used against the French.

One of these got started in a village named Hoa Hao not far from the Cambodian border. The new religion called itself a denomination of Buddhism, and came to be called Phat Giao Hoa Hao, meaning Hoa Hao Buddhists, or Hoa Hao for short. Hoa Hao men grew their hair to their shoulders, preached the pure and simple life, and began arming themselves. Their military leader was a Christlike-looking man named Ba Cut, who could handle a Tommy gun like a professional and claimed he was immortal. The Hoa Hao movement grew like lightning, and became the scourge of the upper Mekong Delta. In the early 1950s, Hoa Hao claimed a million followers, and this may not have been much of an exaggeration. The movement is still very strong.

Another faith called Cao Dai also got started in the 1920s. Its prophet, a colonial province chief named Ngo Van Chieu, was a French-trained intellectual. He used to sit each night in his home holding seances, in which he claimed to be in communication with the departed spirit of Victor Hugo. The ghost of the French master would dictate mystical poetry to the prophet during these seances, which the prophet dutifully transcribed. Victor Hugo, Sun Yat-sen (the leader of the revolutionary Young China movement) and an ancient, classical Vietnamese poet became the three leading saints of Cao Daiism. The religion merged elements of Buddhism, Confucianism, Taoism and Christianity, recognizing the teachings of all four faiths.

Grotesquely impressive pink and green Cao Dai temples went up in areas where the faith took hold, and followers worshiped before gigantic images of human eyes. The Cao Dai cathedral in Tay Ninh is something a sight-seer should not neglect, if he can manage to get through the Viet Cong check points on the road from Saigon. There are huge plaster serpents with neon lights for eyes, exotic tableaus of the steps to heaven, and other attractions.

But the important part about Cao Dai was its army—several regiments in strength, and magnificently trained and armed. Led by Cao Dai General Trinh Minh The, the Cao Dai army held complete sway in several populous provinces in the early 1950s, crushing both French and Viet Minh units that ventured into the Cao Dai Holy See. The French later succeeded in making a deal with the Cao Dais, which kept the Viet Minh out of the Cao Dai area until the end of the Indochina War.

Besides the Cao Dai, the Hoa Hao and the Binh Xuyen, there were many other groups challenging Saigon authority when Diem took over. There was a large residuum of the Viet Minh organization itself, which elected to stay in South Viet Nam rather than go north to the new Democratic Republic of Viet Nam. There were intellectuals, professionals and old-time revolutionaries from the Dai Viet Party, the Vietnamese Kuomintang (VNQDD), and many others who wanted no part of Diem. Unfortunately for themselves, they wanted no part of each other, either.

Diem moved swiftly. He crushed the Binh Xuyen in a pitched battle between his fledgling army and its troops. He cracked down hard on the Cao Dai, and most of its leaders fled to Cambodia. He tried repeatedly to make a deal with Ba Cut, leader of the Hoa Haos, giving Ba Cut a regular commission in the army in exchange for his allegiance.

Ba Cut repeatedly double-crossed Diem, however, so Diem launched Operation Nguyen Hue against the Hoa Haos. Ba Cut was captured in 1957, and publicly guillotined.

Political parties opposing Diem were more or less outlawed, and a lot of their top leaders were locked up or exiled.

By 1958, Diem was in undisputed control of South Viet Nam. The private armies were gone, the dangerous political opponents were neutralized, the streets of Saigon were quiet and more or less free of grenades, and it looked as if Diem had won some peace for his nation.

But as it turned out, this was only a respite. None of the old fighting political organizations had been crushed completely, but had merely been forced to go underground. In later years, American advisors were to cross swords repeatedly with Hoa Hao guerrilla units, under the impression they were fighting Viet Cong.

My reason in going back over this history is to show that there were many groups in South Viet Nam in addition to a lot of peasants and, of course, the communists, who remained violently opposed to Diem. All that was needed to harness a lot of this revolutionary talent into a single channel was some overridingly persuasive new political organization. That organization was not long in forming. It was the National Liberation Front.

The Front began to take shape in 1959. It purported to be all things to all people, and from the beginning, was made up of many dependent front organizations. There was no mention of communism in any of the early organizational work done by the Front, and its leaders made a point of bringing clergymen of all faiths even into the central committee.

A parenthetical note on the relations between Vietnamese communism and religion:

Ho Chi Minh and all his top deputies are old-line communist purists. Ho is currently the dean of international communist revolutionaries (he was born May 19, 1889), and he believes in the Marxist dogma that "religion is the opiate of the people." Nevertheless, he and the others have maintained a certain show of religious tolerance. Even the Roman Catholic Cathedral in Hanoi still stands, and Vietnamese priests officiate there at masses. The cathedral is kept locked up most of the time, and foreign priests are never allowed into North Viet Nam to see what really is going on. But for other visitors, the façade is still there.

At any rate, the fronts included one each for farmers, workers, women, students, professionals, artists and writers, journalists, soldiers (government), clergymen, each of the racial minority groups, and so on. Each front has its own specialized agitprop organization for recruiting and indoctrination.

For government soldiers, the propaganda was particularly interesting. As in all communist-front organizations, the very first precept is class warfare, and a close second is the battle against foreign imperialism. These two themes tie together neatly for use on Vietnamese soldiers. The line to the soldier is this:

"You are a man of the people. You have never had any money, and your family is poor. While you are out spilling your intestines, your commander is probably in Saigon, dressed in white dinner jacket, drinking champagne and watching a Paris fashion show at the Caravelle Hotel [this has happened] or playing tennis with the U.S. ambassador [this also has happened]. You are continually oppressed by your officers, all of whom were trained both by the French and American imperialists.

"As a Vietnamese patriot, you have two duties: To fight for the destruction of a feudal class system that keeps you chained to misery, and to throw out the foreigners and their lackeys who perpetuate this system.

"In the People's Army, there is no class. There is military discipline, but your officer is your comrade and your brother. What you must do and bear, he must also do and bear. We work and fight together, live together, eat together.

"If you cannot join us, your compatriots, you must at least

not fight us. To fight the People's Army is a crime against your own flesh and blood."

This approach is not always successful, but it has demonstrated a powerful appeal. It has done much to undermine the fighting spirit of Vietnamese units. American advisors are constantly exasperated by army units that fail to seek out the enemy, avoid contact, and break off contact, if by chance it is established. Without conscription, the Vietnamese Army would collapse, and the unwilling Vietnamese draftee does not make the most energetic soldier in the world.

All these fronts began to take form in 1958 and 1959, and the first flickerings of guerrilla resistance to the Diem regime began to be felt. The Saigon government saw a familiar hand behind these troublemakers, and the propaganda ministry invented a new and presumably derisive name for them. They were to be called henceforth in all Saigon references as the "Vietnamese Communists," or, in Vietnamese, "Viet Cong." The name stuck, although the rebels themselves have never used it.

Front activity spread rapidly, recruiting heavily from all the anti-Diem factions, and picking up as many peasants as possible.

The main leaders of the front movement were southerners, but they soon were joined by expert advisors in both political and military matters sent down from Hanoi. These advisors kept trickling in. At present, there probably are almost as many "advisors" from Hanoi working with the Viet Cong as there are American advisors working for the Saigon government. A key difference between these opposing groups of foreign advisors is that the overwhelming bulk of Americans are regular army men, while the advisors from Hanoi are mostly political organizers who may also be military tacticians.

From the first few thousand members, the fronts grew rapidly until on December 20, 1960, a national congress of front organizers was convened and formally proclaimed the "National Front for the Liberation of South Viet Nam."

The headquarters of the new national front had to be kept secret and floating because of the danger of Saigon raids. But from the beginning, the front controlled certain "Liberated Zones"—the Do Xa region in the High Plateau, the D Zone jungles north of Saigon, C Zone in northern Tay Ninh Province along the Cambodian frontier, the U Minh Forest near the southern tip of Viet Nam, and so on. Big meetings could be held in these base areas without the slightest danger of serious interference.

The National Liberation Front quickly formed a central committee and a presidium (or politburo), of which lawyer Nguyen Huu Tho was chairman from the beginning. Another key member of the first presidium was a Paris-educated doctor named Phung Van Cung. A former executive of the old Vietnamese communist Democratic Party, Tran Buu Kim, sat on the politburo.

But Western intelligence specialists speculate that the greatest power in the Viet Cong politburo belongs to its secretary-general, a former mathematics teacher named Nguyen Van Hieu. Hieu is certainly the best-known Viet Cong leader outside South Viet Nam. Besides his politburo duties, he is a kind of shadow foreign minister and ambassador without portfolio for the Front, lecturing and attending ceremonies in Indonesia, Czechoslovakia, East Germany, the Soviet Union, China, and other communist or nonaligned countries. He seems to get in and out of South Viet Nam without difficulty, using the various standard infiltration routes, of which there are thousands. South Viet Nam's frontiers are leaky as a sieve, and probably always will be, unless someone decides to station several million sentries continuously along their vast length. Even then, I suspect the frontiers would leak.

Names of all the executives of the National Liberation Front are published and updated regularly by the Front, and there is nothing secret about them. The members of all its committees also are published. I won't bore the reader with a lot of meaningless names, but suffice it to say that each of the committees of the Front leadership is actually a shadow ministry, complete with secretariats, departments and all the other paraphernalia of communist bureaucracy. These shadow ministries function in the jungle, of course, but they still need some of the usual trappings. The Viet Cong makes a point of seizing government typewriters and filing cabinets in its raids.

Similar committees organized by Ho Chi Minh during the Indochina War emerged later as ministries in Hanoi, and this is the same pattern being applied in South Viet Nam.

Along with the development of the National Front committees came the extension of the organization downward, in the form of provincial and district committees. Each subdivision was given an administrative structure patterned after the national committees.

One of the most important of the national committees, the one with which America has been chiefly concerned, is the "People's Self-Defense Armed Forces Committee," or war ministry. It is really this committee and its fighting forces that most Americans think of when they speak of the Viet Cong.

The central army committee is directly in charge of the Viet Cong's "main force" guerrillas, their counterpart of the regular army. These forces operate nationally and are generally involved in the really big fights. Currently, intelligence men estimate their strength at 34,000, but this number has been rising rapidly over the past four years, and presumably will be out of date when this is published.

The war ministry is also linked with the Viet Cong's estimated 80,000 "paramilitary" troops, but does not command them directly. Each province also has its military committee, and this committee commands the "regional guerrillas" in its bailiwick. Below the province level, district military committees control "Hamlet Self-Defense Forces," at the lowest end of the Viet Cong's military totem pole.

All these military forces are co-ordinated from the top, of course, but local military leaders are given a large share of responsibility and autonomy in working out their local problems. This system is similar, incidentally, to the one used by Saigon, which also breaks down its forces three ways: regular army, provincial civil guards, and district and hamlet militia.

There are several reasons for doing things this way, but one of them is that communications in Viet Nam are so poor that local military units must be left largely to shift for themselves.

The main communist reason for the system is based on the idea that fighting forces must be "of, by and for the people," and should be immediately linked to local and presumably popular administrative commissars. Only a local leader knows enough about the situation in his area to command troops intelligently, the Communists reason. Local units should be made responsible by headquarters for carrying out certain missions, but then left alone to work things out for themselves. If they fail, they will have to suffer the consequences, both from the enemy and from headquarters. The consequences may sometimes mean a beheaded district commissar.

A key part of the Viet Cong war ministry is its agitprop section, which is tied to all the other ministries. This section commands the 4,000 or more armed agitprop agents who travel in teams throughout South Viet Nam, raising all kinds of hell for government authorities. The agitprop teams are considered by the Liberation Front (and by growing numbers of Saigon officials and Americans) the real cutting edge of the Viet Cong. All the teams are expert guerrilla fighters, the "special forces" of the Viet Cong. But their main object is not fighting but "agitation and propaganda." Viet Cong recruiting and growth in all fields owes most of its success to these teams. An American officer said of them recently that "they have done us far more damage than all the Viet Cong's main force battalions put together."

I have covered agitprop techniques in several earlier chapters, but a new agitprop team deserving special mention went into operation recently in Quang Ngai Province 300 miles or so northeast of Saigon. The team consists of twenty superbly armed men and their leader, a slim and strikingly beautiful girl about twenty years old. The team sets up along some road with all the men in ambush positions, and the girl standing out in the middle of the road with a pistol in her hand. She stops the first car (if she doesn't, the ambush shoots it to pieces) and directs the driver, normally a man, to come over and sit next to her on a rock near a little waterfall. She lays the pistol down near her, apologizes for this inconvenience, and explains pitifully that she was infiltrated recently from North Viet Nam for this mission. At this point, she pulls up her trouser legs a little, and begins washing her dainty feet in the waterfall, looking fetching as all getout.

"I hate this work," she says softly, "and all I want to do is go back to school, maybe get married and have children sometime. But I have to do it for my country. You poor people of South Viet Nam are under the heel of those American devils, and every Vietnamese—even a helpless girl—must try to help you. That is why I am here and you are here. I hope you don't blame me too much?" she coos.

The driver is kept in conversation until the next car comes along. She sighs, gets up, and says, "Excuse me, but I must leave you now. Someone else is coming, and I have my mission. I hope you will think of me sometimes?"

This routine may strike the reader as corny in the extreme, but American agents in Quang Ngai report that the little girl on the rock has had a profound and dangerous propaganda impact in the area. They are out to get her at all cost.

A complete communist organization normally must have a front which is open to all, an administrative system which is open to some, and a directing party, which is usually secret and open only to the elite.

The Viet Cong had the front from the beginning, evolved the administrative system soon afterward, but gave outsiders no hint of the existence of a party for some time. Obviously, there must have been a party all along, because this is always the core of the whole thing. But it was not until January, 1962, that the Liberation Front announced publicly the formation of the "Vietnamese People's Revolutionary Party." This party, the Front said, was "a Marxist-Leninist party," which henceforth would serve as the "vanguard" of the Front. At last, the Viet Cong was an openly Communist-run outfit.

It is well to note in passing that the average member of the Front and most of its branches is not a Communist member. Party membership is reserved for the elite, who must establish their political credentials over a long period of time. Once they do this, they usually rise fast in the Viet Cong hierarchy. This fairly sharp distinction between party members and nonparty members of the front, coupled with conspiratorial techniques worked out over many decades of communist evolution, makes it fairly easy for an agent to penetrate the Liberation Front itself, but very difficult to penetrate the governing party.

It is safe to say that no one outside a handful of the highest echelon of Viet Cong leaders has an accurate idea how many members the Front has. Fairly good estimates have been made of Viet Cong fighting strength, and intelligence men feel confident about their charts on the Viet Cong order of battle. But the Viet Cong fighting arm is only a small part of its national organization. Guesses have been made that the Front may have something in the vicinity of five million members in South Viet Nam—a nation the total population of which is only around fourteen million.

There is no other party, religious organization, professional or student group or military force in South Viet Nam that can come anywhere near this figure in strength.

Ngo Dinh Diem had a kind of party called the National Revolutionary Movement, and his brothers, Ngo Dinh Can and Ngo Dinh Nhu, organized a secret society called the "Can Lao Nhan Vy Party" ("Personalist Workers Party"). But the combined membership of these two groups never approached anything like Viet Cong membership, and both parties died completely after the deaths of the Ngo brothers.

This leaves the Viet Cong as the only effective political organization in South Viet Nam.

That is the shape of the enemy the Free World faces here.

Chapter 13

Our Image

In the spring of 1964 I came home to the United States for a few weeks' leave, and found myself in Washington, D.C., one warm afternoon with nothing particular to do. It happened that a young Vietnamese woman I had known in Saigon was making her first visit to America at that time. She was a civil service official who had often helped American correspondents and other visitors to Viet Nam by showing them around Saigon, giving them many tips aimed at making their professional tasks a little easier.

I offered to show her around my nation's capital, and we set out on foot. The cherry blossoms no longer were in bloom, but Washington is a handsome city that Americans like myself take some pride in showing off.

We visited the capitol, where I explained our bicameral system, and we stepped into the Senate gallery. The floor was almost deserted, and one senator was giving a long and seemingly pointless discourse on the economy of his state. The Civil Rights Bill was under debate, and Senate business had halted for the long filibuster.

I tried to explain about the Civil Rights Bill and what a filibuster is, but I'm not sure how much of my explanation got across. We continued our walk, and headed up Pennsylvania Avenue.

At the corner of 14th Street and Pennsylvania Avenue, my companion started violently and turned around, just as we were about to cross the street.

A man in his mid-forties with a fat, reddish face had just

yanked the ponytail of lustrous, black hair hanging down my friend's neck, and was now standing two feet from her, glaring. I took her arm and told her the man was just some drunk. We continued walking, but the man apparently was not a drunk. He continued just behind us making quiet catcalls and muttering obscenely. Under different circumstances I would have turned on him, but I felt an ugly scene would just compound the problem, so I led us past 15th Street to within a few steps of the White House, where a policeman was standing. Our pursuer saw what I was doing and turned away, crossing the street.

My friend said she was tired and not interested in more sightseeing. Her black eyes were flashing.

Over a glass of iced tea, I explained, as I have done many times before to other non-Americans, that racist incidents are not typical of my country, and that our government recognizes the problem and is fighting it.

"But how far were we from the White House? Could not President Johnson himself have seen what happened to us if he had been watching?" she asked.

"But you have met thousands of Americans, and you must know by now that most of us are not like that man who followed us," I said.

"Perhaps, after all, racism is just a question of degree among Americans?" she asked with an ironic smile.

A month later, my friend and I were both guests at one of Saigon's diplomatic cocktail parties. I was standing near her when a cabinet minister exchanged greetings with her and asked how she had liked her trip to the States.

"It was all right, but I had an ugly time in Washington," she said, and then told him the details. He clucked sympathetically, nodded his head, and then, noticing that I was within earshot, made some diplomatic remarks in defense of Americans.

The whole episode would be trivial and scarcely worth reporting here, except for the fact that it seemed to be the thing that stood out most prominently in my friend's memories of her trip. She had had a good look at the rural American countryside, had spent most of her time living with an American family, had attended Broadway shows and visited the World's Fair, and in general had had a fair sampling of the American Way of Life.

For the record, I must add that this young woman is not a communist. Her father was killed by Viet Minh guerrillas.

"You don't have to be a communist to be anti-American," another Vietnamese friend once told me.

The Vietnamese are acutely sensitive to matters of race, more so than most Asian nationals.

Ironically, the Vietnamese often treat their own racial minorities atrociously. Cambodians, Chams, and the various primitive tribes of mountain hunters who collectively make up nearly 10 per cent of the population often are termed "the little savages," and are treated accordingly.

Relations between the lowland Vietnamese and the montagnards (tribesmen) are so bad that the late President Ngo Dinh Diem turned the whole project of making peace with the montagnards over to the Americans.

Strangely, the montagnards always have got along better with Westerners than with their lowland countrymen. They looked to French provincial officials to protect them against economic exploitation by the Vietnamese. Many of the mountain tribes never bothered to learn Vietnamese, although most tribes have at least a few members who speak good French.

To this day, lowland Vietnamese provincial officials often communicate with their montagnard constituents in French, their only common language.

A few members of the more advanced tribes, such as the Rhade, have received good educations, and some have studied abroad. Despite this, the montagnards have no representation in the central government in Saigon, and show little interest in Viet Nam as a nation.

From time to time, the chief of state and other ranking Saigon officials visit the montagnards, usually in the mountain town of Ban Me Thuot.

Montagnards are brought into town by truck, and they put on fine shows for the Saigon brass and the ever-present diplomatic corps. Flower leis are hung around the necks of the dignitaries, mountain warriors armed with spears and clad in loincloths parade performing elephants in front of the grandstand, and the visitors are given powerful rice wine, drunk from earthen crocks through long straws. For especially important visitors, a buffalo is usually slaughtered and roasted, and brass friendship bracelets are fastened around the wrists and ankles of the dignitaries.

But it is all just for show. Not long ago, Viet Cong guerrillas, most of them montagnards, wiped out a government post in the mountains. The defenders managed to escape, however, and even took an enemy prisoner. The prisoner had participated in a big, official buffalo roast just a few days earlier.

Hoping to capitalize on the situation, the Viet Cong has long sought the allegiance of montagnards. The Communists have a standing promise that if they win, the montagnards will be given their own autonomous "republic," comprising about one fifth of South Viet Nam. In late 1964, some 2,000 armed montagnards staged an abortive rebellion against Saigon.

In fact, the Viet Cong seems to have had little more success in enlisting the montagnards than have pro-Saigon Vietnamese.

Once I watched a U.S. Army Special Forces officer squatting next to a montagnard hamlet chief talking things over—in French, of course. They had been talking for hours with little tangible result.

Finally, the exasperated American said:

"Oh, come on, help us fight the Viet Cong. The Viet Cong are Vietnamese, after all, and you want to kill Vietnamese, don't you?"

The American got the five pack elephants he had been dickering for.

But Vietnamese do not see any parallel between their own racial problems and those existing in the United States.

"We are all Asians, after all," a friend said to me once. "That means, for instance, that while we hate the Chinese and are willing to fight them to the death, it's not quite the same thing. We and the Chinese can understand each other better, even when we are enemies. When the white and yellow races fight each other, it is a different and terrible thing."

Prince Norodom Sihanouk, the lively potentate of little Cambodia, has often said, "Asia must have an Asian destiny." By extension of this idea, Sihanouk has recognized communist China as by far the most powerful nation in Asia and therefore the destined leader of all Asia.

Sihanouk's own kingdom, with fewer than six million citizens, is less than one hundredth the size of China, a nation that lies only a few hundred miles to the north. That fact in itself is no doubt a practical element in Sihanouk's increasing friendliness to the Chinese.

But another consideration is certainly purely racial. Sihanouk considers his two most immediately dangerous enemies Thailand and South Viet Nam, two of his neighbors. In fits of anger, he often refers to the peoples of his two neighbors as "the Siamese and the Cochin-Chinese"—words that have extremely objectionable connotations with racial overtones to Thais and Vietnamese.

But Sihanouk's feelings about the West in general and the United States in particular are even less agreeable.

The Cambodian ruler felt himself badly slighted by U.S. protocol officers on a visit to New York City once in the late 1950s, and has always viewed Americans as potential imperialists. To this day the name of John Foster Dulles, U.S. Secretary of State during the Eisenhower administration, is a dirty word in Cambodia. Sihanouk feels that Dulles was exercising "Yankee Imperialism prejudicial to the interests of Asians" in organizing the Southeast Asia Treaty Organization (SEATO).

Sihanouk's distrust of Westerners extends almost as much to Russians as it does to Americans.

One day Sihanouk had held one of his periodic press conferences at the Royal Palace in Phnom Penh, under the majestic, upturned roof of one of the gorgeous state buildings adorning the palace grounds. On this occasion, Sihanouk had spoken entirely in Cambodian, and since there were no interpreters available, foreign correspondents (including myself) were without a story. (Sihanouk speaks fluent French and English, and has been learning Russian.)

As the Prince left the building and stepped into his waiting limousine, correspondent Yuri Kurutschkin of the Soviet news agency *Tass*, dressed in a bright sport shirt, decided to beard the lion.

Leaning an elbow on the princely limousine, Kurutschkin politely asked "Monseigneur" if he would go over the main points of his press conference in French, for the benefit of the foreigners. Sihanouk obliged politely, and without further comment drove off.

The following day, Cambodia's government-controlled press carried blistering editorials that said, in effect:

"One would expect that the great Soviet Union, leader of the Socialist bloc, would have sufficient funds to purchase a tie and jacket for its correspondent Mr. Kurutschkin, and would teach him better manners than to lean on the limousine of His Majesty, the Chief of State."

Kurutschkin was recalled from his post a short time later. But the thing that struck me at the time was that another correspondent also dressed in a sports shirt that day had entirely escaped editorial notice—the correspondent from communist China's New China News Agency.

In contrast to Sihanouk's rather humdrum reception in New York, he has received a hero's welcome in Peking on various visits. Tens of thousands of Chinese were lined up to cheer his passing motorcade, and the top brass—Chou En-lai, Liu Shao-chi and others—gave flowery speeches about "our Asian brother, Prince Norodom Sihanouk, an inspiration to oppressed peoples everywhere."

Sihanouk's current love affair with France is only partly the result of an eight-million-dollar aid program Paris extended to Cambodia in 1964.

A more important reason is that France has made its peace with Red China, an indispensable condition Sihanouk attaches to relations with any Western power.

Cambodian ties with France, particularly cultural relations, remain much stronger than relations between France and other Indochina nations. Hundreds of French technical advisors, teachers and "political experts" are on the official Cambodian payroll. But Sihanouk does not like press attention to the French presence in Cambodia.

I was expelled from Cambodia, presumably permanently, after writing several articles on the influence four pro-Chinese-communist French adventurers hold on Prince Sihanouk. I regretted the expulsion, both for professional and personal reasons. I like Cambodia, and had always been on cordial terms with the Prince.

Underlying most of the developments in the Indochina nations is an element of racism.

Vietnamese communists avoid racism as a propaganda peg, since this runs counter to the communist theme that "all workers and peasants are brothers."

Instead, Viet Cong pamphlets play on the theme that the "Yankee Imperialists" are racists, and should be hated accordingly.

Hanoi's leading daily newspaper, *Nhan Dan,* regularly publishes photographs of racial incidents in the American South. Such pictures are easily pirated from American news agencies by monitoring their radiophoto transmission frequencies.

Sometimes racial differences between Vietnamese and Americans engender more curiosity than emotion. An American friend of mine, an army captain, told me once of his experiences in moving into a tiny hamlet in the Mekong River Delta, newly liberated from the Viet Cong.

The hamlet had been occupied and administered by the Communists for more than five years, and my friend was the first American most of the villagers had ever seen. He was assigned to stay there several weeks.

"I used to get up in the morning and shave over a tin pan behind the hut I was sleeping in," he said.

"Vietnamese don't do much shaving because they don't have much facial hair, and I was an object of great curiosity. Every morning sixty or seventy youngsters and housewives would gather round to watch intently while I went into my routine. Every once in a while I'd get rattled by all this attention and cut myself. They'd see the blood and everyone would say 'ah!' Can you imagine what it's like to have seventy people say 'ah' at a time like that?"

Nevertheless, American racism has been a major subject of communist propaganda throughout the world for more than a generation, and Vietnamese communists have been hearing their share of it.

As early as 1924, Ho Chi Minh was writing essays on the Ku Klux Klan and related subjects.

(Ho felt, in 1924, that the KKK itself was doomed. In his essay No. 74 of *La Correspondance Internationale,* he wrote: "Finally the Ku Klux Klan has all the defects of clandestine and reactionary organizations without their qualities. It has the mysticism of Freemasonry, the mummeries of Catholicism, the brutality of fascism, the illegality of its 568 various associations, but it has neither doctrine, nor program, nor vitality, nor discipline.")

Vietnamese have noticed that Negro and white U.S. Army officers and men work together but rarely play together, and tick this off as further evidence of the truth of charges of American racism. They have been impressed seeing Negroes of field grade officer rank commanding white officers and men, but have also noticed that Negroes and whites generally go to bars or out strolling on a segregated basis.

"That's one thing about the French," a Vietnamese told me once. "They treated Viet Nam as a nation like dirt, and they were far more brutal in every way than the Americans. But there was never any question of racial discrimination. A Vietnamese soldier in the French army was treated by his French comrades exactly like any other soldier. Black Africans, Europeans and Asians worked and played together without any racial separation. The Frenchman might rape our women, but he would also marry them."

There are strong racial overtones to some of the Viet Cong terror bombings in Saigon.

For years, the American community here has maintained a PX, a hospital, movie theaters, recreation halls, swimming pools and other facilities on an "Americans only" basis. Reasons given are that "indigenous personnel" must be kept out to avoid damaging the local economy, to give soldiers and diplomats a relaxed atmosphere, and so on. There is nothing unique in the system, which has pertained in every nation where large numbers of American troops have been stationed.

But it is keenly resented by most of the Vietnamese I have talked to, regardless of their political inclinations or feelings about Americans in general. There is a wide feeling that these installations have something in common with racially exclusive establishments in America itself.

The American Capital Kinh-Do Movie Theater in Saigon has been bombed twice, once resulting in three killed and more than fifty wounded. It closed down permanently. The bleachers at an American baseball park have been bombed with heavy U.S. casualties, and other installations have been damaged.

In nearly every instance, bombings have been traced to Vietnamese students in their late teens or early twenties. All were recruited by the Viet Cong in the heat of their misplaced idealism. At least one young terrorist has said he was striking a blow for racial and political freedom against the Yankee Imperialists.

Recently, barbed wire, sandbags and touchy guards placed around American installations have added fuel to the general resentment.

Having to step off the sidewalk into the street to skirt barbed wire surrounding an American office contributes to a sense of irritation.

Effective guards against terror bombings are almost impossible in Saigon, and bombings are no doubt destined to continue for many years to come.

As an American security officer said recently, "There is really no protection from a fanatic determined to kill someone at any cost."

As much as anything else, this kind of fanaticism can be sparked by real or imagined racial slights.

Driven to desperation by the lethargy of Vietnamese methods and tactics, American military and civilian advisors lose their tempers often.

One afternoon, at a helicopter pad in the remote, jungle-covered highlands of Central Viet Nam, I saw an American helicopter pilot order a field grade Vietnamese officer off a helicopter at pistol point.

The Vietnamese had been riding from one point to another, and the American needed extra space in his machine to pick up some wounded Vietnamese soldiers for evacuation. The Vietnamese officer refused to yield his seat until threatened.

The Vietnamese grudgingly stepped down, and dust kicked up by the whirling rotor blades spewed over his starched, khaki uniform. "*Colon*," he muttered at the pilot, as he walked off.

Colon, a French word meaning "colonist," has unpleasant connotations in Viet Nam, linked with Caucasian imperialism.

Not far from the place where the helicopter incident occurred, another AP correspondent ran into more bad blood. The AP man was riding in a U.S. Army jeep past a Vietnamese Army camp, when a volley of rocks sailed over the barbed wire fence. One of the rocks smashed the jeep's windshield, and the driver accelerated fast.

The usual friction that often develops between U.S. troops stationed abroad and local populations sometimes compounds itself into incidents with far-reaching consequences in Viet Nam.

A few years ago, a young U.S. Marine Corps guard at the U.S. Aid mission headquarters in Saigon took a shine to one of the Vietnamese secretaries who worked there.

The Marine and the girl began going out on dates, and their relationship grew warmer. One day she told him she was expecting a baby, and she asked him to marry her. He said he'd have to broach the idea to his parents.

The day the baby was born, the Marine visited the girl at the hospital to tell her the bad news. His mother, he said, disapproved of his marrying an Asian girl, whom she felt would not fit in at home. The young man rotated back to the States a short time later, and the last I heard, the girl had found another job, with which she was supporting her baby and herself.

The incident would be scarcely worth mentioning, except for the fact that Saigon is a small town, and a relatively small group of leading Vietnamese families hold most of the white collar jobs. It happened that this girl was a very close relative of Le Cang Dam, who at the time was director of the Vietnamese Immigration Service—a man with power to issue or withhold visas from Americans seeking to enter the country.

There is no evidence that Dam's unpleasant personal experience with Americans in any way influenced his work, although it is a fact that official Vietnamese-American relations never reached a lower ebb than they did during the time he was in office.

Miscegenation is even more severely condemned by most Vietnamese than by most Americans. A Vietnamese girl seen walking in the streets of Saigon with an American man is apt to draw disapproving clucks or worse from passersby.

Periodically, the Vietnamese government tries to crack down on prostitution in general and an estimated 3,000 bar hostesses in Saigon in particular. Such attempts have been notable failures, as have been attempts by General Paul D. Harkins and other American military commanders to prevent Vietnamese-American liaisons.

Mme. Ngo Dinh Nhu, Diem's strong-willed sister-in-law, tried some drastic approaches to curbing "creeping Americanism." For a while, police under her orders were picking up all women seen walking with Americans.

Once, two young members of Mme. Nhu's women's militia wandered into my office asking if they could have copies of a picture I had taken at one of their parades. I agreed, and asked them a few questions about their life in the Women's Paramilitary Corps. They told me some amusing anecdotes about barracks routine, and said they had joined partly because this was the only way they could get into college.

Several days later, I wrote what seemed to me a completely harmless news story about the two girls, and forgot the incident. I carefully avoided identifying the two girls, however.

I learned two months later that Mme. Nhu had been incensed. Apparently she had been angered not so much by anything I had written as the fact that two of "her" girls had talked to an American. She instituted a police investigation which, using the scant personal facts I had included in the story, was enough to pinpoint the two girls.

Both girls and their families underwent a long police interrogation, and the families were placed under surveillance.

Mme. Nhu herself was the frequent target of miscegenation charges by her many enemies. Viet Cong propaganda sometimes portrayed the Vietnamese first lady in an obscene pose with a grotesque Uncle Sam, lying on a pile of dollar bills. There is no indication how much impact such propaganda may have had, but obviously the Viet Cong at least thought it effective.

In any event, communist propaganda thrives on real or imagined Vietnamese-American sex relations, and trivial incidents can develop into full-blown diplomatic crises.

But Vietnamese-American relations are by no means uniformly hostile.

One night, a group of Vietnamese and American paratroopers were drinking together at one of Saigon's rougher establishments, known as the Playboy Bar. This bar had been bombed twice by communist terrorists, with heavy casualties both times.

As the evening wore on, the Saigon police commissioner in civilian clothes happened to stop by, and decided the bar should close down early because of the danger of bombings. The paratroopers threw him out. He returned a short time later with a small army of Vietnamese and American military police.

The paratroopers, outnumbered four to one, decided to make a stand, and a full-scale street brawl quickly erupted. The MPs were pushed back, pummeled and bloodied. The American and Vietnamese paratroopers, their arms around each other, burst into song, their common enemy vanquished. It must have been a touching instance of hands-across-the-sea friendship, despite the unsavory circumstances.

(The paratroopers were all arrested later when reinforcements arrived.)

On a more worthy level, I have seen many real friendships blossom between American and Vietnamese troops fighting in the field. At least one American officer has died in a valiant effort to save the life of a Vietnamese comrade under fire, and many Vietnamese have died doing the same kind of thing for Americans.

"I had a rough time last night," a young U.S. officer told me once.

"My counterpart [the Vietnamese officer to whom the American had been assigned as an advisor] invited me around to his place for dinner. He served big, hard-boiled duck eggs with sort of blackish yolks that had baby ducks inside. Then we had roasted chicken chopped up into little pieces, bones and all, and tough as leather. Then we had some kind of shrimp paste wrapped around sugar-cane sticks and dunked in a sauce made out of fermented fish. We washed it down with huge bowls of rice, all stuck together, and water glasses of some kind of booze that tasted like diesel fuel.

"I had a real rough time getting all that stuff down, but it was worth it. My counterpart is too great a guy to offend."

Such is the stuff of real friendship.

Every U.S. military advisory detachment throughout South Viet Nam, however small and however remote from a base camp, normally has its own 16-millimeter movie projector and a rotating stock of films representing the latest from Hollywood. Most detachments get replacement reels often enough so that they can show different movies five or six times a week.

While Vietnamese are excluded from the American theater in Saigon, scores of Vietnamese children swarm to the American field movies, staring intently at the makeshift projector screens while Americans ply them with chewing gum and Coke.

It is difficult to know what a child of the Mekong River Delta thinks as he watches Elizabeth Taylor romp through a love scene. But he is always eager for more, except at certain times.

When the Viet Cong are planning a bombing, the children are rarely around.

"If you go into a hamlet and everything's quiet and there are no kids running around screaming 'okay!' and 'how you!' watch out," a seasoned American advisor said. "It always means that Old Joe is around somewhere, laying for you."

Just before two large bombs exploded under the bleachers of an Americans-only baseball field, killing three Americans and injuring more than a score, everyone noticed something unusual: the children who always played around the bleachers, picking up empty bottles and cans, and yelling "how you," were not there.

So far, no U.S. field detachments have had any ugly incidents involving children, but a few veterans of this war are none too sure about the intention of all the happy, swarming kids and their seemingly innocent friendship with Americans.

Too often, veterans have seen just such children planting deadly land mines in roads.

"One of the tragedies of this place," an American said, "is that the little fellow having such a nice time with us watching the movie tonight may spend tomorrow night booby-trapping my jeep. It's enough to make a man a cynic."

Americans do learn the pitfalls of Viet Nam, and surprisingly many U.S. field advisors have learned passably good Vietnamese. Little by little, perhaps they have made the beginnings of a bridge across the vast cultural, social, political, linguistic and racial gulf between Viet Nam and the United States.

By the end of his one-year tour in Viet Nam, the average field advisor (as opposed to officers and officials who spend all their time in Saigon) has begun to learn a great deal about Viet Nam. But then he goes home, and a new man arrives, who must start from scratch.

Some American servicemen are repeaters in Viet Nam. I know one man, Sergeant Al Combs of Brooklyn, New York, who is currently on his fourth tour in Viet Nam. By pulling every military wire in the books, he has managed to spend all but a few days of the past six years in the Far East, most of it in Viet Nam.

But Combs' case is probably unique. Some other repeaters turn up here, but relatively few Americans are eager to come back for more. It's an arduous, frustrating job, and the danger of death from some unexpected quarter becomes greater each year.

"The constant rotation of Americans has one desirable feature," a Vietnamese officer told me, with tongue in cheek. "It gives the maximum number of Americans an opportunity to learn some interesting things from us Vietnamese. But I hope your country will hurry with its education, because time seems to be running out on us all, doesn't it?"

Chapter 14

Americans and
the New Face of War

A radically unorthodox American experiment on a very small scale began in 1964 in the high, Viet Cong-controlled valleys of Quang Ngai Province. The experiment, which for the moment, at least, has official blessing, may peter out or it may prosper. The man running it is a twenty-six-year-old American field agent of the U.S. Information Service. This young man, Frank Scotton of Needham, Massachusetts, is shot at constantly, he carries and uses a submachine gun, and he speaks fluent Vietnamese. He comes closer to being an American agitprop leader than any official I have ever met, and the program he administers relies almost entirely on pure communist guerrilla tactics.

"After all," Scotton says, "they stole atomic bomb secrets and all kinds of other things from us. Why should we be squeamish about stealing 'people's warfare' from them? It works better than anything we've come up with to match it, so why not give it a try?"

The men Scotton and a handful of other American, Australian and Vietnamese experts train are given pledge cards when they graduate as "Special Government Commandos." The pledge cards are printed with four general rules, all copied right out of works by the North Vietnamese defense minister, Vo Nguyen Giap, and eight specific rules, all copied directly out of the standard text by Mao Tse-tung.

The first four rules (out of Giap) are:
1. Respect the people.
2. Help the people.

3. Protect the people.

4. Follow orders.

The second eight rules (out of Mao) are:

1. Speak politely and truthfully.

2. Pay fairly for what you buy.

3. Return everything you borrow.

4. Pay for anything you damage.

5. Don't mistreat the people.

6. Don't damage crops.

7. Don't rape women.

8. Treat captives well.

To an American, this may sound like a litany of Boy Scout injunctions. But looking back over the bloody history of the human race, are there any wars in which any of these injunctions were made the primary teaching of front-line troops, much less taken seriously?

The men in Scotton's teams are all killers. They are recruited from the cream of the local militiamen, and they are accustomed to using terror in a general way. Scotton and his helpers are teaching them to use controlled terror in a new and restricted way—the Viet Cong way.

One of the commando recruits turned agent for the Viet Cong recently. The squad of which he was a member set up its own field tribunal, condemned the man and beheaded him. Both the head and body were politely returned to the man's family, however, for proper burial.

The teams Scotton trains, thirty-nine men each, are patterned exactly on Viet Cong agitprop teams. Their training consists largely of group political discussion and politico-military agitation tactics. All this training and practice is out in certain target hamlets, not at any camp.

From the first day, each trainee must spend all his time among the people who are his targets, always in Viet Cong-contested areas. He eats with the peasants, lives with them and works with them. He is required to know personally every family in every hamlet in which he works.

During the day, the trainee dresses in black, baggy blouse

and trousers, just like the other hamlet residents—and the Viet Cong. He sleeps, talks, and helps out with hamlet chores, making himself as agreeable a guest as possible. He buys all his meals and anything else he needs (except weapons) right there.

At night, he puts on a loose camouflaged uniform, and goes out to spread terror. He patrols and ambushes. Each time he kills, he leaves a slip of paper printed in black with a sinister human eye on the body. (Fifty thousand of these papers were printed by the U.S. Information Service, which is enough of a supply to last for some time.)

He learns to know many of the National Liberation Front members living in the hamlets in which he works, and some of them die violently in their beds. Other Viet Cong functionaries find black eyes pasted to the doors of their huts at night. The eyes are ripped down in the morning, but mysteriously reappear the next night.

The new commandos are paid directly with American funds, not by the Vietnamese government. Each commando earns about $15.00 a month, $5.00 more than he would make as a regular hamlet militiaman. He gets no extra money to pay intelligence tipsters, and is ordered to gather intelligence the hard way. So far, only five of these teams are in operation. But on June 9, 1964, at Tu Thuan Village, one of them killed a Viet Cong courier, and found the following letter in the corpse's pocket:

District 1
To: Mr. Ba at C16

I herewith inform you about the present situation of villages in our district and the results of winning the people's hearts.

There are a number of people who look to us, but they are still unsure of the present situation. Therefore we must work hard. When we broke into Tu Thanh Village, policemen came later and arrested some of our underground, but the situation is not too dangerous.

Concerning the military situation of the enemy, they have organized one special section with the assistance of American invaders. Most of the soldiers in this unit are outstanding. They are commanded by Nguyen Duy Be, who is very active and arrested a party man in 1956. He was also a battalion commander under

Diem's regime. The plan of operation of this unit is good. They usually launch ambush right in our control zone with a small unit, based on information furnished by spies.

I am studying the method of reaction to this unit. Its activities aimed at Tu Binh and Nguyen Villages have caused difficulties for us, and you'd better direct C6 [a regional Viet Cong guerrilla unit] to be careful. It is dangerous to meet this section.

I will return to meet you on the occasion of the anniversary at father's, to discuss with you many questions, especially our reaction to the above, because if the situation is not corrected our activity will be hurt.

This letter will be sent to you through Mr. Hoang.

Good luck, Viet

An American reader has grounds, perhaps, for objecting to such tactics. For one thing, there is a cold-blooded ruthlessness about them, even in the careful politeness with which they are carried out, that bespeaks something alien to the whole texture of American tradition. In any case, the reader may argue, this kind of thing should be the work of regular soldiers, not of civilian officials who are supposed to be spreading the good word about the American Way of Life. Perhaps. But I'm afraid the record shows that almost everything else the United States has tried in South Viet Nam has failed. Time has just about run out, and I think those who are trying some radical departures should be excused.

A certain mystique has begun to grow around Americans serving in Viet Nam, I think. I have had the feeling on occasional visits to my native land that Americans have an image of their compatriots in South Viet Nam as dashing young men with green berets, roaming through the jungles on elephantback, and raising hell deep behind enemy lines.

There is some justification for this image. There actually are a lot of dashing young men in green berets (and other kinds of headgear) doing a dangerous and competent job. It has even happened on occasion that a few of them rode elephants. As for enemy lines, there aren't any, and every American in Viet Nam is in enemy territory to one degree or another. The very first rule of communist guerrilla warfare, as enunciated by Mao Tse-tung, is that "the guerrilla must be to the people as a fish is to water." Hence, no front lines, only infiltration.

How do they live, these 23,000 American military men and couple of thousand civilian officials?

They deserve a book in themselves. They can be colorful, funny, brave, resourceful, honest, dedicated and very hard working. They also can be unimaginative, deskbound, gullible, comfort loving and bigoted. In short, they are Americans.

They have their foibles and even their status symbols. Officers' wives have "arrived" when they become committeewomen of certain social service groups, especially the Viet Nam-America Association.

Fighting men have "arrived" when they own a Swedish "K" submachine gun. This gun is a much uglier-looking collection of nuts and bolts than the American Thompsons and "grease guns," and is practically indestructible. It looks like a he-man's weapon, and it is also hard to get, which makes it a perfect status symbol for the well-dressed American in Viet Nam.

For the thousands of Americans living in Saigon, even including the helicopter pilots and field advisors who face death in the field every day, life has its comfortable side. This is possibly the first war in American history in which most of the fighting men can get home for a 5 P.M. martini at the end of a day of bloodshed, have an excellent hot meal, take a shower, see a movie, perhaps read or write a few letters in a private or semiprivate room, and go to sleep on a soft bed. This pattern of existence is almost as true at every American field detachment in South Viet Nam, however remote, as it is in Saigon.

The big PX commissary store in Saigon is indistinguishable from any small-town supermarket in America, and is just as crowded with women and kids doing the weekend marketing.

Officers' families live in villas in Saigon, the luxury of which could not possibly be equaled for them in the USA.

Excellent servants are paid $20.00 a month or less to work seven days a week, doing all the washing, cleaning, cooking, baby-sitting and local marketing. The average military family has at least two such servants, leaving the wife without much in the way of chores. She generally joins the "Cercle Sportif," where she can swim in an enormous and beautiful pool, or play tennis. Others who play tennis there have included Major General Duong Van Minh, the former Chief of State, and U.S. Ambassador Maxwell D. Taylor.

Inevitably, there are wives who complain of "wretchedly primitive conditions."

If I speak mostly of officers, it is because, on the American side of things, Viet Nam is an officer's war. One out of four of the 23,000 servicemen here is a commissioned officer. An even dozen of them are generals. Most of the enlisted men are in the higher noncommissioned officer grades. And the overwhelming majority of American servicemen killed or wounded here are officers. The reason is that there is no American infantry in Viet Nam, and this is not the kind of dirty, exhausting "GI Joe" war that Americans have fought in the past.

Most Americans in Viet Nam realize that this is a very peculiar kind of war, in which it isn't enough to shoot the enemy. You go on shooting him, and he just keeps getting stronger. There is a mysterious new glossary of military terms, like "infrastructure," "counterinsurgency," and so on. There is something puzzling and frustrating about the whole thing, and the Americans here resent it.

More needed to be known about this peculiar enemy, and American intelligence organizations began to proliferate. First, there was the CIA. From its headquarters on the second floor of the embassy in Saigon, the CIA's 200 or so agents were divided into three groups: administrators and analysts, field observers, and infiltrators. The infiltrators were (and are) the only secret operatives of the agency. They have joined every other American official agency, they have assumed covers as civilian contractors, and for all I know, there may even be a CIA foreign correspondent.

Closely allied to the CIA was the military Combined Studies Group, which administered the whole Special Forces program.

The U.S. Aid mission set up an intelligence group, working with its civilian police advisors. The U.S. Information Service set up an intelligence group. The U.S. Army set up the 704th Military Intelligence Detachment, which dabbles in all kinds of things. The Provost Marshal's office had an intelligence outfit. The army created another intelligence unit for "strategic intelligence." At a lower level, the army has put into operation a "sector intelligence" unit at every one of the scores of American advisory detachments throughout South Viet Nam. Even the U.S. Navy, which has only a minuscule role in South Viet Nam (partly advising the Vietnamese armed junk patrol fleet) brought in a little intelligence unit. And the U.S. Embassy's security section was involved all along in political intelligence.

Scores of airplanes—twin-engine German Dorniers, American C46s, single-engine L28 "Heliocouriers," and others, all of them completely unmarked—fly this army of spooks around the country.

But it is not one big, happy family. American competitive free enterprise prevails, and none of the agencies I have named is willing to co-operate with the others on a regular basis.

Each maintains fierce unit esprit, and takes enormous pride in its intelligence scoops. Information is very often closely concealed from competing American agencies, because of the danger that the competitors may pirate the material and report it to headquarters first, getting the credit.

This is not just a diverting game. Official and military careers very often are made or broken in Viet Nam, and from the career standpoint, a Vietnamese tour is critical.

The same applies to regular military officers. Friction between American officers is especially noticeable when regular army officers and army special forces officers are working in the same area. A lot of regular officers resent the glamour and irregularity of the special forces men, and many of the special forces men feel the regular army just doesn't understand the problem in Viet Nam.

The long-standing feud between the U.S. Air Force and the U.S. Army often flares up in Viet Nam, which is a vital proving ground for each branch of service. At this writing, a peace pact still has not been signed between these two branches in Viet Nam that would enable an Army helicopter pilot to ask for help directly from an Air Force fighter in the area. This defect in co-operation has very nearly cost American lives on several operations at which I have been present (eavesdropping on a radio headset).

U.S. civilian and military officials often resent each other.

I doubt that the Viet Cong has problems like this. Inter-service rivalry in that outfit is punishable by beheading.

Superficially, Vietnamese-American personal relations are often good, but I think the relationship is skin deep. At times, Vietnamese hostility can flare out of control, and American patience frays badly.

All generalities are open to challenge, including the one I am about to make. But I think most Vietnamese not only dislike Americans but hold them in contempt. As a nationality, we are most disliked for things we cannot help—the color of our faces and the length of our noses. We are disliked because we are of the same racial stock as the French, and, ironically, because we do not seem to have the *savoir vivre*, the polish, of the French. We are disliked for being rich while Vietnamese are poor, for living in villas surrounded with barbed wire, while they live in huts, and all the other things that are part of the vast gulf between two cultures.

All this can be overcome, and often is.

But there are some even more serious obstacles. Most Vietnamese regard Americans as extremely gullible, politically infantile, and hypocritically softhearted. For these things, they hold us in contempt, which in Viet Nam is much worse than mere dislike.

I cannot give you any conclusive proof of these observations, and I offer them only on the basis of having lived a long three years among Vietnamese of every social caste. It is more a cumulative impression than anything else. It comes out in dropped remarks, innuendoes, reactions to situations, and even sometimes in frank statements from one's closest friends. Here is a sample, coming from a highly educated and worldly friend of mine:

"You Americans have poured money into South Viet Nam blindly, and through your policies, you have armed and equipped the Viet Cong with the best weapons made.

"You have come here to teach us how to fight a war we might never have had to fight if it hadn't been for you. You have brought us no new ideas, only new gadgets coupled with the tired old military ideas of the French. You are beginning to find that we Vietnamese know more about people's warfare than you, and it is we who are the advisors, not you.

"You have always managed to back the wrong men here, the ones whose only qualification is being anticommunist, the ones who think like you because they have been rich enough to spend most their lives in the West, and who will lose the most if the Viet Cong wins. They are not Vietnamese, except their faces.

"You have staked your military reputation on Viet Nam, and yet you refuse to jump in with both feet by sending in armies and maybe even running the country as a colony for a few years. You won't do this, because you're afraid to take the responsibility. Your advisors actually order our troops, but only through the façade of your own officers. Your government is running our country, but only through its CIA—not openly. We know you are not here because you love Viet Nam (as you say) but to protect American international interests.

"And on top of all these things, the Viet Cong is beating you—not us, you. This is why we despise you."

That was, word for word, what my friend said. I offer it not as a pearl of enlightenment, because nearly every point in his thesis can be argued. But it is the view of one Vietnamese, and I suspect of many Vietnamese. This person is a South Vietnamese, incidentally. A North Vietnamese would never have used such blunt phrasing, even to a close friend.

I can think of a few Americans who are not held in contempt by the Vietnamese. One is Henry Cabot Lodge, who was the American ambassador to Saigon in the fall of 1963 and early

1964. He was blunt, skeptical and decisive. He also surprised a lot of people by taking an extreme interest in the political heart of the nation, which seemed to concern him even more than the shooting war.

He was not fooled by the "teatime bomb," a diplomatic gambit applied to many an unsuspecting American official by Vietnamese officials. Vietnamese tea, served hot and clear in little glasses, has a strong diuretic effect, and causes pressure to make a trip to the john to build up rapidly. All Vietnamese know this.

Lodge arrived at a time when Saigon was under martial law and American-Vietnamese official relations had never been worse. It was necessary to talk to President Diem as soon as possible. The last man Diem wanted to talk to just then was the American ambassador—any American ambassador.

Diem had to receive Lodge, but applied the tea trick. In the sweltering hot palace reception room, servants brought glass after glass of tea to Lodge while Diem rambled on for hours about his grandmother, his childhood in Hue, and almost anything but the crisis in hand. Diem was presumably counting on the tea to take effect so Lodge would excuse himself and hurry back to the embassy. The trick worked, but Lodge never fell for it again. Subsequent meetings were brusque and pointed.

Ever since Vietnamese independence, American intelligence officials had relied on the Vietnamese intelligence system for most of their information. This was not for lack of qualified, Vietnamese-speaking Americans, but because of Diem's touchiness about American spooks wandering around on their own.

This touchiness was always respected by the Americans, in the interest of preserving Vietnamese-American harmony, and somehow the intelligence reports always had it that the war was going well. Lodge was the first ranking American in Viet Nam to ignore the niceties and send out his own crews—without notifying any Vietnamese authorities. He sent one team into Long An Province and another into Kien Hoa, both south of Saigon, and among the most critical provinces in the nation. The conclusions of these teams, in substance, was that the situation in both provinces was worse than even the fears of the most confirmed pessimists (who included a number of resident American newsmen).

Lodge called for a crash program in Long An. One of his ideas was that emphasis should be laid on development of political structure, precinct by precinct, with many of the aspects of the time-honored American ward system. Toward the end of his tour here, he was out in the countryside much of the time, literally stumping for support for the new Vietnamese leader, Nguyen Khanh.

Lodge had lots of ideas and painted with a broad brush. He thoroughly shook up the whole American official community, and alienated a lot of people along the way. He made undying enemies of the survivors of the Ngo family, particularly Mme. Ngo Dinh Nhu, who charges periodically that Lodge was behind the coup of November 1, 1963, in which both her husband and brother-in-law were slain. Actually, Lodge's only tangible contribution to the coup was in tightening down on American economic aid to the Diem regime, as a means of bringing pressure to stop the repressive measures Diem was using on Viet Nam. This aid cut probably was a major factor in squeezing the hair trigger that sets off coups in Saigon.

When Lodge left, a broad segment of Vietnamese regarded him as something of a Vietnamese national hero. One of the few genuinely spontaneous demonstrations I have ever seen in Saigon turned out at the airport for his departure. There were a good many thousand people there, cheering the slightly stooped, six-foot-four-inch American, and some of them had tears in their eyes. Lodge may not have been liked any better than other Americans, but he was a symbol of authority, imagination and courage who, if nothing else, commanded respect. He was, in Vietnamese eyes, a politician at least as able as the French, and a statesman.

It would be nice to report that since then things have improved, at least in Long An and Kien Hoa Provinces, where Lodge put so much effort. Unfortunately, the situation even in those two provinces has continued to deteriorate. Basically, Viet

Nam must find its own destiny, no matter how much good advice it gets.

What of the future?

South Viet Nam is certain to have more political upheavals, and probably coups. I see no prospects of real political stability in the foreseeable future.

The United States is not likely to give up, and neither is the Viet Cong.

I have the impression that the three Gulf of Tonkin incidents in the late summer and fall of 1964, in which American naval forces and North Vietnamese naval forces clashed directly, were little more than incidents. They were probes and shows of force, but from the standpoint of the war in South Viet Nam, they seemed to have some of the character of historical aberrations.

This entire book has dealt with various aspects of the war in Viet Nam, which is something entirely new to American experience. American officers are generally agreed that the experiences of both World Wars and the Korean War are almost totally inapplicable in South Viet Nam.

Communists in general realize they have a good thing going in South Viet Nam. The Vietnamese communists in particular believe they have refined the art of "people's warfare" far beyond the early teachings of Lenin and even those of the Chinese master, Mao Tse-tung. The Vietnamese war machine has admirers all over the world.

During a brief period near the close of World War II, Ho Chi Minh's guerrillas, who at the time were working in southern China, co-operated up to a point with Chiang Kai-shek's nationalist army against the Japanese. Chiang recognized the Vietnamese as masters of guerrilla warfare, and asked to borrow some Viet Minh advisors for some of his units. Ho obliged. Unfortunately for Chiang, when his final showdown with the Chinese communists came, the Viet Minh advisors were now his enemies, working closely with Mao Tse-tung.

A lot of the things I have described in this book are peculiarly Vietnamese, or at least peculiarly Asian. But there are some striking similarities between the social, economic and political situation in South Viet Nam and the situation in scores of countries that dot the African and South American continents.

The international communist movement, particularly the Peking part of it, has a close eye on all these countries. Asia is pretty much gobbled up, the Soviet Union is out on its own, and Europe is settling down into a stability that does not make an apt setting for revolutionary activity.

The United States is an enormous fortress, against which a frontal attack might prove suicidal. In any case, Korea proved that the vast hordes of China in themselves are not enough to overcome American arms in conventional battle. Nuclear war with America remains a possibility, but only as a last resort.

But Africa and Latin America are up for grabs.

The National Liberation Front of Viet Nam is not the only such organization in the world. The National Liberation Front of Algeria has already won its war for independence, partly because of a new French policy enunciated by De Gaulle, which did away with the old patterns of French colonialism.

Fronts are forming in many new African nations, and most of them are getting help from China.

Fidel Castro's entire "26th of July Movement" followed the whole front pattern. Castro's flashing success only ninety miles from the homeland of the Yankee Imperialist has brought him great prestige with Asian communists.

It seems also that the Viet Cong has a certain prestige in Latin America. On October 9, 1964, two Venezuelan Liberation Front agents kidnaped a U.S. Air Force colonel from his home in Caracas. Their ransom demand was a subject of great interest in Viet Nam. They would agree to send back the American, they said, if the Americans in Saigon would arrange for the pardon of a nineteen-year-old Viet Cong terrorist who was scheduled to be shot October 15. This particular young Viet Cong was caught red-handed on May 9, 1964, trying to blow up U.S. Defense Secretary Robert S. McNamara, who was due to visit Saigon in a few days.

It happens that the American was released with no deal, and

Troi, the Viet Cong, was shot anyway. But it shows that the Viet Cong has friends in faraway places.

In any case, Viet Cong methods of making trouble for the United States are likely to become a pattern for many years to come in many parts of the world.

The mastermind of Vietnamese communist "people's warfare," General Vo Nguyen Giap, became North Viet Nam's defense minister after crushing the French at Dien Bien Phu. His hand is markedly visible in the direction of the Viet Cong, and he regards himself as a teacher. In *People's War, People's Army,* he suggests that while great Russia and China have found their own communist solutions, Vietnamese tactics may be more applicable in small, underdeveloped countries. He adds, somewhat smugly:

"In combining the invaluable experience of the Soviet Union and People's China with its own, our Party has always taken into account the concrete reality of the revolutionary war in Viet Nam, and thus is able in its turn to enrich the theories of revolutionary war and army."

Giap's book was published in many languages in Hanoi, in 1961. It carries a publisher's note so sinister in its implications that I think its republication here is appropriate:

We are very pleased to publish the English translation of a series of articles by General Vo Nguyen Giap, member of the Political Bureau of the Central Committee of the Viet Nam Workers' Party, Vice-Premier and Minister for National Defense of the Democratic Republic of Viet Nam, Commander-in-Chief of the Viet Nam People's Army.

In these articles, the author introduces the liberation war waged by the Vietnamese people, the features of that war and deals with the reasons for victory:

Mobilization of the entire people, setting up of a people's army, merging of all patriotic organizations and people into a united national front, clearsighted leadership of the Party of the working class. It lays particular stress on the problem of organization and direction of the revolutionary armed forces of Viet Nam. In a word, it is the combination of experiences gained by the Vietnamese people in the course of a long struggle against colonialism, for national independence, a struggle which ended in 1954 with the brilliant Dien Bien Phu victory and the signing of the Geneva Agreements.

Publication of this book is most timely.

It is true that since the end of World War II, the maps of Asia, Africa and Latin America have been subject to radical changes, other countries will soon be independent and colonialism is unquestionably doomed to collapse. It is no less true that great obstacles still stand in the way of the peoples struggling for their liberation. The Algerian war has just entered its seventh year. The so-called "U.N. action" in the Congo has turned out to be an imperialist plot against Lumumba's motherland. Cuba is subject to daily provocations by the U.S.A. Half of Viet Nam's territory is still under the heel of a new type colonialism "made in U.S.A."

We hope that all our friends who, like us, are still suffering from imperialist designs and threats will find in *People's War, People's Army* what we ourselves have found: Further reasons for confidence and hope.

Viet Nam may or may not eventually fall to the Viet Cong. In any case, America is on trial there.

The challenge of a new kind of war has been thrown down to America. The weapons by which this war is fought include politics, diplomatic blackmail, interference in the domestic affairs of other nations, propaganda and controlled terror, all of which have somewhat dirty connotations in the American mind. It is a war in which a clever adversary can turn military defeat into political victory, ending up on top.

Even the military tactics of this kind of war are somewhat loathsome to most Americans. They involve ambushes, sniping, and murder in bed. Seldom if ever does it involve the vast, noble battles of the past in which American arms covered themselves with glory. The only glory anyone is likely to get out of it is the satisfaction of carrying a bundle of human enemy heads, suspended by wires stuck through their ears. There will never be the handing over of a sword by a beaten general to his victor. If there is victory, the fighting merely will die down to a few isolated incidents.

It is a war fought as much at a union meeting, a rural threshing party (in which singing farmers lead an ox over a pile of rice all night long to knock the grains loose), or in a coffee shop, as it is in battle. It is fought also in churches, temples and pagodas. No institution, no social class, no sex and no age group is exempt. It is total war, in a sense far more profound than that intended by Hitler, when he used the phrase.

It is a war fought with lies and counterlies.

To use a phrase coined by a different kind of American fighter, it is a war in which "nice guys finish last."

To carry the baseball allusion a little further, I'm afraid it is a kind of war in which America will have to pick up a new kind of bat to stay in the game.

Perhaps, in the end, America will find it can put Marx, Lenin, Mao and Giap to work for it, without embracing communism itself.

Perhaps some still unseen approach will be found.

Perhaps America will fail to meet the threat.

It would be much more entertaining to watch if there were not so much at stake.

Index